*Greater Good*
*The Case for Proportionalism*

# Greater Good
# The Case for Proportionalism

Garth L. Hallett

Georgetown University Press / Washington, D.C.

Georgetown University Press, Washington, D.C.
©1995 by Georgetown University Press. All rights reserved.
Printed in the United States of America

10  9  8  7  6  5  4  3  2  1      1995

**Library of Congress Cataloging-in-Publication Data**
Hallett, Garth.
    Greater good : the case for proportionalism / Garth Hallett.
        p.   cm.
    Includes bibliographical references and index.
    1. Christian ethics—Catholic authors.     I. Title.
BJ1249.H294   1995
241'.2—dc20                                                    95-5698
ISBN 0-87840-590-9 (hard)

241.2
Hal

# Contents

**Acknowledgments**    **vii**

**1  A Christian Criterion of Right and Wrong    1**
Value-Maximization (VM) 2    Overview 18


**2  A Major Objection    20**
The Finnis-Grisez Dilemma 20


**3  The Positive Case for VM    30**
Philosophical Considerations 30    Theological Considerations 34


**4  Natural Law: Aquinas    52**
An Aristotelian and Christian View 53    The First Principle of Practical
Reason 56    Comparison with VM 60    Other Possibilities 62


**5  Divine Commands: Adams    64**
Adams's Theory 64    Possible Convergence 65    Conflicting
Identifications 67    Comparative Utility 71


**6  Respect for Persons: Donagan    74**
Similarities and Dissimilarities 74    Further Dissimilarities 76    Reasons
for the Principle's Narrowness 81

**7   *Inviolable Goods: Grisez*   89**
*Value Inviolability 90      An Implicit Challenge 91      An Illustration:
Contraception 93      Assessment 95      The Larger Lesson 98*


**8   *"Proportionate Reason": Knauer*   100**
*The Standard Version 100      The Revised Version 107      The Moral/
Nonmoral Dichotomy 109      Overview 112*


**9   *Irreducible Rights: Thomson*   113**
*A Hard Case 114      A Countercase 122      The Cases Compared 125*


**10   *A Single Supreme Norm?*   128**
*Ross and McCloskey 129      Gewirth's General Claim 132      Gewirth's
Solution 134      Lewis's Alternative 135      The Final Question 138*


**11   *The Norm's Significance*   139**
*VM's Theoretical and Practical Significance 140      VM's Comparative
Significance 145*


**Notes   161**
**Works Cited   189**
**Index   205**

# Acknowledgments

This work has profited greatly from the comments of many people—Scott Berman, Russell Hittinger, Gerard Hughes, Peter Knauer, Richard McCormick, Martin Palmer, Philip Quinn, William Rehg, Eleonore Stump, Judith Thomson, the reader for Georgetown University Press—and from the fine stylistic editing of Jeannette Batz and Helen Mandeville. Warm thanks to them all.

*Greater Good*
*The Case for Proportionalism*

# 1

# A Christian Criterion of Right and Wrong

The "moral systems" of the seventeenth and eighteenth centuries addressed the question: "When may we act on a doubtful conscience?" More recent systems have focused on the query: "What should we do?" Prominent among these is the type of response which Christian ethicians have christened "proportionalism."

The positions so labeled vary notably. Some would be better called by another name, since, unlike the majority, they do not judge right action by the proportion of good and evil. Of those that do, some look only to the good of human happiness or pleasure (utilitarianism), some only to consequences (consequentialism), and some only to nonmoral values and disvalues as determinants of right action. Other versions of proportionalism impose no such restrictions but admit all values—human and nonhuman, consequential and nonconsequential, moral and nonmoral—to consideration.[1] Given these and other divergences, the merits of different forms of proportionalism vary considerably, and the strongest case for proportionalism is the case for its strongest, most plausible version.

The version I still favor is the one proposed in an earlier work, *Christian Moral Reasoning* (CMR). "If we wish to be both consistent and true to our Christian heritage," CMR inquired, "what criterion of right and wrong should we adopt?"[2] After sorting through a mass of Christian moral reasoning, from New Testament times to the present, CMR replied: "If Christian moral reasoning is to be both consistent and true to its past, it must be based on the balance of values; value-maximization must be its logic and its law."[3]

Within its broad inquiry, CMR did not develop and defend this maxim as fully as its importance warrants and current discussion requires. Indeed, there has been no thorough, systematic exposition and defense of a proportionalist position in Christian ethics. The present study's purpose is to remedy this lack.

1

Exposition, here in chapter 1, will precede evaluation, in later chapters. Other Christian ethicians have endorsed quite similar forms of proportionalism,[4] but none has advanced the precise version here to be proposed and put to the test—the one I shall label VM (for Value-Maximization).

### VALUE-MAXIMIZATION (VM)

In first approximation, VM may be formulated as follows: *Within a prospective, objective focus, and in the sense thus specified, an action is right if and only if it promises to maximize value as fully, or nearly as fully, as any alternative action, with no restriction on the kind of value concerned, whether human or nonhuman, moral or nonmoral, consequential or nonconsequential.* Explication of this norm can proceed in stages. After the present chapter's account, further light will come from the next chapter's answers to objections and later chapters' comparisons with alternative viewpoints. Not everything can be said at once, or needs to be. Let me start with a first, fundamental point of clarification, then move through this thumbnail formulation, term by term.

### Criterion, Not Method

VM may be viewed as a *norm*, directing conduct, or as a *criterion*, defining right action; but it is not a method or procedure. The distinction between a norm or criterion, on the one hand, and a method or procedure, on the other, is often noted but as often ignored, with unfortunate consequences. I shall therefore need to dwell on it.

Prescinding from the complex philosophical discussion of criteria, suffice it to say that a criterion of X, as here understood, is constitutive of X and not an external clue or symptom; and that what counts as a criterion and what as a mere symptom is determined by the meaning of X, and specifically by the term's truth-conditions. Thus the customary criterion of rain, as determined by the customary use of *rain*, is drops of water falling from clouds, and not thunder or lightning; for these latter do not pertain to the term's truth-conditions: there may be thunder and lightning without rain, and there may be rain without thunder or lightning, but not without drops of water falling from clouds. That is what rain consists in.[5]

Moral terms like *right* and *wrong* differ importantly from a descriptive term like *rain*. No one can discover whether it has rained, or will rain, simply by examining the term *rain* and distinguishing criteria from symptoms. But a person can learn what rain consists in—namely, drops of water falling from clouds—by unpacking the meaning of *rain*. This general knowledge is decisive for particular inquiries. Determining what counts as rain, it determines what evidence and reasoning are probative or even pertinent in establishing the occurrence of rain. The like does not hold for right and wrong. Not only can no one discover whether a given course of action is right or wrong simply by analyzing the word *right* or *wrong*; neither can anyone discover what right and wrong consist in by unpacking these terms. No constant standard of right and wrong exists, language-wide, by which individual cases might be decided. Neither does such a criterion appear, for all times, places, and topics, in Christian moral discourse. Hence the criterial question, as decisive in Christian ethics as it is elsewhere, must take the form: What criterion *should* establish the meaning of *right* and *wrong* for Christians?

At this point I might suggest why moral criteria do not exhaust the truth conditions of moral terms,[6] why the truth conditions of moral terms do not exhaust their meanings,[7] and why, accordingly, people need not talk at cross purposes, or engage in constant equivocation, when, despite their differing criteria, they employ the same moral expressions. However, the only point I wish to stress here is that criteria, whether moral or other, are not methods, in any sense known to Webster (e.g., "a systematic procedure, technique, or mode of inquiry").

Yet criteria are decisive for method.

*What* we seek determines *how* we seek. For microbes I use a microscope and focus on a slide. For birds I use binoculars and look, say, in the trees. For stars I use a telescope and wait till dark. For sea shells I patrol the seashore and use my own two eyes. The kind of thing I seek determines the place, the time, the instrument, the procedure. And so it is when people investigate the "right" thing to do. Their common terminology should not deceive us. If their criteria differ, so does the object of their search, and with it the appropriate procedures.[8]

Note the singular "object" and the plural "procedures." Rain may be a single thing (drops of water falling from clouds), but the methods and clues for determining its occurrence—past, present, or future—are many (aches in the joints, satellite photos, weather reports, patter on the roof, wet sidewalks, distant thunder, meteorological calculations, etc.). So it is for right and wrong. A single valid criterion may define right and wrong, but the clues that correlate with the criterion, and the corresponding methods of discerning right and wrong, may vary widely. Thus, VM leaves room for head and heart, custom and explicit thought, reasoning and imagination, calculation and intuition, Scripture and tradition, authority and private judgment, rule-following and case-by-case assessment, discernment of spirits and value-tables, imitation of Christ and personal directives from God. Not all methods and procedures are compatible with VM—for example, consulting *Mein Kampf* as a moral oracle is not—but a great many are.[9]

Norms, too—the Golden Rule, Kant's Categorical Imperative, the Ten Commandments—are not methods. Thus, whether VM be termed a criterion (defining right action) or a norm (directing conduct), it is important to distinguish it not only from a clue or symptom, but also and especially from a procedure, "structure of moral reasoning,"[10] or "method for making moral judgments."[11]

Norms and methods are easily confused, since they are closely related.[12] People's methods may reveal their criteria or norms, and their criteria or norms largely determine what methods are appropriate. Given the norm of utility, utilitarian calculations may be appropriate. Given the norm of value-maximization, value-balancing may be appropriate. It need not be suitable, however, for every issue or on every occasion; and the balancing may take varied forms, as do utilitarian calculations.

If the distinction between criterion and method, norm and procedure, is not kept in view, as it often is not, unsound criticisms are likely to result. A criterion may be criticized in ways that apply only to a method.[13] Or a single criterion of right and wrong may be mistaken for a single, invariant method of determining right and wrong, and may therefore be rejected.[14] Or discussion of a criterion may be faulted for slighting various procedural issues.

Proportionalism, it has been objected (in reference to positions like VM), "is all prudence with little emphasis on the joy and enthusiasm of being in love with God—or anyone else, for that matter. It resolves tensions of competing loyalties rather than exulting in such tensions. It downplays symbolism, art, wonder, music, and poetry."[15] How so? What does proportionalism play up while playing down symbolism, art, wonder, and the like? No doubt it is thought to emphasize reason, order, and careful calculation—in a word, "prudence." But it does not. It is not that kind of theory.

Certainly VM is not. It may be, for example, that much love of God with little value-calculation permits surer discernment of right and wrong than does much value-calculation with little love of God; but that does not signify that right conduct consists in loving God. Neither does right conduct consist in the careful calculation of values. The path is not the destination; the seeking is not the thing sought. What *makes* action right or wrong? What does the rightness of conduct *consist in*? This question is the issue that VM addresses.

## Prospective Focus

The issue must be stated more precisely than merely in terms of actions' "rightness," for ethical terms like *right* and *wrong* have a quicksilver quality. Their meanings vary more, for example, with temporal perspective than do those of most physical expressions. The definition of *snow* is unaffected by the fact that the snow is reported or predicted; the word retains the same sense in both backward-looking and forward-looking contexts. The like does not hold, however, for terms such as *right* and *wrong*; nor should it. Different settings call for different senses, suited to the needs of the occasion.

To the retrospective query, "Was that the right thing to do?" the answer may be: "No, look what happened." To the prospective question, "Should I do it?" there can be no such reply. Not only do the action and its consequences lie in the future. Not only are they impossible to determine fully in advance. But depending on the nature and reality of freedom, human and divine, there may be no matter of fact as to what *will* occur. "If determinism is not true (i.e., persons have free choice) there simply is no such thing as 'the totality of what will happen if one decides in a certain way.'"[16] At the very least, a norm which claims to be Christian must allow the possibility that determinism is not true, for God or for us. So VM, which looks to the future, does not say, "Those actions are right or wrong which *did or did not* maximize value,"[17] or "Those actions are right or wrong which *will or will not* maximize value," but "Those actions are right or wrong which do or do not *promise to* maximize value."

In this perspective, probabilities are important. Assessing individual values and disvalues of a contemplated course of action, one must note not only their specific kind and extent but also the likelihood that they will be realized by the action.[18]

Granted, likelihood is problematic. As Max Black has remarked: "Certainly we use probability notions successfully, and sometimes with great accuracy (as in actuarial forecasts), but there is no general agreement on the *analysis* (or definition) of probability."[19] There is no agreement on the analysis of physical probability, nor of human probability, nor of whether the latter reduces to the former.

And yet, some physical and human transactions are indeed more likely than others. If, for instance, I look out my window here in St. Louis, I am more likely to see people walking across Grand Boulevard than crawling across on their hands and knees, or leaping all six lanes in a single bound. I am more likely to see cars going forward than backward; more likely to see snow falling in January than in May. Thus, despite the lack of theoretical consensus, VM can legitimately suppose a probabilistic understanding of the term *promise*.

It might seem that VM, with its prospective focus, leaves out not only some varieties of retrospective judgment but also the kind of abstract, atemporal questions—"Is euthanasia wrong?" "Is lying ever permissible?" "May the starving take what they need?"—that predominate in ethical inquiry; and it might appear that the norm's importance is thereby much reduced. On the contrary, such queries highlight the norm's significance. Like ethics generally, they serve a practical purpose; they are meant to guide conduct. But past conduct cannot be guided; only prospective action can be. So what does such guidance require? How are right and wrong most appropriately conceived within a prospective perspective? This focused query sharpens considerations that more abstract discussions often leave unclear. It calls attention, for example, to the distinction between actual and probable outcomes. It also directs attention to several important respects in which a prospective focus typically needs to be "objective."

### Objective Focus

Looking forward to what is likely should not be confused with judging what *looks* likely, for then the query would arise: looks likely to whom? Omniscient observers? Present-day humans, collectively considered? Whoever the agent happens to be, whether adult, adolescent, or child?

The first perspective, VM's, is objectively prospective; the second is subjectively prospective.

To illustrate, consider the decision to drop the atomic bomb on Japan. Subjectively, Truman and his advisers saw no other way to prevent a bloodbath far worse than the recent one on Iwo Jima. Objectively, we now know they were mistaken. From internal Japanese accounts we know, for example, that abandoning the demand for unconditional surrender was definitely worth a try before resorting to atomic arm-twisting. Thus, what looked the most promising course of action was not in fact the most promising. In VM's objective sense, it did not promise to maximize value.

A decision based on misinformation might qualify as "objectively right" in C. I. Lewis's acceptation: "An act is objectively right if, on all the data open to him when he must decide, the doer believes that the consequences of it will be good, or better than any alternative, *and* this expectation is a *justified* belief."[20] Prospective moral judgment generally reveals, and requires, a more fully objective sense of *right* and *wrong* than the one Lewis indicates. What we wish to know is whether a contemplated act is right in view of the actual facts of the case: we wish to know, for example, whether dropping the atomic bomb really is the only way to shorten the war. Hence VM abstracts from how good our reasons are or how justified our beliefs appear. For a fully objective judgment, the facts are what matter, not our limited, fallible beliefs about the facts.

Attention to the needs of prospective agents dictates that VM's focus be objective in three further respects. First, VM prescinds from how people *believe* they should act, and considers how *in fact* they should act. As Richard Swinburne remarks:

> Brutus may have thought it right to kill Caesar, and for that reason we may judge him an honourable man who acted in accordance with the dictates of his conscience. In so far as this latter, that he followed his conscience, is the only criterion for the rightness of his action, you and I may agree that he did what he ought to have done. If we do say this, we are using "ought" in a subjective sense. We may however go on to discuss whether in fact, whatever Brutus' own view on the matter, he ought to have killed Caesar. You being pacifist may say that he ought not to have done; I may say that he ought. Our disagreement

is about whether he did what he ought to have done in an objective sense.[21]

It is in this objective sense that VM's criterion of "right" and "wrong" should be understood.

Second, what holds for acts holds also for values. As thinking an act right does not make it right, so thinking something good does not make it good. Likewise, as desiring an act does not make it right, so desiring a thing does not make it good. So saying, I wish to distance myself not only from relativistic views, but also from relational views of the kind enshrined in Thomistic tradition: "'Good,' in the widest sense in which it is applied to human actions and their principles, refers to anything a person can in any way desire. 'Good is any object of any interest.'"[22] Value is not—at least not as VM understands it. Treachery, for instance, is not a value, no matter how highly the Sawi of New Guinea may have prized it.[23]

It may be, as Thomas Nagel suggests, that "most of the apparent reasons [to do or want something] that initially present themselves to us are intimately connected with interests and desires, our own or those of others, and often with experiential satisfaction."[24] Aesthetic perfection, aimed at by the artist, is intimately connected—causally—with human interests and desires, and may bring great satisfaction. Likewise, treachery is intimately connected—causally—with human interests and desires, and may bring great satisfaction (as it did to the Sawi when told of Judas's masterpiece). But being desired or approved does not make the artistic accomplishment good and the treachery bad; being desired or approved does not make enjoyment of the treachery bad and enjoyment of the artistic accomplishment good. Such discriminations, prescinding from interests, desires, or personal evaluations, further exemplify the sense in which VM's perspective is objective.[25]

Finally, the norm also abstracts from the agent's motive or intention. Motive or intention is typically decisive for a judgment of culpability, but typically irrelevant for a judgment of what should be done. Should I enlist? Should we marry? Should they block the abortion clinic? Such queries make no mention of motive or intention, nor need they. If the action is right, and is done for the reasons that make it right, right motive or intention is assured. Prospective judgment can safely center on whether the action itself—enlisting, marrying, blocking the clinic—is the right thing to do; it need not and should not confuse this objective question with the subjective question of how well the agent's inner dispositions match the goodness of the act. So VM, looking to the future, is objective in this further sense; it prescinds from motive or intention.[26]

It prescinds from actual motive, and it prescinds from prospective motive. As an agent may have a bad motive in doing the right thing, so, in advance, an agent may find the right thing appealing for a bad reason. Or, as an agent may have a good motive in doing the wrong thing, so, in advance, an agent may find the wrong thing appealing for a good reason (e.g., may find euthanasia attractive as a remedy for suffering). To determine the rightness or wrongness of the prospective action, a person must therefore abstract from motive, possible as well as actual. The question "What should I do?" need not and should not be complicated by the query "How should I be motivated?"

Intention, as well as motivation, drops from consideration within VM's prospective focus. For contrast, consider the following explication (not endorsement) of a traditional viewpoint.

Suppose a surgeon is about to perform a hysterectomy on a pregnant woman. He is scrupulous and asks himself how he can discover whether he actually only permits and does not intend this operation to result in the child's death. He may say to himself: "I would not be prepared to carry out the operation if it were possible to save the mother's life without acting in a manner which brings about the child's death." Unfortunately this statement, though sincere, leaves his question open. Also, a surgeon who carries out a craniotomy may say to himself: "I would not be prepared to do so, if it were possible to save the mother without the further consequence of the child's death." And there is agreement at least among traditional theologians that this latter surgeon *intends* to kill the child as a necessary means to saving the mother. In the case of the hysterectomy, the mother's survival and the child's death are, so to speak, *collateral* effects of the operation. Thus our scrupulous surgeon can be reassured that he does not intend to kill the child as a means to an end because in the given circumstances he is factually unable to do so. At the same time he is sure that he does not intend to kill the child as an end, because he would not be ready to carry out the operation if he only knew how to save the mother without putting the child to death. Thus he has established two premises which allow him to draw the conclusion that in fact he does only permit this operation to result in the death of the child.[27]

Poor man! How confusingly complex such reasoning appears, even when neatly laid out. And concern for his true subjectivity, if taken seriously, might call for the services of a psychiatrist. The surgeon's decision would be greatly simplified if he could ignore the complexities of his intentionality, actual or possible, and center on the act to be performed. And he can. Whatever the objective norm of right conduct may be, if he makes it his own and chooses accordingly, his will is rightly ordered. VM is for people's genuine needs, within a prospective focus.

The four senses I have indicated for the word *objective* need to be distinguished from a fifth. "Objective" often means: "expressing or involving the use of facts without distortion by personal feelings or prejudices." It stakes a claim to superior cognitive status. Such is not the meaning stated or implied at any point in the preceding exposition. "Subjective" features such as those I have excluded from consideration—estimates of outcome, judgments of rightness, assessments of value and disvalue, motive, intention—can be as objectively considered as any other features, and often should be (for instance in judgments of culpability). They just do not fall within VM's focus.

### Action

To explicate this term I shall not proffer any dubious "theory of action." Still, what will count as an "action"? Roughly: any response to the moral query, "What should I (we, you, they, she, he) do?" Accordingly, the term's scope needs both narrowing and broadening.

First, the narrowing. Since people do not deliberate about the morality of actions that are wrong by definition, or by inclusion of a wrong intention, such actions drop from consideration. People may ask, "Should I kill this man?" or "Should I say these disrespectful-sounding words about God?" but it would make no sense for them to inquire, "Should I murder this man?" or "Should I blaspheme?" If the "should" has a moral sense, the answer is self-evident. Dispositions or attitudes—though sometimes called "actions"—likewise fall outside VM's ambit (save perhaps as values counting for or against an action). Thus VM does not apply to "acts" such as "love and honor and pity and pride and compassion and sacrifice."[28]

Broadening is also required; for prospective, objective moral inquiry may take the form, "Should I or should I *not* do X?" Doing X counts as an answer, and so does not doing X. More specifically, the question may be: "Should I respond to this attack or keep quiet?"; "Should I accept this job offer or stay where I am?" "Keeping quiet" or "staying where I am" sounds more like inaction than action; yet it answers the question, "What should I do?" Keeping quiet or staying put may be the preferable "course of action" for me. It is in this broad sense that VM's reference to "action" should be understood.[29]

The term also embraces composite, comprehensive deeds. If driving a nail is viewed as a paradigmatic action, building a house may appear no action but a congeries of actions. Yet a person is more likely to ask "Should I build this house?" than "Should I drive this nail?" VM is meant for the questions people actually ask. Accordingly, it extends not only to "Should I build this house?" but also to "Should I be a carpenter?" or "Should I live in Chicago?" Being a carpenter or living in Chicago may sound strange as an "action," but less strange as a "course of action," and not strange at all as an answer to the question "What should I do?" In any case, such is the term's intended sense; in VM, it has this further breadth.

## Right and Wrong

Like many other moral terms, *right* and *wrong* have both conditional and unconditional senses.[30] Without contradiction a person may say that it is right to keep promises, yet right for X to break her promise, given the circumstances. In VM, *right* has the latter, absolute sense. The norm indicates what makes actions right, all things considered.

Talk of "making actions right" calls for further distinctions. VM might be worded to determine what, if anything, is *the* right thing to do, or what is simply *a* right thing to do; or it might determine both, more comprehensively. It might say, as VM does: An action is right if and only if it promises to maximize value as fully, or nearly as fully, as any alternative action. If an action is the only one that satisfies this description, it is the right thing to do; if it is one of two or more that satisfy the description, it is a right thing to do; if it is one of the many that do not satisfy the description, it is a wrong thing to do.

This comprehensive version of the norm is preferable, partly because it is broader and partly because, being broader, it conforms better to the typical questions we pose prospectively. "What should I do?", we ask, or, "What should we do?" Sometimes the answer may be: "Since it promises to maximize value notably, this one action is the right one; it is what you should do." Sometimes the answer may be: "There is no single thing you should do; but in view of their roughly equal value-prospects, you would act rightly if you did x or y or z. Otherwise you would act wrongly."

So understood, VM occupies a middle ground. In comparison with morality in general, the norm is narrow: it does not encompass subjective morality as well as objective. Yet in comparison with objective duty, obligation, precept, or counsel, the norm's coverage is broad. A single right thing to do coincides, roughly, with duty, obligation, and precept; plural right things to do coincide with the permissible, including whatever is better but not required (since it is not notably better than all alternatives). VM leaves some room for supererogation—that is, for going beyond the call of strict duty—but less room than traditional precept ethics does, which, stating obligation generally, abstractly, and minimalistically, relegates important areas of conduct to the realm of mere "counsel."

Just how much leeway VM leaves depends on how elastically one reads the words "or nearly as fully." Read the phrase tightly, and VM will appear too demanding. Read it more loosely, and VM will appear more reasonable—especially if one recalls that obligations may be slight. Here, then, is the key to interpretation. Rather than read the phrase tightly or loosely, then decide whether VM is satisfactory, take the opposite tack: decide where at least minimal obligation begins, then read the phrase accordingly.

Where, then, does the border lie? At precisely what point does the disparity between an act and its rivals become so great that the act becomes morally mandatory? To such a query no answer is possible, or necessary. If different criteria applied on both sides of the divide between required and not required, it might be possible to trace a definite border. However, they do not; and at no precise point along the continuum from negligible to enormous value-imbalance has any authority, human or divine, posted the advisory: "You are now leaving the land of counsel—of the preferable or better—and entering the realm of precept, duty, and obligation." Besides, such a posting would be superfluous. All we need to know is that a contemplated action is superior to alternatives, and how notably.[31]

## Values and Their Range

My chief reason for preferring the word-pair *value* and *disvalue* over *good* and *evil* is that *evil* too readily suggests just moral evil, whereas VM is broader. A disvalue may be the mere absence of some good (e.g., artistic ability), or the privation of "due" good (e.g., health), or a positive, non-privative evil (e.g., physical pain). Similarly, three kinds of value might be distinguished: the mere absence of positive evil (e.g., pain); "due" good (e.g., health); and any positive good that is not "due" (e.g., artistic ability). Though all of these values and disvalues count for or against prospective conduct, they do not count doubly or redundantly (e.g., the presence of health plus the absence of sickness; the presence of knowledge plus the absence of ignorance).

Values and disvalues would count twice if extrinsic worth weighed in the balance along with intrinsic. For example, if an action was likely to foster love between a couple, and that love was likely to increase their happiness, both the love and the happiness might count in favor of the action; but if both the intrinsic and the extrinsic worth of the love counted in favor of the action, then the greater happiness would count twice—once in itself and once as a consequence of the greater love. If consistently extended, such doubling might balance out; all alternatives might gain proportionately, and the verdicts between them might be unaffected. Preferable options might still be preferable; tied options might still be tied. However, I cannot see that this result is guaranteed. The issue is complex and requires closer scrutiny than *CMR* accorded it.

Here I shall not seek a solution, since, whatever the verdict, there is no need to exclude extrinsic or instrumental values from the understanding of VM. The couple's love counts, and so does their prospective happiness. It is just needful to note how they count—nonredundantly. More serious are other kinds of restrictions, commonly proposed, which VM explicitly resists.

One is consequentialist. Though intrinsic value is more discernible in a whole dance than in a single step, or in a whole concerto than in a single bow-stroke, even in these more comprehensive actions some theorists would distinguish between the actions and the values they entail. Some actions may be full of value, they would say, as a sponge may be full of water; but squeeze the sponge hard enough and the sponge alone remains, bone-dry. Extract every last drop of aesthetic, emotional, intellectual, social, religious, physical, or psychological value, and the action alone remains, devoid of intrinsic worth. This process, if carried through completely for all actions, would show that their value lies solely in their consequences.

The closer one examines this abstractive enterprise, the less feasible and realistic it appears.[32] Besides, why bother? Even if all actions, or all actions as envisaged by prospective agents, were intrinsically value-free, VM would not be falsified; there just would be no values of the kind it allows for but does not require. By contrast, if even a single prospective action harbored a trace of intrinsic value, a strictly consequentialist version of the norm would be falsified. So VM has good reason for its amplitude; it takes account of values intrinsic to actions as well as of those likely to result from the actions. Accordingly, it makes little difference where the line is drawn, in general or in particular cases, between actions and their consequences. The verdicts come out the same.

Similar remarks apply to moral and nonmoral values. The attempt might be made to reduce all moral values to nonmoral, so as to define right action uniquely in terms of nonmoral values. For example, the value of justice might be equated with the value of its consequences. Or, as a mere state of affairs, it might be denied classification as "moral." With regard to the irreducibly, incontestably moral value of choices and attitudes, it might be argued that these are impervious to outside influence. Nothing we do or say can affect another person morally. Indeed, nothing we do or say can affect our own future morality.

Overall, these stratagems look both desperate and dubious.[33] And again, why go to all this trouble? Even if there were no irreducibly moral values, or none relevant to value-maximization, VM would not be falsified; there just would be no values of the kind it allows for but does not require. By contrast, if even one such value escaped elimination, a more restricted version of VM, citing only nonmoral values, would be falsified. So again, VM has good reason for its nonrestrictive range. I shall return to this theme in chapter 8.

## Alternatives

"Under what conditions is one action an 'alternative' to another?" asks Lars Bergström. "And what should be meant by 'the alternatives' to a given action?"[34] In order to provide at least a partial answer, he introduces the notion of an "alternative-set," as follows:

> DEFINITION: The set $A$ is an *alternative-set* if, and only if, (i) every member of $A$ is a particular action, (ii) $A$ has at least two different members, the members of $A$ are (iii) agent-identical, (iv) time-identical, (v) performable, (vi) incompatible in pairs, and (vii) jointly exhaustive.[35]

A minimal set of this kind would consist of contradictory alternatives (e.g., living in St. Louis and not living in St. Louis). A maximal set would include countless contraries (e.g., living, at a given time, in St. Louis or Omaha or Dallas or London or Rome). No set would include combinations of members (e.g., living in Omaha and in Dallas), since all members are incompatible in pairs. And no set would include versions or variations of any member differing from it only in their greater specificity (e.g., living on Lindell Boulevard in St. Louis), since their inclusion would violate the same stipulation, that members be incompatible in pairs.

A maximal set, abstractly stated, may exhaust all possibilities at its level of generality, and thereby satisfy condition vii; but no such set exhausts all possibilities, at all levels. One set may consist of living in the U.S. or Peru or China or. . . ; another of living in Missouri or Alaska or Texas or. . . ; another of living in St. Louis or Kansas City or Independence or. . . ; another of living on Lindell Boulevard or Grand Avenue or Manchester Road or. . . ; and so on, down to the street address, the floor, the precise apartment.

The possibility of specifying alternatives in ever greater detail poses a problem for VM. Relative to its contradictory, an action is right, according to VM, if and only if it promises to maximize value as fully or nearly as fully as its contradictory. Relative to contraries, an action is right if and only if it promises to maximize value as fully or nearly as fully as any contrary. However, in some of its more specific versions an action may satisfy these conditions, and in others it may not. The same may hold true at each new level of greater specificity. How, then, can an alternative be judged unless spelled out in ultimate detail—that is, more fully than any alternative ever actually is?

Consider the same illustration. It may be a good idea to live in the U.S.—but not if that means living in the Badlands. It may be a good idea to live in St. Louis—but not if that means living underneath an overpass. It may be a good idea to live on Lindell Boulevard—but not if that means living in this shack or that expensive mansion. It may be a good idea to live in a given house—but not if that means sharing it with ten other people or with an eccentric uncle. And so forth.

How fully must an action be stated before a verdict becomes possible? Does the answer differ from action to action and from situation to situation? Can an action ever be stated fully enough to permit a verdict? Can't we always imagine some specific version that negates an apparently favorable verdict? Is an answer ever possible short of the full concreteness of an action as actually performed? If nothing less than full concreteness will suffice, VM may still be valid, but can it be applied? Is it ever usable?

Let us consider, realistically, how we reach decisions. When, for example, we opt for a given apartment, we take many things for granted—that we will furnish it, that we will not share it with several other families, that we will not pay ten times the reasonable rent, and so forth. Thus, when we ask "Should we live in this apartment?", the implicit sense of the query is this: Are there reasonable ways of carrying out this decision which are preferable to reasonable ways of carrying out alternative decisions? To this query the answer may be positive, even though the verdict on some unimagined perversion of the general proposal would have to be negative.

The problem thus resolved is partly practical, partly theoretical. For fully particular actions, no theoretical problem would arise. However, the actions VM judges are never fully particular. Being prospective, not actual, they derive their specificity from the fullness with which they are stated in the "should" questions VM answers; and these questions always fall far short of full particularity. Nonetheless, VM can retain its validity if the "action" it refers to is understood to be any reasonable version (that is, any reasonably value-maximizing version) of a more abstractly stated course of action that determines the alternative-set.

Practically, a course of action can be stated with sufficient precision to permit a judgment on reasonable versions, globally considered, in relation to the action's alternative-set. There is no need to envisage all possible aberrations (e.g., removing the apartment's radiators, replacing the carpets with pebbles, piping in rock music night and day). There is no need, and no possibility: in "Should I (we, they, she, he, you) do x?" x is never stated in full detail. VM is meant to answer the questions people can and do ask.

### Value-Maximization

The phrase "maximize value" is shorthand. An action might promise more value than any alternative and still not be the right thing to do. Indeed, it might be a wrong thing to do. Right action promises not merely to maximize value but to maximize it *relative to disvalue*. Either it promises to maximize value over disvalue or, where no favorable outcome looks possible, it promises to minimize disvalue over value.

The words "or nearly as fully" add a further refinement. If, in some option, the proportion of value to disvalue is superior to that in any alternative, that is the better thing to do; if it is notably superior, that is the obligatory thing to do; and if the difference is great enough, the obligation is serious. It may be, however, that no prospective course of action is notably superior to all others; there may be a tie or near-tie.[36] In that case, no course of action merits endorsement as *the* right thing to do.

A detailed, fully specific response to the question "What should I do?" would never merit such endorsement, since such a response would not indicate *the* right thing to do. Thus, relative to all alternatives, repaying a debt may be the only right thing to do—but repaying it in full, in two installments, in person, in cash, at 9:35 a.m. next Thursday and 2:13 p.m. on Friday, with so much in the first installment and so much in the second, using these or those words, standing at this or that spot, and so forth, is not. No equally specific version of the action would be.

Whereas there may be just one right thing to do within a given maximal set of alternatives, there is always more than one wrong thing to do. For instance, given my abilities, inclinations, circumstances, and opportunities, there may be just one thing I should do with my life: I should be a concert pianist. But there are many things I should not do with my life (sell junk bonds, vegetate, join the Foreign Legion, create computer viruses, offer my services as a hired gun). Thus right and wrong are not symmetrical. In a maximal alternative-set, there is never just one option, abstract or concrete, which is *the* wrong thing to do, whereas there may be just one option which is *the* right thing to do in comparison with all rival, incompatible alternatives.

According to VM, there is never more than one such option. Hence, in a strong sense, there can be no moral dilemmas. We may encounter dilemmas of value (when unable to avoid disvalue whichever alternative we choose), dilemmas of choice (when unable to decide between equally legitimate alternatives), and dilemmas of judgment (when unable to determine which alternative, if any, is the right one to choose). But in no instance need we fear being obliged to perform incompatible actions. No more than one rival course of action is ever *the* right thing to do.[37]

Enough details for now; it is time to step back and take a larger view.

## OVERVIEW

Synoptically, VM may be gotten in clear focus by contrasting it, point by point, with the following characterization:

> According to the simplest consequentialist theory of moral reasoning the moral good or evil of human acts is determined by the results (consequences) of these acts . . . If one can add up the good results expected of each possible course of action and subtract in each case the expected bad results from the good, then according to the simplest form of consequentialism the morally right choice is that alternative which will yield the greatest net good—or, in an unfavorable situation the least net harm.[38]

VM differs from this simple view in six respects. First, it more carefully distinguishes between a theory of moral reasoning and a theory of right conduct. Second, it does not pose as the sole correct theory of moral conduct; it assesses acts prospectively not retrospectively, and objectively not subjectively (e.g., by motive and intention). Third, it does not consider only the consequences of acts; the acts themselves weigh in the balance. Fourth, it does not assess what action *will* yield the greatest net good, but what action *promises* to. Fifth, it does not require that the best alternative be "the morally right choice"; it may just be preferable. Sixth, it does not specify any such procedure as this adding and subtracting, nor limit moral reasoning to any single procedure. Value-maximization should not be confused with value-calculation. The next chapter will have occasion to examine this difference more closely.

The plan of what follows, from here to the end, is simple. Having unpacked VM, I shall now assess the norm's philosophical and theological validity, in itself (chaps. 2 and 3) and in comparison with alternative viewpoints (chaps. 4 to 10); then I shall assess the norm's significance, in itself and in comparison with alternative perspectives and concerns (chap. 11). Briefly: Is the norm sound? Is it important? Answers for VM can serve as answers for proportionalism generally, if, as I hope to show, VM enunciates the most plausible form of proportionalism.

# 2

# A Major Objection

It would be tedious to answer all actual and possible objections to VM. Some will receive attention in subsequent chapters; others I can let the reader resolve, in the light of explanations offered in this study or elsewhere.[1] One set, however, whose importance later chapters will attest, I shall consider here at the start.

## THE FINNIS-GRISEZ DILEMMA

Repeatedly and at length, John Finnis, Germain Grisez, and like-minded thinkers have urged a pair of objections which, on examination, form a dilemma on whose horns they believe proportionalism (which they sometimes call "consequentialism") is hopelessly impaled. The painful alternatives are these: if the goods to be considered are disparate, they cannot be compared; if they are not disparate, there can be no choice between them but the greater good, if seen as such, will be chosen necessarily.[2] "My criticism of consequentialism," writes Grisez, "is that it is inconsistent to hold both that the goods involved in various alternatives are commensurable and that a person can deliberately adopt an alternative which promises a lesser good than the alternative which ought to have been adopted."[3]

Grisez and fellow critics believe that basic human goods are in fact too dissimilar for evaluative comparison but that even if they were wrong on this point, the error would provide no comfort for proportionalists: they would still be impaled on the dilemma's other horn. The greater good would be irresistible;[4] thus a dictum like VM would serve no purpose. What use is a norm that no one can knowingly violate? In my view, neither horn of this dilemma is sharp enough to damage proportionalism.

As a first indication of my reasons, consider a tragic case.[5] A prominent European philosopher, happily married for years, is strongly attracted to a younger woman. If the appeal were weaker, there would be no temptation. If the appeal were to a greater, higher good, there would be no temptation. But such is not the man's situation. He is conscious, perforce, of his loving wife, of their long and trusting relationship, of the great good he would be betraying and the evil infidelity would represent. But the young lady is so charming and vivacious, her admiration so gratifying, the newness of the relationship so invigorating, the promise of pleasure so enticing, that the lesser good—the one he recognizes as lesser—is the one he chooses, and he regards himself as a monster ever after.

Here, I suggest, the good betrayed and the good preferred, though disparate, are comparable as greater and lesser; they are commensurable. Nonetheless, the lesser good, being so attractive, can be chosen, and it is. Finnis and Grisez would disagree on both counts. Disparate goods cannot be compared as greater or lesser. If they could be compared, a lesser good, recognized as such, could not be preferred; the greater good would be chosen of necessity. Hence proportionalists' dilemma.

## No Choice

The claim of necessity has one likely source whose influence may be decisive. Conflate the desirable and the desired—define the good, subjectively, as "anything a person can in any way desire"—and this horn of the dilemma looks sharp. Whatever a person finds attractive—say, revenge—is ipso facto good. Whatever a person finds more attractive is ipso facto better. Perceived value and felt attraction cannot conflict.[6] However, in the objective sense of *value* prescribed by chapter 1, perceived value and felt attraction can indeed conflict, and often do.

Suppose that five men are suffering from migraines. Suppose that one of them has the choice of protracting his own pain and relieving the others' or of relieving his own pain and protracting theirs. The competing evils are comparable, and it is clear that five migraines are a greater evil than one. So does the sufferer feel an overwhelming inclination to relieve the others' agony and prolong his own? Is he compelled to do the altruistic thing?[7]

Consider a real-life case:

As his huge construction crane began to tip, its too-massive load swinging out of control nearly twenty stories up, Tom O'Brien tensed to leap through his cabin door to safety. Every nerve in his body screamed: *Jump!* But an image flashed before his mind of shattered buildings avalanching into the street, crushing pedestrians, flattening autos and buses, killing scores of people. By staying at the controls, he might, just might, be able to prevent such carnage. And he did. When the crane's boom, cab, and monster tractor-treads followed the 53,000-pound load into the excavation where O'Brien had managed to guide it, he was the only person hurt.[8]

O'Brien was a hero. Not everyone would have acted as he did. Despite the risk to others—many others—another man might have chosen to save his own skin. His freedom would not have been cancelled by the realization that death or injury to many was a greater evil than death or injury to one. When his nerves, too, screamed "Jump!" he could have obeyed their urging.

Grisez anticipates this rejoinder. "Someone might object that one can know what will produce the greater good for everyone concerned, but choose a lesser good which happens to be a greater good for oneself."[9] Such a person, he replies, would be an egoist; and for an egoist, personal good and the good of others are not commensurable. "If the supposedly greater good does not promise an egoist every benefit for himself or herself which an alternative promises, then the egoist can choose the so-called lesser good, because, at least for the egoist, one's own good and the good of others are not commensurable."[10] Though the good of thousands were at stake, the egoist would perceive it as neither a greater nor a lesser good than his own, but as a basically different kind of good: other people's good.

The key move in this response is to assume that anyone who jumped, knowing the threat to others, would ipso facto be an "egoist." With this label attached, it becomes plausible to suggest that the person wears egoistic blinkers. He can have no inkling that others have an equal claim to life or that sacrificing himself might be the better thing to do. Any such comparison becomes impossible.

For this response to work, the population must be sharply divided. There can be no halfway altruists or mitigated egoists, capable of comparing their good with others' but sometimes tempted to prefer their own lesser good. An egoist may choose altruistically once, twice, ten times, but he does not gradually become an altruist. A gradual transition would entail gradually becoming aware of others' good as comparable to one's own while still being capable of egoistic choices. And that, for Grisez, is impossible.

This sharp dichotomy, required by Grisez's argument, sounds unrealistic.[11] Even were the argument more plausible, the truth of its conclusion would still need to be shown; a mere possibility does not incriminate VM. Besides, mine-thine options are not the only kind to consider.

A lesser good may have a stronger appeal not only because it is one's own, but also because it is immediate. Thus C. I. Lewis speaks of "one who yields to the solicitations of a present gratification, and in so doing, wittingly prejudices his own further interests."[12] The alcoholic knows what misery for himself and others taking a drink will occasion; the drug addict or cigarette smoker knows the habit's likely consequences. But the tug of the immediate, powerful craving may win out over a person's judgment of what is better.

Other instances of disparity between recognized value and felt attraction might be cited,[13] explaining the possibility of choosing a lesser good. "But how are such choices possible?" someone may ask. "How can a person prefer an alternative known to be less good?" The answer is that human beings are not constituted as the question assumes. They are not value-maximizing machines, automatically acting on VM's—or their own—value verdicts. They do not always do what they know to be best.[14] If it were otherwise—if felt attraction could never conflict with a person's judgment of what is better, or a person could never yield to such a conflicting attraction—it is difficult to see how sin (subjective wrongdoing) would be possible.

## Incommensurability

The second horn of the Finnis-Grisez dilemma looks sharper, given the right illustrations. How difficult it appears, for instance, to compare justice and truth and assign one the higher value.[15] Yet, notes Grisez:

> If a consequentialist admits that justice and theoretical truth, or any other two goods, are fundamental and incommensurable, then the consequentialist also admits that "greatest net good" is meaningless whenever one must choose between promoting and protecting or impeding and damaging these two goods in

some participations. For if these goods really are incommensurable, one might as well try to sum up the quantity of the size of this page, the quantity of the number nineteen, and the quantity of the mass of the moons as to try to calculate with such incommensurable goods.[16]

This argument contains a kernel of truth, one which *CMR* spells out more fully than Grisez does. Yet the truth it contains does not warrant Grisez's conclusion. Yes, values like justice and theoretical truth are incommensurable. No, comparisons of the kind VM requires are not therefore meaningless. For the values cited are general and abstract, whereas the needed comparisons are specific. Let me explain.

If asked whether justice is superior to truth, one's first response should be to request the sense of the query. Does it concern justice and truth in themselves, abstracting from their implications, or does it concern their total worth, extrinsic as well as intrinsic? If the former, does the query suppose the existence of an essence of justice and an essence of truth? If so, does it request comparison of only the essences, prescinding from all else? If it does, how are the essences to be understood and identified? If it does not, is the desired judgment to be quantitative, qualitative, or both? Should it, for example, consider only the highest forms of truth and justice and ignore the rest? Should it consider the highest actual forms or the highest possible? So doing, should it disregard how frequently or fully the various forms are realized? Instead of weighing only the most perfect varieties, should it assess the mean, or perhaps the average level, of the two values' realization?

Without these and further specifications, the requested comparison makes no sense. But such specifications are seldom furnished, so the comparisons seldom make clear sense. Context must come to the rescue, and often does not. Here is an important element of truth in Grisez's critique.

But what about his conclusion? Which of these possible senses should such queries have for VM's purposes? The moment we consider the question of application, we see that none of the variants is preferable, for all are equally useless. In a concrete case no abstract rating, whether extrinsic or intrinsic, quantitative or qualitative, existential or ideal, would provide any guidance.

Suppose, for example, that I am considering the best recipient for some extra cash. Esthetic values suggest the local art museum, truth values suggest my alma mater, and justice values suggest a social-justice lobby. All are worthy causes. But how effective is the lobby? How well run is the university? How badly strapped for funds is the museum? These and many other details are pertinent to my choice; yet on none of them can I receive any light from a rating on esthetic values, truth values, or justice values in general. Neither average nor median nor any other such calculation contributes even minimally to the requisite concrete estimate of the alternative choices.[17]

But suppose we do become more specific: What comparisons does VM call for, and are such comparisons possible? Matthew 10:31 furnishes an example from which much can be learned. Speaking to specific persons, Jesus says: "You are worth more than many sparrows." The standard objections to transcategory comparisons—the lack of any "principle" or "method," the absence of any "common scale" or "common denominator," the impossibility of "measuring," the reliance on mere "intuition"—would rule out this and similar gospel comparisons. So either the objections are invalid or the comparisons are invalid. I think it is clear which alternative we should prefer. We are, indeed, worth more than many sparrows. Accordingly, if the choice is between a person and a sparrow, preference goes to the person.

With dubious consistency,[18] some opponents of commensurability admit the possibility of such a value-comparison. "Realities higher in the chain of being are greater goods than inferior realities," write Finnis, Boyle, and Grisez; "persons are greater goods than animals; the gods are better than earthlings; the death of one's pet is a lesser evil than the death of one's child."[19] Furthermore, "it is clear that such non-moral and moral uses of 'greater good' and 'lesser evil' are meaningful. But none of them is the use the consequentialist needs."[20]

Why not? The few cases cited in confirmation illustrate that such uses may sometimes be irrelevant, but indicate no reason why the comparisons just admitted could not ground proportionalist verdicts. Whenever one such value or disvalue is pitted against another—for instance, the death of one's pet versus the death of one's child—the preference goes to the greater good or the lesser evil.[21] However, choices are seldom so simple; more complex comparisons are generally demanded. So let us reflect further on this gospel paradigm.

The stated relation between persons and sparrows is ordinal, and ordinal relations may be multiplied. Suppose A is more valuable than B, and C more valuable than D; then, regardless of how great the gap is between A and B or between C and D, and regardless of the unstated relation between A and C or A and D, in a choice between A + C on one side and B + D on the other, the verdict clearly goes to A + C. VM is applicable.

Since values are combined on both sides and their combined worth is then compared, one might here speak of "addition" and "sums." No measuring occurs, however; and no units are then added or subtracted. The question is: Are such adding and subtracting also needed?

Clearly something more than just ordinal comparison is necessary if VM is to be generally valid or applicable. Ordinal comparisons, simple or complex, suffice in many cases, but not in all. Suppose, for example, that A is more valuable than B, and D more valuable than C: is A + C more valuable than B + D? There is no way of telling unless we know *how much* more valuable A is than B and D is than C. It would suffice, for example, to know that A is much more valuable than B, and D only slightly more valuable than C, or that A is only slightly more valuable than B, and D much more valuable than C. In the first combination the decision would favor A + C, in the second B + D. Again, it would suffice to know that the difference between A and B is slightly less than that between D and C, or that the difference between D and C is slightly less than that between A and B: B + D would prevail in the first case, A + C in the second. In another variation, the differences between A and B and between D and C might be roughly equal, hence comparison would yield a tie between the two combinations. Or A and B, and D and C, might be roughly equal in value, in which case, too, A + C and B + D would be of roughly equal value.

Theoretically, all combinations can be covered this way. All we need is the additional notion of *degree* of difference, and this our paradigm provides. If one person is worth more than many sparrows (one translation says "hundreds"), then one person is worth *much more* than a single sparrow. Matthew 12:12 makes this further step explicit: "Surely a person is worth *far more* than a sheep!"

All combinations can *theoretically* be accounted for this way. In all there is a verdict, one way or the other, whether or not we can make it out. I therefore agree with Nicholas Rescher: "It is infeasible, in general, to reduce questions of preferability to matters of measurement."[22] Criterion and method—*preferability* and measurement—

should not be confused. But I do not agree that "where there is no measure, there can be no maximization either."[23] Again, method and criterion—measure and *maximization*—should not be confused. Pain has degrees, and can be maximized, but how can it be measured?

The distinction between theoretical adequacy and practical facility can be illustrated nicely by means of a comparison with tug-of-war. The direction the rope moves is not determined solely by the numbers pulling on each side, nor by the fact that some pull more strongly than others, but also by how much more strongly they pull. With this factor added, the result becomes determinate. The forces exerted and the differences between them are precise, and they yield a definite result. Yet onlookers may be in no position to predict the result with any sureness. Pit one sturdy adult against five weak five-year-olds and the outcome may be easy to predict. ("You are worth more than many sparrows.") Pit two strong adults against one, and there still may be no problem. But multiply and mix the contestants on both sides, and the outcome may be anybody's guess. Nonetheless, whether they are difficult or easy, right or wrong, the comparisons and predictions make sense.

Calling pullers "strong" and "weak" resembles calling values, or value-differences, "great" or "slight": in both instances, the terminology looks grossly inadequate for the task of calculation. Even if we had exact words, how could we make exact estimates, either of how much harder one person pulls or of how much more valuable one good appears? We may imagine attaching gauges to each of the pullers (without affecting the force of their pull) and connecting the gauges with a computer to sum up the forces on both sides. But this is fantasy. Onlookers have no instruments; instead, they must rely on knowledge, or surmises, of such factors as the number of contestants on each side; their weights; their strength; their grip; their condition (healthy or sick, tired or fresh, hungry or well-fed); their motivation; the tightness of their clothes; the treads or spikes on their shoes, or the lack thereof; the smoothness or roughness of the terrain. Even if all such details were known, person by person, how could the relative importance of each be exactly assessed, and how could forces be totaled, person by person, on each side?

How fantastically complex! How impossible to state the varied factors in terms of a common measure, or calculate the result with any precision! Yet even when tug-of-war comparisons prove most perplexing, the theory behind them makes good sense—just as good as when the outcome is readily foreseeable (for example, when an adult tugs, with all his might, against a toddler).

The like holds for value estimates. By reason of various factors—our severely limited factual knowledge; the difficulty of achieving an experiential or imaginative grasp of even many values that lie within our ken; the difficulty of tracing the ramifications of a given value and of clearly distinguishing one value from another; the abstractness and indefiniteness with which value questions are often posed; the varying sensitivity, objectivity, and reliability of human appraisers; the lack of any standard value-measure (understandable in view of such facts as the preceding)—value calculations are often uncertain and imprecise. Yet even when value comparisons prove most perplexing, the theory behind them makes good sense—just as good as when the verdict is more evident ("You are worth more than many sparrows"). Theoretical validity should not be confused with practical facility.[24]

Incommensurabilists' objections have taken many twists and turns, which an earlier response of mine tried to follow.[25] The present exposition, complementing that one, replies explicitly or implicitly to all the objections I have encountered against the comparability of disparate values.[26] From a single sample, of a kind many critics admit, I have elicited sufficient justification for the comparisons VM needs.

Rejoinders might focus either on the sample or on its analysis (ordinal relationships, degrees of difference) or on the analysis's adequacy for VM's purposes. The first approach looks most promising. Scrutinizing the gospel paradigm more closely, one might suggest that humans and sparrows are indeed disparate but that the bases of Jesus' comparison are not. Humans' superiority derives from their possession of attributes that sparrows lack (e.g., freedom, intelligence, morality, religiosity); and these attributes, when added to what humans share with sparrows (e.g., life, movement, sensation), yield a clear value verdict in favor of humans. Thus the gospel comparison requires no confrontation of disparate values but simply addition and subtraction.

This response errs in supposing both qualitative and quantitative sameness in what humans share with sparrows; the life, movement, appearance, and sensations of sparrows differ greatly from those of humans. Thus mere addition and subtraction are not possible—unless one can judge that, despite their differences, the "shared" attributes are of equal worth as realized in sparrows and in humans. Not only would this assessment be dubious, but it would violate critics' veto on comparing disparate values.

Besides, this example stands for countless others.[27] Tom's friendship with Florence, in itself, is worth more than many sparrows, in themselves. Brenda's faith is worth more than the delectation conferred by many chocolate chips. One Brandenburg Concerto is worth more than many indifferent sketches. Jesus' sacrifice on Calvary is worth more than many children's understanding of a proof in geometry. On examination, the denial of such judgments proves sophistical. Yet any one of them yields the same conclusions as the gospel paradigm.

Let this sampling of objections to VM suffice for now. Others will surface in subsequent chapters. To establish VM's title to serious consideration, a positive apologia must now complement this initial defense.

# 3

# *The Positive Case for VM*

VM meets the Finnis-Grisez objection. It also meets other objections, and in this respect fares better than rival positions, as we shall see. However, it does not merit acceptance merely as the sole survivor once it and its competitors have been put to the test. A positive case, both philosophical and theological, can be made for the norm's validity.

## PHILOSOPHICAL CONSIDERATIONS

The positive philosophical rationale for VM can be summarized in the words of Robin Attfield: "What is intrinsically valuable, after all, is what there is irreducible reason to promote, desire or cherish, and thus where an action (or an omission) would optimise the balance of intrinsic value over disvalue, it will be the action (or omission) which does what there is most reason to do, all things considered. But what there is most reason to do, all things considered, must surely be what it is morally right to do."[1] Implicit in the notion of value is a claim on action; implicit in the notion of greater value is a stronger claim on action; implicit in this stronger claim is the general norm of value-maximization (VM in embryo). More fully, the basic philosophical case for VM can be stated in six points—five substantive and one linguistic.

### 1. *Objective values and disvalues exist.*

Like many another philosophical starting point, this one cannot be grounded in anything more ultimate. Theologians can go back to *Genesis*, where God contemplates creation and sees that it is good. Philosophers can go no further back than human perceptions of the good. Neither deductively nor inductively can they prove or disprove the existence of values independent of human valuation (any more than they can prove or disprove the existence of the past, the constancy of nature, other minds, or an external world).

True, they may proffer sample values—life, love, peace, joy, friendship, beauty, understanding—in demonstration. And if somebody, citing "organic unities," questions the inclusion of a value such as love or joy, they can distinguish, say, between joy at another's suffering and joy at another's good fortune, then drop the former and retain the latter. If somebody rejects peace as a value and touts the virtues of war, they can counter by noting war's agony, terror, slaughter, and destruction. But if their interlocutor recognized no objective value in any kind of love or joy, and no objective disvalue in death, destruction, agony, terror, or anything else, the mere citing of examples would do nothing to convince him.

From such instances as this we learn that logic alone can settle nothing.

> We do *not* have to be shown that the denial of some kind of objective values is *self-contradictory* in order to be reasonably led to accept their existence. There is no constraint to pick the weakest or narrowest or most economical principle consistent with the initial data that arise from individual perspectives. Our admission of reasons beyond these is determined *not* by logical entailment, but by what we cannot help believing, or at least finding most plausible among the alternatives.[2]

Thus, "someone who, as in Hume's example, prefers the destruction of the whole world to the scratching of his finger, may not be involved in a *contradiction* or in any false *expectations*, but he is unreasonable nonetheless (to put it mildly), and anyone else not in the grip of an overly narrow conception of what reasoning is would regard his preference as objectively wrong."[3]

In confirmation, a pragmatic case—indeed, the most radical kind of pragmatic case—can be made for objective values. Were values purely subjective, life would not be worth living; nothing would be worth doing—or debating. As C. I. Lewis observed: "Those who would deny the character of cognition and the possibility of truth to value-apprehensions, must find themselves, ultimately, in the position of Epimenides the Cretan who said that all Cretans are liars. Either their thesis must be false or it is not worth believing or discussing."[4]

To place this brief discussion[5] in proper perspective, notice that our inability to prove the existence of objective values does not disadvantage VM vis-à-vis its rivals. If nothing—persons, natural fulfillment, human happiness, obedience to God, basic human goods, rights—held any objective value, alternative accounts of right conduct would also stand on shaky ground.

*2. Objective values and disvalues make positive and negative claims
on prospective action.*

This idea has been variously expressed.[6] I agree with Attfield that there is a necessary link between intrinsic value and reasons for action.[7] "Values, though not wholly realizable, *clamor for realization.*"[8] More specifically, I agree with Peter Geach and R. M. Hare "that 'good' is an action-guiding word, for it belongs to the idea of *goodness* that normally and other things being equal people should choose things that they call good."[9] This being a weak, prima facie "should," the link with "good" is analytic. Mutatis mutandis, the like holds for "evil" and "should not." More is needed, however, to establish unequivocal rightness or wrongness.

*3. All objective values and disvalues, without restriction, make
such claims on action.*

"Surely," writes Henry Veatch, "any and every sort of good—indeed, anything that is of value at all—needs to be reckoned with somehow, somewhere, in men's counsels and plans and choices aimed at achieving the good life."[10] If there are moral values as well as nonmoral, nonconsequential as well as consequential, nonhuman as well as human, they too have a claim on action, by virtue of their being values. The like holds for disvalues.

*4. Only objective values and disvalues make such claims
on action.*

Veatch's saying can be reversed: "Surely nothing need be reckoned with in people's counsels and plans and choices that has no value or disvalue." Thus, for likes and dislikes to count for or against action, there must be value or disvalue in acting on one's likes. For divine commands to count for or against action, there must be value or disvalue in obeying divine commands. For the dictates of "nature" to count for or against action, there must be value or disvalue in following nature's dictates. Whatever speaks validly for or against action is, *eo ipso*, an objective value or disvalue.

5. *The greater the prospective value or disvalue of alternative actions, the stronger is the claim for or against them.*

This assertion follows from 2 and 4. Given the link between value and action, additional value or disvalue makes a further claim, positive or negative, on action. Given the absence of any counterclaim—from something other than value or disvalue—nothing disturbs the stated correlation.

This fifth point is the heart of VM. To generate a norm of value-maximization, the point needs only to be clothed in the right words. A further, semantic observation links it with chapter 1's formulation.

6. *The term "right" aptly characterizes any action whose claim is not notably weaker than that of any incompatible alternative.*

Within the preceding framework, there can be little quarrel about calling an action "*the* right thing to do" if its claim is notably stronger than that of any incompatible alternative; or about calling it "*a* right thing to do" if its claim is equal to that of one or more alternatives and inferior to none. As for an action whose claim is not notably inferior to that of its strongest rivals, such an action would commonly be termed permissible; and what is permissible is likewise right to do. An idealizing tendency might label this terminology loose, inaccurate, or minimalist. However, such a reaction would result, I suggest, from supposing a precise, rigoristic meaning for moral terms, unsupported by actual usage.[11]

Beyond this step in VM's vindication, chapter 1 takes over. Its detailed explanations and justifications of the general formula, together with the underlying rationale just stated, constitute a positive philosophical case for VM.

## THEOLOGICAL CONSIDERATIONS

Most Christians would agree that Christian moral theory must maintain continuity with the Christian past. Yet the past by itself cannot answer new questions. For their solution, discernment is necessary—discernment which, in Gustafson's words, "learns from, and is thus informed and directed without being determined by, the past."[12] VM is a case in point.

Seeking an answer to its central, criterial question, *CMR* consulted a wide range of Christian sources. In varied authors on varied topics—in the gospels, Paul, Aquinas, Loyola, Rahner, Chesterton, Niebuhr, Teilhard, and others—it first noted intimations of VM (chap. 4). In equally varied sources, it then cited evidence apparently opposed to VM (chap. 5), and from this evidence picked out two norms in genuine opposition. One stressed natural form (e.g., of sexual intercourse); the other vetoed evil of any kind as a means to good, however great. Comparing these two norms with VM, *CMR* found them qualitatively and quantitatively inferior. Were they valid, they would prohibit actions no one condemns. Were they born of genuine moral insight, they would be more widely, consistently applied. On both scores, VM is preferable (chap. 6).

In its sampling, *CMR* focused on modes of thought it judged both relevant to widely varied issues and prevalent among Christians; only from approaches satisfying both of these conditions can a general, Christian criterion of right and wrong emerge. A candidate criterion need not be explicitly articulated, but must at least be implicit in a mass of Christian moral reasoning. VM satisfies this requirement. However, given the extensive sifting—and possible gerrymandering—of evidence required to discern VM in Christian sources, it may be wondered whether all rivals would do worse if judged by similar standards. A more searching scrutiny of Scripture and tradition than *CMR*'s is called for.

### Scripture

The New Testament does not speak of "values" and "disvalues." It does not enunciate a norm of "value-maximization." Indeed, the criterion thus expressed may seem foreign to its thinking. To counter this impression, I shall first sketch a case for VM which falls short of demonstration but does at least make clear that VM's scriptural strangeness is more terminological than substantive.

Paul Ramsey has remarked: "Jesus' words: 'Love one another *as I have loved you!*' are the commandment, the model, the organizing principle of all New Testament ethics."[13] But how did Jesus love? "The blind receive their sight, the lame walk, the lepers are cleansed, the deaf hear, the dead are raised, the poor have good news brought to them" (Luke 7:22). As dozens of gospel incidents attest, Jesus "went about doing good and healing all who were oppressed by the devil" (Acts 10:38). His mission and his mind are captured in the saying, "I have come that they may have life and may have it to the full" (John 10:10).

Hence VM's message comes to this: "Let this same mind be in you which was in Christ Jesus."[14] Be as dedicated as he to the good, and as opposed to any sophistries, confusions, or misconceptions that, like the scribes and pharisees' objections, restrict or impede the service of the good. In agreement with scriptural indications such as Genesis 1, Jonah 4:10–11, and Matthew 10:29, VM looks beyond human welfare and makes room for the rest of creation. In agreement with evidence such as 1 Corinthians 13, it looks beyond benefits and recognizes values intrinsic to acts themselves: "There are forgiving, mild, humble, friendly, devout *ways of doing the things* we do and of leading our lives in pursuit of varied values."[15] In agreement with the whole of Scripture, VM looks beyond love of neighbor and includes the love of God, nonreductively: "Biblical morality is above all a *'morality of the alliance.'* The good is there defined in the setting of a dialogue: it is an affective interchange, religious in nature, between God and human persons called to become his people."[16] It is achieved not only through but also *in* their living the alliance.

To summarize: there is a wholeness in VM that matches the wholeness of Scripture, and a narrowness in restrictions on VM that is not backed by Scripture. "Let your goodness have no limits, just as the goodness of the heavenly Father knows no bounds" (Matt 5:48).

This quick, panoramic view may dissipate the impression of strangeness, but what does it prove? How much support can VM derive from such a sampling? How much weight will the individual texts bear? For example, John 10:10 may furnish an apt motto—"I have come that they may have life and may have it to the full"—with which to evoke the full range of human values and commend their fullest realization. Yet how legitimate is such an application?

Of the Johannine conception of life, central to the fourth gospel, Rudolf Schnackenburg writes: "Here, too, John owes more to Jewish thought than first appears. This is shown importantly by his retention of a total view, which knows no philosophical opposition between body and soul, no emphasis on a 'higher' part of man, no retreat to a deeper, essential core of man and therefore also no reference to the immortality of the *soul*."[17]

This assessment applies to our text, John 10:10. So may Leon Morris's holistic reading of John 1:4: "There is probably a characteristic Johannine double meaning here. The life of which John writes is in the first instance the kind of life that we see throughout this earth. But this will call to mind that spiritual life which is so much more significant that John can speak of it as 'the life.'"[18]

Neither John 1:4 nor John 10:10 points solely to a future life. "Coming from the synoptics," notes Schnackenburg, "one is struck above all by the reworking of the term 'eternal life.' In the synoptics its orientation is strictly to the future; in John it is placed firmly in the present."[19]

Though *life* is thus broadly inclusive in John, it appears to have a more transcendent focus than does, for example, the judgment scene of Matthew 25, with its multiple references to humble human needs. This passage, not cited in my sampling, might seem strongly to support VM's general thrust. And so it does, in some interpretations.

Three readings form a dialectical triad. In the first, Jesus identifies himself, unrestrictedly, with "those in desperate need of the basic necessities of life."[20] In the second, he identifies himself with needy disciples; hence "Matthew XXV 31–46 *cannot* provide a legitimate basis for Christian concern for the poor and needy of the world."[21] In the third, he identifies himself with disciples, but "what is done positively *for* them is not limited *to* them."[22] The test is still a test of mercy, and Vatican Council II can rightly conclude:

> Wherever there are people in need of food and drink, clothing, housing, medicine, employment, education; wherever [people] lack the facilities necessary for living a truly human life or are tormented by hardships or poor health, or suffer exile or imprisonment, there Christian charity should seek them out and find them, console them with eager care and relieve them with the gift of help.[23]

However one takes Matthew's judgment scene, it does not stand alone. The love repeatedly enjoined in the New Testament is universal, like that of the Father, who makes his sun to shine and his rain to fall on all alike; like that of Jesus, who died for all; like that of the Good Samaritan: "The point of the story is summed up in the lawyer's reaction, that 'a neighbor' is anyone in need with whom one comes into contact and to whom one can show pity and kindness, even beyond the bounds of one's own ethnic or religious group."[24] As the same tale shows, the need to be met and assistance to be given may be earthly, not heavenly: the man lies half-dead by the roadside; the Samaritan tends his wounds, finds him lodging, cares for him. Thus Luke 10:29–37 complements John 10:10 as well as Matthew 25:35–46. Even if these latter texts do not, on close inspection, reveal the full richness which Christians would wish to read into a formula like VM, the New Testament does.

The chief difficulty for ascribing VM a scriptural basis comes, not from the New Testament's narrowness, but from its indefiniteness. True, VM itself is very general and abstract. However, it speaks not only for the fullness of value but also against restrictions such as those imposed by Finnis, Grisez, and other ethicians. None of the scriptural evidence just cited speaks against the rival, incompatible theories here considered. What, if anything, does? What, if anything, counts against VM? To pass beyond the mere injunction "Do all kinds of good, avoid all kinds of evil"[25] and favor one opposed theory over another, comparative assessment is needed.

This assessment can be selective. It can disregard Aquinas's First Principle of Practical Reason (chap. 4) and Robert Adams's divine-command theory (chap. 5), which reveal little conflict with VM. It can also disregard Judith Thomson's insistence on individual rights (chap. 9), which lacks scriptural backing. The chief Christian challenge to VM comes from the representative views of Alan Donagan, Germain Grisez, and Peter Knauer, examined in chapters 6, 7, and 8 respectively. Underlying their theories, and largely accounting for their divergence from VM, is their common insistence that disparate values cannot be compared as VM requires. On this, Scripture does have something to say. New Testament data to consider fall into three categories:

*Possibly pertinent.* Examples are Matt 5:19 ("'one of the least of these commandments'");[26] Matt 5:29–30 ("'It is better for you to lose one of your members than for your whole body to go into hell'");[27] Matt 6:25 ("'Is not life more than food, and the body more than clothing?'");[28] Matt 12:6 ("'There is greater than the temple here'");[29] Matt 12:41 ("'Something greater than Jonah is here'");[30] Matt 12:42

("'Something greater than Solomon is here'");[31] Matt 18:6 ("'It would be better for you if a great millstone were fastened around your neck and you were drowned in the depth of the sea'");[32] Matt 22:38 ("'This is the greatest and first commandment'");[33] Matt 23:17 ("'which is greater, the gold or the sanctuary that has made the gold sacred?'"); Matt 23:19 ("'which is greater, the gift or the altar that makes the gift sacred?'");[34] Matt 23:23 ("'you tithe mint, dill, and cummin, and have neglected the weightier matters of the law'");[35] Mark 9:45–48 ("'It is better for you to enter life lame than to have two feet and to be thrown into hell. . . it is better for you to enter the kingdom of God with one eye than to have two eyes and to be thrown into hell'");[36] Luke 10:42 ("'Mary has chosen the better part'");[37] Luke 11:31 (cf. Matt 12:42); Luke 11:32 (cf. Matt 11:41); Luke 12:23 ("'Life is more than food, and the body more than clothing'");[38] John 5:14 ("'Do not sin any more, so that nothing worse happens to you'");[39] John 10:29 ("'What my Father has given me is greater than all else'"); 1 Cor 7:9 ("It is better to marry than to be aflame with passion");[40] 1 Cor 12:31 ("Strive for the greater gifts"); 1 Cor 13:13 ("and the greatest of these is love");[41] Phil 1:23 ("My desire is to depart and be with Christ, for that is far better");[42] 1 Tim 5:8 ("He has denied the faith and is worse than an unbeliever");[43] Heb 1:4 ("Having become as much superior to angels as the name he has inherited is more excellent than theirs");[44] Heb 11:40 ("God had provided something better");[45] 1 Pet 1:7 ("Much more precious than perishable gold is faith which stands the test");[46] Rev 2:19 ("'your last works are greater than the first'").[47]

All these texts, as here translated, contain value comparisons; in some there are indications of degree ("much more precious," "far better," "as much superior. . . as"); and in others there can be little doubt about the authors' willingness to state degree (life is worth *much* more than food; it is *far* better to lose one member than to be thrown into hell; and so on). All, however, suffer from indefiniteness. In one instance (Luke 10:42), there may be no comparison. In others, the things compared are ill-defined. Even when these are clear, the nature of the comparison is not. (Is one value means and the other end? Is one value partial and the other total? Are the values compared at least somewhat disparate or fully homogeneous?) It is probable, therefore, that a number of these texts do not exemplify the contested kind of comparison that VM has need of. It is possible that none does. However, that is less probable. And even one or two would tell in favor of VM and against its incommensurabilist critics. The rest would simply exemplify other kinds of comparisons without counting either way.

*Implicitly pertinent.* Here 1 Cor 8:13, on eating food offered to idols, can serve as illustration. In chapter 8, discussing Knauer's views, I note that there was no need for Paul to consider whether eating the food would, in the long run, defeat the aim of the eating. I can state with equal assurance that though Paul was aware of the reasons people might have for the eating, he applied no such test. He did not estimate the long-term consequences for pleasure or for nourishment and thereby reach a verdict. He was concerned about the spiritual welfare of those who might be harmed, and found that value more weighty than any pleasure or nourishment the eating might provide. Or so one may reasonably surmise. One may also surmise that Paul judged the prospective harm to be *far* more important than the possible nourishment or pleasure. Further, these opposed values are of the pertinent type: they are not homogeneous, or related as part and whole, or as means and end. Thus everything VM needs—disparate values, greater and less, degree, preference for the greater—is present implicitly.

*Explicitly pertinent.* To this category belong the passages chapter 2 scrutinized: Matt 6:26 ("Look at the birds of the air. . . Are you not of more value than they?"); Matt 10:31 ("You are worth more than many sparrows"); Matt 12:12 ("Surely a person is worth far more than a sheep"); and Luke 12:24 ("Of how much more value are you than the birds!"). These combine the strong features of the other two categories, minus their weaknesses. As in the first category, the comparisons are explicit. As in the second category, the comparisons are not plausibly viewed as same-type, part-whole, or means-end. The sparrows, for example, are not regarded simply as food. "Without your father's leave, not one of them can fall to the ground" (Matt 10:29).

Though the weight of this collective evidence is hardly crushing, I think it can at least be said that with respect to value-commensurability, scriptural evidence favors VM over its most important Christian rivals. This point is crucial. If the pertinent value-comparisons are impossible, VM is invalid; if they are possible, theories based on their impossibility are invalid. Scripture suggests that they are possible.

It also suggests something more. A first look at the evidence just cited reveals values, value comparisons, and judgments of degree.

A second look at the same evidence reveals the connection between value and action, and between greater value and action preference (cut off the member, pluck out the eye, forgo the food, do as Mary did.) Thus, of my six-step philosophical demonstration, the chief thing still lacking, it seems, is the final formulation. The ingredients lie ready at hand. However, this impression may result from selective reading of the evidence. What counter-indications can be found in the New Testament, which perhaps tell against VM, as the texts above tell against its chief rivals?

Against proportionalist positions, two main objections have been urged from the Christian past—weakly from Scripture and more strongly from subsequent tradition. One objection concerns evil means, the other exceptionless precepts.

First, the biblical passage most frequently cited by opponents of proportionalism is Romans 3:8: "And why not say (as some people slander us by saying that we say), 'Let us do evil so that good may come'? Their condemnation is deserved." Finnis interprets Paul's words as follows:

> Some people, in the first ferment of belief in humankind's definitive redemption through Christ by grace, opined that wrongdoing is tolerable or even desirable because it affords occasion for God to accomplish his redemptive work. . . . That good effect is surely greater than the evil in the actions! How then (v. 7) can God, in his final judgment on those actions, regard them as evil? Indeed, why should not those who notice this connection between their actions and God's glory pursue that greater good directly, by choosing to do what would otherwise be sin as a *means* of bringing about that greatest good?[48]

Having so construed the issue, Finnis concludes: "Since St. Paul does not dispute that sin brings about the incomparably great good of God's glory, his teaching entails that the question whether an act is wrongful is *not to be settled* by trying to show that in a given case it would bring about consequences greater in goodness, or lesser in evil, than the goods attained or evils avoided by alternative acts."[49]

If the genuine sinfulness of merely putative sins were the question Paul addressed—if the sinfulness of the contemplated conduct were at issue—Finnis's inference might work. But such a supposition contradicts Finnis's own statement of the situation—that some people "opined that *wrongdoing* is tolerable or even desirable," that "*sin* brings about the incomparably great good of God's glory." To reject such a suggestion manifests no conflict with VM. No proportionalist would disagree with Paul's reply or its evident justification: wrongdoing is wrong; sinning is sinful.

This response may seem too quick; so consider the possible alternatives. (1) If the sin Paul had in mind was genuine sin as judged by nonproportionalist standards, there would of course be a problem for proportionalism, in virtue of this initial supposition and not merely of a contrary proportionalist verdict. But why make this question-begging supposition? (2) If the sin Paul had in mind was genuine sin as judged by proportionalist standards, there would be no problem for proportionalism, since the judgment, if accurate, would have to take account of all consequences, including God's glory: the sin would still be a sin. (3) If, as seems more likely, Paul had no specific, uniform moral standard in mind when he spoke of doing evil, he could argue as he did without impugning proportionalism. All that his ready verdict requires is that genuine sin, however defined or conceived, be genuinely wrong; and with this requirement there should be no problem for anyone.

It might be suggested that only a proportionalist would reason in the way Paul rejects, that only for a proportionalist would such reasoning make sense, and that therefore Paul had proportionalism implicitly in his sights. However, neither of this argument's premises is true. Proportionalists are not the only ones to cite notable advantages (e.g., God's greater glory) as supporting a course of action; and this particular reasoning, in Rom 3:7–8, would make no better sense for a proportionalist than it would for anyone else (see 2 above). So let us pass on.

A second line of critique appears in the recent papal encyclical *Veritatis splendor*. On the one hand: "*The teleological ethical theories (proportionalism, consequentialism), while acknowledging that moral values are indicated by reason and by Revelation, maintain that it is never possible to formulate an absolute prohibition of particular kinds of behaviour which would be in conflict, in every circumstance and in every culture, with those values.*"[50] On the other hand: "In teaching the existence of intrinsically evil acts, the Church accepts the teaching of Sacred Scripture. The Apostle Paul emphatically states: 'Do not be deceived: neither the immoral, nor idolaters, nor adulterers, nor sexual perverts, nor thieves, nor the greedy, nor drunkards, nor revilers, nor robbers will inherit the Kingdom of God' (*1 Cor* 6:9–10)."[51]

In first response, I suggest that the list is Paul's but the doctrine is not. Of the concept "*intrinsically evil* acts," as of the concept "*exceptionless* norms," one might observe with Thomas Deidun: "This obviously supposes a level of reflection which we should not expect to find in any New Testament writer, any more than we should expect to find developed reflection on concepts like 'conscience' and 'natural law.' The New Testament is not, as has sometimes been supposed, a heavenly preview of the history of moral theology, but God's word incarnate in time."[52]

Consider: Why did the encyclical cite Paul's list, rather than that of the Council of Jerusalem: "It has seemed good to the Holy Spirit and to us to impose on you no further burden than these essentials: that you abstain from what has been sacrificed to idols and from blood and from what is strangled and from fornication. If you keep yourselves from these, you will do well" (Acts 15:28–29)? This listing of "essentials" sounds as absolute as Paul's. The Council does not inquire, for example, as contemporary ethicians might, whether a starving person could legitimately eat meat sacrificed to idols. So are all these acts "intrinsically evil"? The subsequent fate of this catalog, in comparison with Paul's, suggests the need for fuller theological reflection. The texts, on their own, do not readily yield a verdict against VM.

And yet, if, despite Scripture's indefiniteness and the frailty of individual texts, I have managed to make a case for VM, might not similar attentiveness reveal a scriptural basis for this second critique? I think not, but shall leave a fuller account of my reasons till the next section. Subsequent tradition provides more plausible grounds for the encyclical's objection than does Scripture, and much of what I say about these grounds will apply to Scripture.

## Tradition

Subsequent Christian tradition speaks for VM much as Christian Scripture does. This tradition does not spell out the norm, but it does show constant concern for values. Countless instances of value-balancing, by the most varied authors on the most varied topics, betray a preference for greater value. Such preference can be discerned in traditional reasons for "indirect" abortion, for permissible falsehoods, for legitimate disobedience to laws or those in authority, for capital punishment, for dispensation from Sunday observance, for legitimately breaking a promise, for Old Testament dispensations from divine law, for exceptions to positive precepts such as repaying a debt. A similar preference appears in arguments for private property, the principle of subsidiarity, monogamy, the indissolubility of marriage, government and laws, particular forms of government, the preferential treatment of those nearest and dearest; in arguments against fornication, marriage with close kin, mixed marriages, and the legal prohibition of immorality; in the doctrine of just war; in the teaching on circumstances that change the moral species of an action; in all sorts of "slippery slope" arguments; in laws justified by the common danger or the common good; in Ignatian value-tables; in the double-effect requirement of commensurate reason; in casuists' countless discriminations when treating complex moral cases; in other typical evidence soon to be cited.[53]

Only a comparably widespread restriction on value-maximization would negate this general thrust toward greater good and tell against VM. But tradition backs neither of the restrictions proposed by utilitarians, excluding moral values and values intrinsic to conduct from consideration. It backs neither of the rival norms—naturalness and the ban on nonmoral evils used as means—which *CMR* weighs and finds wanting. And the positions examined here in chapters 4 to 9 point to no more convincing evidence; historically as well as theoretically, they fail to impeach VM.[54] To cite an example already seen, the doctrine of value-incommensurability that underlies Donagan's, Grisez's, and Knauer's positions is a recent innovation: Christians in times past did not hesitate to compare disparate values as greater or less, to varying degrees, and to draw practical inferences from the comparisons.[55]

Nonetheless, objections from Christian tradition have been urged against proportionalism. The chief two are those already mentioned. One is more focused, the other more diffuse; so one answer can be relatively brief, while the other will have to be longer.

The focused objection cites long-standing resistance to the saying "The end justifies the means." Christian tradition, it is said, condemns the use of evil means to good ends, no matter how good, whereas VM does not. So VM clashes with Christian tradition, and must be rejected.

In reply, it is necessary to distinguish different senses of the ban on evil means and discern which of these senses conflict with VM, then note which senses traditional resistance reveals. How has the phrase "evil means" been understood? How might it be?

*1. Morally evil means.* This sense is common. "Those things which are clearly sins," writes Augustine, "ought not to be done under any pretext of a good reason, for any possible good end, with any seemingly good intention."[56] "The Christian religion," Grosseteste insists, "declares and holds that sin must not be committed, whether for the sake of pursuing good or of avoiding loss."[57] Aquinas concurs: "Whatever is intrinsically sinful may not be done for any purpose however good—as Paul says in Romans 3:8."[58] As already noted, if the rejection of evil means is understood this way, it does not clash with VM.

*2. Nonmorally evil means.* Some recent formulations of the principle of double effect specify this sense. Yet according to *CMR*, "love not only permits but repeatedly requires non-morally evil means: disagreeable medicine, distressing criticism, painful punishment, fatiguing labor, and so forth."[59] A ban on all such means would conflict with VM. If standard among Christians, it would constitute a strong argument from tradition against the norm.

*3. Nonmorally evil means making instrumental use of the evil.* Disagreeable medicine does not cure by means of its disagreeableness, whereas painful punishment does correct by means of its painfulness and bitters on the breast do wean by means of their bitterness.[60] A veto on all such means would clash with VM as clearly as does the preceding interpretation.

*4. Evil means in an indeterminate sense of "evil."* In many of its occurrences, the prohibition of evil means makes no distinction; no clue indicates one or the other of the preceding three interpretations. Often, in moral argument, sense 1 would assure the truth of the ban on evil means but beg the question at issue (e.g., the legitimacy of organ transplants), while sense 2 or 3 would not beg the question but would cast doubt on the ban's truth. Thus the reader or hearer is left uncertain of the prohibition's sense. Such straddling reveals no clear conflict with VM; still less would sense 1, which often seems the more likely reading of such indefinite sayings.

With these four varieties of the traditional veto distinguished, it can be said in historical summary that 1 and 4, which do not conflict with VM, predominate in Christian tradition, whereas 2 and 3, which do conflict with VM, have slight historical standing. Version 2 arrived on the scene only recently and has been widely challenged. Version 3 is still more recent, and still rarer.[61] Thus, this particular argument from tradition dissolves when scrutinized. The traditional condemnation of evil means to good ends does not tell against VM.

And yet, there is something to this first, focused objection. The evidence cited does reveal conflict with VM, but of a different, more general kind. Consider the words I have quoted from Augustine. They exemplify sense 1, and sense 1 does not clash with VM. However, Augustine becomes more specific: "When the works themselves are already sins, such as theft, impurity, blasphemy, and the like, who would say that they should be done for good reasons so as either not to be sins or else, still more absurd, to be just sins?"[62] I would not, nor would VM. But it would question whether, for example, telling a falsehood, for even the best of reasons, was always wrong in itself, as Augustine supposed.

Here in Augustine, more clearly than in Paul, we can spot the beginnings of the tradition to which *Veritatis splendor* appeals. There are acts, the encyclical insists, "which, in the Church's moral tradition, have been termed 'intrinsically evil' (*intrinsece malum*): they are such *always and per se*. . . Consequently, without in the least denying the influence on morality exercised by circumstances and especially by intentions, the Church teaches that 'there exist acts which *per se* and in themselves, independently of circumstances, are always seriously wrong by reason of their object.'"[63]

Quotations like those above—from Augustine and 1 Cor 6:9–10—suggest that the encyclical speaks for more than just Catholic tradition or Catholic concerns. And Catholic readers, especially, will doubtless wish to know how VM relates to the encyclical's critique. In the encyclical's discussion of "The Moral Act" there appears the most prestigious presentation of a type of criticism commonly urged against proportionalism. To what extent is VM implicated?

In reply, I shall indicate why VM is implicated less than most versions of proportionalism, then why proportionalism in general is less implicated than the encyclical might suggest. It will then be possible to assess more accurately the nature and extent of the conflict critics allege between proportionalism and Christian tradition.

Several features of "proportionalism" highlighted in the encyclical are foreign to VM:

1. VM agrees that "the weighing of the goods and evils foreseeable as the consequence of an action is not an adequate method for determining whether the choice of that concrete kind of behaviour is 'according to its species,' or 'in itself,' morally good or bad, licit or illicit."[64] Indeed, VM agrees doubly. First, it looks to acts themselves and not just to consequences. Second, it does not propose any method—this weighing or another—but enunciates a criterion compatible with a variety of complementary methods (see chap. 1).

2. Further, looking to the act itself, VM is ready to recognize moral evil there, as perhaps a decisive determinant of the action's overall moral status. As chapter 1 noted and chapter 8 will stress, the norm's focus is not confined to what the encyclical terms *"the premoral order,* which some term non-moral, physical or ontic."[65]

3. Again, VM does not look beyond the action to the agent, as do some (see chap. 1), and incorporate motive and intention as essential components of any moral judgment. Neither does it link the objective and the subjective as Knauer does (see chap. 8). Thus it does not fit the encyclical's description: "Certain *ethical theories,* called 'teleological,' claim to be concerned for the conformity of human acts with the ends pursued by the agent and with the values intended by him."[66]

Even proportionalist theories that differ from VM in these respects clash less squarely than one might think with the tradition the encyclical evokes. For this, too, several reasons may be cited. Whether given acts are "intrinsically evil," hence never to be done, depends largely on how the acts in question are stated—evaluatively or neutrally, broadly or narrowly, sharply or loosely—and on how their "intrinsic evil" is understood. Let me explain.

*Evaluative versus neutral.* No Christian ethician, proportionalist or other, would question the absolute, exceptionless validity of many a moral verdict cited in lists such as Augustine's or those the encyclical quotes from St. Paul and Vatican II (*Gaudium et spes,* 27). To be sure, "robbery" and "theft" are always wrong, for the terms are value-laden; but what about taking another's property? A long tradition has sanctioned taking what one needs and cannot otherwise obtain in order to stave off death by starvation. To be sure, "mutilation" is always wrong, for this term, too, implies a negative verdict; but what about removing an organ from one person to save another's life? To be sure, "impurity" is always wrong, and "adultery," "murder," "idolatry," "arbitrary imprisonment," and so forth: the very names proclaim the fact. Any act, so labeled, is indeed "intrinsically" wrong. Its being "impurity," "theft," "mutilation," "murder," "idolatry," "adultery," or "arbitrary imprisonment" assures its wrongness. But the labeling does not preclude the most varied explanations of the wrongness. The "absoluteness" of the tradition which these listings represent, hence its clash with proportionalism, is largely a verbal mirage.

*Broad versus narrow.* "Acts" may undergo another sort of inflation, giving rise to the verdict "intrinsically evil." In simple illustration, consider these remarks of Grisez:

> Consequentialism implies that there are no intrinsically evil acts. This view can seem attractive if one considers kinds of acts one holds to be morally acceptable. Most college students today easily accept consequentialism in the field of sexual ethics. But consider: Would it ever be right for a professor to assign grades in a course, not according to the work the students have done, but rather according to the extent to which they agree with him? Confronted with this question, students usually begin to see that acts of some kinds are always wrong.[67]

Ignoring the possible conflation of "intrinsically evil" and "always wrong," let us ask: How far does the grade-giving act extend? To the student's seeing the grade? To anyone else's reading it? Granted: students', parents', and others' perusal of the grade is not something the teacher does; so it might be said not to belong to the teacher's act. But if nobody ever reads the grade, where is the harm of "grading" in the manner described? Some marks have been written on paper; some digits have been entered in a computer. If, as Grisez says, students see such an action as always wrong, they clearly have something more in view than just the teacher's scribbles or the computer entries. If that something more is included in the "act," consequentialists and other proportionalists might acknowledge that the act, thus extended, is "intrinsically wrong."

Thus the contrast Grisez draws looks illusory, in this and similar cases. Cut an act thin, and it may look innocuous. Cut it thick, and it may look "intrinsically evil." Blur the distinction between thick and thin, as Grisez does, and the thin act may seem intrinsically evil— wrong regardless of consequences, wrong in a way that proportionalism cannot account for. This, too, exaggerates the impression of conflict between the tradition Grisez speaks for and the theories which he, like *Veritatis splendor*, opposes.

*Loose versus sharp.* Abortion, it may be said, is always wrong. But then special cases are cited, and the prohibition is hedged: "indirect" abortion is always wrong. On examination it turns out that indirect abortions are of kinds backed by proportionalist reasoning: better to save the mother than to lose both mother and child. Hence the impression of conflict with proportionalism, which the initial statement might create, is removed or greatly reduced by the more careful formulation.

For fuller illustration of this contrast between blanket prohibitions and more carefully stated versions, consider the question of divorce. Scripture, tradition, and the whole magisterium have agreed, writes Grisez, that one should never divorce and remarry.[68] And yet, starting with the so-called Pauline privilege[69]—if not already with Matt 19:9[70]—a steady stream of exceptions have been admitted to this apparently unconditional scriptural proscription. So Grisez might modify his shorthand formulation. It is sacramental marriage, he might suggest, that is, and has always been judged to be, absolutely indissoluble. However, this would not be accurate for the early church,[71] nor for Eastern and Protestant churches[72]—nor even for more recent Catholic teaching. To accommodate a further exception, Grisez would have to specify that *consummated* sacramental marriage is absolutely indissoluble—or, more precisely, sacramental marriage consummated as sacramental (*matrimonium ratum et qua ratum consummatum*).

And what is *sacramental* marriage? Just which marriages are indissoluble and which not? Well, marriages between a woman at least 14 years old and a man at least 16 years old, who have both been validly baptized (according to specific conditions), who have sufficient knowledge of what they are doing (further conditions), and give their free consent (more conditions), without this or that type of mental reservation, in the presence of such and so many witnesses, using this or that formula, provided they are free of various impediments (of consanguinity, impotence, orders, previous union, religious profession and so on), unless (in this or that type of case) a dispensation has been obtained.[73]

Scores of conditions that have accumulated through the centuries presently define what marriages get treated as indissoluble within the Catholic Church. Attach the tag "indissoluble" to the class defined at any moment in the process and it would soon have to be removed. The border would be redrawn.

As I have noted, the successive modifications that have been introduced are neither arbitrary nor morally irrelevant:

Age by age, refinements have been added, in various ways (legislation, interpretation, theological reasoning) and for varying reasons. Sometimes biological considerations have been operative (as with regard to degrees of consanguinity), sometimes psychological considerations (as with regard to age or consent), sometimes sociological reasons (as with respect to the presence of witnesses), sometimes exegetical ones (as with respect to fidelity) and at still other times more directly religious or ecclesial considerations have been uppermost (as in the case of the Pauline privilege).[74]

Viewed macroscopically, indissolubility may look like an exceptionless rule affirmed without change from apostolic times. Viewed microscopically, it alters its appearance and reveals concern for values constantly at work. In this instance the tradition Grisez alludes to speaks for VM rather than against it. When, for example, the unmodified norm is seen as impeding a Christian partner's living of the faith (Pauline privilege) or a non-Christian's entry into the Church (Petrine privilege), the norm is modified.[75] The norm is for people—that they may have life—and not the other way round.

*"Intrinsically evil."* The preceding distinctions reveal three ways in which actions can appear "intrinsically evil": their very description (e.g., "murder" or "theft") may make the acts wrong by definition;

expansion of the acts may make evil consequences intrinsic to them; and loosely defined acts may be equated with whatever specific versions are deemed illicit. Recognition of these three sources greatly reduces the impression of conflict between proportionalism and Christian tradition. So does examination of a fourth potent source of the same impression.

For Pius XI, as for Pius VI, if a marriage is so contracted as to be a true marriage, "it carries with it that enduring bond which by divine right is inherent in every true marriage."[76] The bond is intrinsic to the marriage; its violation is intrinsic to divorce and remarriage. Hence the latter is intrinsically evil, "opposed of its very nature to the divine law."[77] For,

> although before Christ the sublimity and the severity of the primitive law was so tempered that Moses permitted it to the chosen people of God, on account of the hardness of their hearts, that a bill of divorce might be given in certain circumstances, nevertheless, Christ, by virtue of His supreme legislative power, recalled this concession of greater liberty and restored the primitive law in its integrity by those words which must never be forgotten: *What God hath joined together, let no man put asunder.*[78]

How, then, shall we conceive this "supreme legislative power"? Voluntaristically, so that whatever an arbitrary, all-powerful God commands is right, or agapistically, so that whatever a loving God commands is right? Despite tension in the tradition, I think it is evident, in general and in detail, where Christian emphasis has fallen. God's commands are not arbitrary. His command of marital permanence, for example, has excellent reasons to support it, which Christians have sought to divine and apply.

To label actions "intrinsically" evil in virtue of commands extrinsic to the actions could beget confusion. It could suggest that the actions are wrong regardless of circumstances, regardless of consequences, regardless of whatever values and disvalues the actions entail. This suggestion is not warranted. The God who commands may be concerned for value, and the commands may betray that concern. (See chap. 5.)

As predicted, my response to the second objection from tradition has proved lengthier. Focusing on the most prestigious formulation of this criticism, I have noted pertinent differences between VM and the proportionalism targeted by *Veritatis splendor*; then, for proportionalism generally, I have indicated important ways in which the impression of conflict with Christian tradition is illusory. I might now go further. I might note that for VM and perhaps other versions of proportionalism, even neutrally stated acts might always be wrong; or that proportionalist grounds might support the exceptionless wording and unquestioning application of certain negative precepts.[79] And yet, given the vagaries of Christian moral thinking, the impression of *some* opposition between VM and tradition is surely not illusory. (Think of the present study, with its many conflicting views; then multiply them.) My question has not been "What criterion of right and wrong is consistent with *all* of Christian tradition?" but "What criterion of right and wrong is *most* consistent with Christian tradition?" VM answers this question better than any conflicting norm I know of.

# 4

# Natural Law: Aquinas

Chapter 1 provides a fair idea of the norm I have labeled VM, but not the sharp understanding that can come from discerning just where, how, and why this position differs from others. Chapter 2 shows VM unscathed by one major criticism, but others remain to be considered. Chapter 3 suggests the strength of VM's position, but only partially; full, accurate assessment of the norm's credentials requires that other viewpoints also be examined. So the time has come for comparisons.

As the positions I shall review, in representative thinkers, all differ notably from VM, they are possible rivals. Whether they differ massively or in detail, in content or in formulation, their differences from VM might give them an edge. In my judgment they do not; chapter by chapter, VM will survive each comparison. This outcome should occasion no surprise. If I judged some theory or formulation preferable, it is the one I would have proposed, in place of VM. Still, as critique follows critique readers may receive the impression of an exercise in refutation, unless they keep in mind the need for such a series.

Comparative scrutiny may proceed differently, it is true. I might have worked toward a final formulation, rejecting, correcting, and refining as I went, thereby conveying the impression of greater openness and more disinterested striving for the truth. However, substantive reasons suggested the reverse ordering. To permit fuller, clearer comparison with each alternative position, I have introduced the favored theory—VM—at the start rather than at the end, and am now ready to work toward final confirmation rather than final formulation. To initiate comparison, I have chosen a long-standing tradition, natural-law ethics, and a still influential spokesman of that tradition, St. Thomas Aquinas.

## AN ARISTOTELIAN AND CHRISTIAN VIEW

"In so far as any common core can be found to the principal versions of the natural law theory," writes D. J. O'Connor, "it seems to amount to the statement that the basic principles of morals and legislation are, *in some sense or other*, objective, accessible to reason and based on human nature."[1] VM fits this description, as do most of the other positions I shall consider. Clearly, however, the paradigm Christian viewpoint to examine under the heading "natural-law ethics" is that of Aquinas.[2]

St. Thomas's ethics, like Aristotle's, is teleological: human beings are to find fulfillment by realizing their potentialities, especially the capacity that sets them off from other animals, namely, their intelligence. For Aquinas as for Aristotle, speculative intelligence is superior to practical, and the highest object of speculative, contemplative knowledge is the divine.[3] "It is in seeing God," writes Thomas, "that intelligent beings find real happiness. In this vision all desire comes to rest, and in it is found that true sufficiency of all values which, in Aristotle's view, is required for happiness."[4]

Adding a vision of God, in a future life, Aquinas's thought seems to remain continuous with Aristotle's. The Stagyrite's views have simply been "baptized." It is not so, however; for the terminus of human striving is now no longer a human achievement, as is speculative understanding, but a reward conferred for a life well lived, in accordance with some other standard. Aristotle could say: Living well, as a human being, consists above all in developing one's intellectual powers and achieving understanding of that which is highest. Aquinas could say: "The highest perfection of human life is that man's mind be occupied with God."[5] But he could not and would not say: Living well, as a human being, consists in so developing one's intellectual powers as finally to achieve direct contemplation of God.[6] In his view, the goal to which all should aspire is right-rewarding, not right-making.[7]

It cannot be maintained, however, that Aquinas always kept this distinction clearly in view. Nor have his expositors.[8] Odon Lottin writes: "The moral value of every intermediate end is determined by the last natural end. Hence action is morally good in the measure that it brings us to that last end."[9] It would be less misleading to say that human action brings us to the last end in the measure that it is morally good, and it is morally good in the measure that it satisfies some criterion other than that of approaching the last end. It is similarly misleading to state, as others have: "Morality is the agreement or disagreement of a human act with the norms that regulate human conduct with reference to man's Last End."[10] In a sense, any valid moral norm "regulates human conduct with reference to man's last end," but not in the sense that it determines actions' morality by their relation to that end.

What, then, in Aquinas's view, does make actions objectively right or wrong? What test must Christian conduct satisfy? One Aristotelian answer is: "right reason." "In human actions, good and evil are predicated in reference to the reason; because as Dionysius says, *the good of man is to be in accordance with reason,* and evil is *to be against reason.* . . Acts are termed human or moral in so far as they obey reason."[11]

What, though, does reason dictate? Reason is a faculty, not the norm it follows; the measurer, not the measure it applies.[12] By itself, the formula *"right* reason" is merely a blank check, ready to be filled in as one pleases: teleologically, deontologically, or otherwise. It does not conflict with VM—not because it answers the same question the same way, but because, without further specification, it gives no answer to the question.

A second Aristotelian answer is "natural tendency."[13] "Since good has the nature of an end," writes St. Thomas, "and evil, the nature of a contrary, hence it is that all those things to which man has a natural inclination, are naturally apprehended by reason as being good, and consequently as objects of pursuit, and their contraries as evil, and objects of avoidance. Wherefore according to the order of natural inclinations, is the order of the precepts of the natural law."[14]

Various objections may be urged against this answer, but in the end it, too, appears a blank check, awaiting further specification. "Natural" tendencies are good tendencies whose goodness needs to be explained.

Observing human beings as they are, we discover few universal, uniform, unchanging inclinations on which precepts of natural law might be based.[15] Even if we discovered a handful, they would not suffice to ground a general norm of right action. And even if they were more numerous, the gap between *is* and *ought* would still have to be bridged:

> Granted that these are "natural inclinations," why *ought* we to strive after them? How does the obligation follow from these facts, if facts they are? St. Thomas answers that it is because those things to which we have a natural inclination are "apprehended by reason as being good and consequently as objects of pursuit." But why are those things which are good in the sense of being sought after necessarily also good in the sense of being the right kind of things for us to choose?[16]

In this pertinent sense, what many seek may be bad and what few seek may be good.

Consider the case of children and the obedience they owe their parents. Mothers and fathers would receive with incredulity the suggestion that children have a natural inclination to do as they are told— to clean up their rooms, turn off the TV, go to bed, or stop playing and come in for supper. Thomas, aware of original sin and children's nature, made no attempt to base his case for obedience on an inherent tendency, but argued instead: "A son's debt to his father is so evident that one cannot get away from it by denying it: since the father is the principle of generation and being, and also of upbringing and teaching."[17]

In Aquinas's moral demonstrations, such silence about natural inclination is the rule rather than the exception. As P. J. McGrath remarks:

> St Thomas himself does not seem to have taken this part of ethical theory very seriously, since if he had, he should have appealed to it in all his ethical arguments; an action for him should be morally good only if it accords with a natural tendency and morally bad only if it frustrates a natural tendency. But in fact he uses several other forms of ethical argument in his writing and I have been able to find only three instances where he uses this type of ethical argument explicitly—to show that love of one's neighbour is morally good, to show that sexual intercourse is morally good and to show that suicide is morally wrong. So

I think we can conclude that St Thomas was aware of the difficulties in his own position.[18]

If, then, something comparable to VM is to be found in Thomas's
ethics, it will have to be both more broadly applied and more fully
spelled out than conformity to natural inclination. So let us turn,
without further beating about, to the norm which most readily invites
comparison with VM.

### THE FIRST PRINCIPLE OF PRACTICAL REASON

In reply to the query "Whether the natural law contains several precepts, or only one," Aquinas writes:

> As *being* is the first thing that falls under the apprehension sim-
> ply, so *good* is the first thing that falls under the apprehension
> of the practical reason, which is directed to action: since every
> agent acts for an end under the aspect of good. Consequently
> the first principle in the practical reason is one founded on the
> notion of good, viz. that *good is that which all things seek after.*
> Hence this is the first precept of law, that *good is to be done and
> pursued, and evil is to be avoided.* All other precepts of the natural
> law are based upon this: so that whatever the practical reason
> naturally apprehends as man's good (or evil) belongs to the
> precepts of the natural law as something to be done or avoided.[19]

Although this passage is one of the most discussed in Aquinas's
writings,[20] two basic questions have received slight attention from
commentators.

First: Is this "first principle of the practical reason" a moral principle, followed by those who act morally and violated by those who do
not, or does it state a practical necessity conformed to willy-nilly
by all human agents, moral or immoral, since they all seek some good
in whatever they do? In this latter interpretation, "the first precept
does not say what we *ought* to do in contradistinction to what we *will*
do."[21] "Just as the principle of contradiction is operative even in false
judgments, so the first principle of practical reason is operative in
wrong evaluations and decisions."[22]

There is something to be said for both interpretations, the moral and the nonmoral. The latter connects better with the notion of the good as that which all seek, whereas the former connects better with the "other precepts of the natural law," allegedly based on this first principle. However, in view of the general and immediate setting, of other passages (especially *Summa theologica* 1, q.79, a.12; 1–2, q.90, a.2, ad3; 1–2, q.94, a.6,c; and *In Psalm.* 36:19), and of the tradition to which this discussion belongs,[23] a moral reading of the principle, which many commentators have taken for granted,[24] seems clearly preferable.[25] It is also the only reading that would make Aquinas's principle at all comparable to VM. Just how comparable the principle is, even when so understood, depends on a second neglected question.

If the principle "Good is to be done and pursued, and evil is to be avoided" is taken as a supreme moral principle, how are the terms *good* and *evil* to be understood: in the comprehensive sense suggested by the dictum "Good is that which all things seek after," or in the narrower, strictly moral sense suggested by other evidence? In this more restricted reading, the norm would signify: "Whatever is right to do should be done; whatever is wrong to do should not be done" (call this Reading 1). In the broader interpretation, the norm would signify: "Good of whatever kind—nourishment, life, pleasure, knowledge, virtue, God—should be pursued; evil of whatever kind—pain, hunger, error, war, sin—should be avoided" (call this Reading 2). Whereas Reading 2 is broadly teleological, Reading 1 is purely formal and compatible with any moral theory, whether teleological or other. Thus the interpretive issue posed by these two readings is basic.

Exegetes regularly assume one sense or the other, without noting these two options or assessing their respective merits.[26] I shall therefore have to do some spadework of my own. My immediate aim will be to clarify this passage and norm, but the same evidence will also reveal Aquinas's thought more fully, thereby permitting broader, surer comparison of his views with VM.

Evidence for Reading 1 includes the following considerations:

1. A similar passage of St. Albert, Thomas's teacher, focuses on just moral good and evil.[27]

2. A narrowly moral sense is the one suggested (though not imposed) by the single place where Aquinas employs the norm syllogistically to derive a moral conclusion. In the early commentary on

the *Sentences* his reasoning runs: Evil should be avoided; but adultery is evil; therefore it should be avoided.[28]

3. A broader, nonmoral reading would make normative derivations much shakier. As one expositor remarks: "No man can fail to recognize that food is good, that society is good, for all men are moved by natural appetites to food and society. . . . This does not mean, however, that the pursuit of the objects of these appetites is always good."[29] So if the injunction to do good is expressed without qualification, must not moral good be meant?

4. Aquinas concludes his account with the gloss: "so that all the things which the practical reason naturally apprehends as man's good belong to the precepts of the natural law under the form of things to be done or avoided"; and things "said to belong to the natural law," as subsequent samples show, are actions, for instance preserving one's life, perpetuating the race by sexual intercourse, educating offspring, learning the truth about God, living in society, shunning ignorance, avoiding offence to those with whom one has to live. That is, they are things which it is right to do, since nature inclines us to them.

5. A variety of specific developments—for example, Aquinas's treatment of suicide (see below), lying[30], counsels,[31] contraception,[32] and other sins against nature[33]—point away from the broad teleology of Reading 2, hence favor Reading 1.[34]

6. The principle that "the same thing cannot be affirmed and denied at the same time," with which Aquinas compares the first principle of practical reason,[35] is as empty and formal as Reading 1.

7. Both these principles, he says, are self-evident, to us and in themselves. But "any proposition is said to be self-evident in itself, if its predicate is contained in the notion of the subject."[36] This can be said more surely of Reading 1 than of Reading 2. It is true, I believe, that even the general notion of goodness is action-oriented as well as appreciative;[37] and St. Thomas might agree. However, from the assertion that "the good is what all seek,"[38] that "any appetite is only of the good,"[39] that "what is good for something is suitable for it,"[40] and the like,[41] it does not strictly follow that the good *should* be done or pursued. Reading 1, on the contrary, leaves no doubt about its analyticity. "Should be done" is contained in the notion "morally good" or "morally right."

The weight of this last point is lessened by Aquinas's readiness to label assertions "self-evident" which are no more manifestly analytic, in themselves or in his thinking, than is Reading 2;[42] for example:

"The commandments of God must be obeyed";[43] "Thou shalt love the Lord thy God";[44] "Thou shalt love thy neighbor";[45] "One should do evil to no one."[46] Furthermore, persuasive reasons tell in favor of the second reading:

1. The norm's link, in the same passage, with the dictum "Good is that which all things seek after," which is general,[47] and with the words already quoted: "all those things to which man has a natural inclination, are naturally apprehended by reason as being good, and consequently as objects of pursuit, and their contraries as evil, and objects of avoidance."

2. Close parallels with *Summa* 1–2, q.10,a.1,c, on the "principle of voluntary movements" ("Now this is the good in general, which the will naturally tends to as any power does to its object; it is also the ultimate end, which is related to all desirable things as the first principles of demonstration are to all intelligible things; and universally it is all the things which belong to the one who wills according to his nature").

3. Precedents in Aristotle, such as "Practical wisdom is the disposition to reach true and reasoned conclusions about actions concerning human goods."[48]

4. Other precedents in Hugh of St. Victor[49] and in Anselm of Laon and his influential school ("the obligation of doing others good and avoiding their harm").[50]

5. Occasional indications of a more than merely moral sense in the comparable, usually ambivalent formulas that abound in earlier and contemporary discussions of synderesis.[51]

6. The explicit presence of some nonmoral goods (life, knowledge of the truth) among those Aquinas cites in illustration, and the implicit presence of others.

7. The doubling in the phrase "to be done and pursued" (*faciendum et prosequendum*), which nicely accommodates right actions to be done and nonmoral goods to be pursued, or instrumental good to be done and final good to be pursued,[52] but sounds less natural and needful with regard to moral good alone.[53]

8. Considerable evidence that Aquinas accepted the thought expressed by Reading 2.[54] "We plainly see," he writes, "that as anything has more perfect power and stands higher in the scale of goodness, the broader its desire for good and the wider its quest to realize good."[55] Thus he states, for instance, that all law, human and divine, aims at the common good;[56] that it is subject to the law of charity,

which enjoins doing good to others;[57] that prudence, the guide to all virtue, chooses the greater good;[58] that "God is not offended by us except insofar as we do something against our own good."[59]

In view of this eighth point, it may not make much difference what meaning we accord Aquinas's precept, or whether the precept has some single sense. Scholars often call attention to such difficulties in determining "the" sense of a text, but seldom see the difficulties as telling against the existence of a sense. Surely the author meant one thing or the other, and what the author meant is what the text means. It may be doubted, though, whether Aquinas, unlike his commentators, clearly envisaged both readings, recognized how importantly they differed, and intended just one sense rather than the other,[60] yet made no clearer than he did which sense he had in mind. However, whether he meant one thing or the other may matter little if, as seems the case, he accepted what both readings say.

## COMPARISON WITH VM

At first glance, an exegetical verdict may look important in order to understand the role assigned this "first principle." All other precepts of the natural law are based on this one, Aquinas says; all others "flow from" it.[61] However, in neither Reading 1 nor Reading 2 can Aquinas's precept serve in the manner these sayings suggest.

Take the question of self-defense. One argument employing Reading 1 might go: Moral evil should be avoided; but defending oneself is morally evil; therefore it should be avoided. Another, contrary argument might run: Moral good should be done; self-defense is morally good; therefore it should be done. Both times, the conclusion follows immediately from the second premise; the first premise is superfluous. Reading 2 does no better. One argument employing it might say: Evil of any kind should be avoided; but the death or injury of an attacker is an evil; therefore it should be avoided. Another would reach the opposite conclusion: Evil of any kind should be avoided; but the death or injury of the person attacked is an evil; therefore it should be avoided. The conclusions thus cancelling each other, no verdict would be forthcoming.

Aquinas's views suggest that this would always be the case. Every human action contains some good, he said, both objectively and subjectively. So a norm that simply enjoined doing good could not decide between alternatives. And a norm that enjoined doing good and avoiding evil, without further stipulation, could not determine whether to avoid the evil present in evil acts or to pursue the limited good they also contain. Further guidance would be needed. Clearly, then, Reading 2 would be as useless as Reading 1 for purposes of moral discernment or demonstration.[62]

The point I am making is stronger than that often made by commentators. It is evident that specific moral verdicts cannot derive directly from Aquinas's norm, by itself, no matter which way it is read. It cannot function as does, for example, the single premise in the argument: No one should be harmed; therefore Jim should not be harmed. However, this is to be expected. No substantive general norm—Kant's, Mill's, Moore's, or any other—could do better; none could function as a single premise to beget specific moral verdicts. Each has need of a further premise, stating what shows respect, what maximizes happiness, what maximizes benefits, and so forth. The stronger thing I am saying is that Aquinas's norm, read either way, cannot function even as these other norms do and therefore does not compete with them. Specifically, it does not compete with VM.

"If, however," *CMR* suggested, "we wish to make the maxim truly operative, and thereby validate Aquinas's claim," we can understand "good" and "evil" "as designating values and disvalues to be maximized or minimized through action. Explicitly or implicitly our reasoning would then run: 'Good is to be maximized, evil minimized; but this line of conduct (general or particular) does maximize good in relation to evil; therefore it should be followed.' Here there is no tautology, no idle repetition, but a supreme norm operates as a supreme norm should."[63]

Evidence like that already cited might be adduced in support of this richer reading. "It is the role of prudence," Aquinas wrote, "to prefer a greater to a lesser good."[64] And when good and evil conflict, the evil should be minimized, so that the greatest remainder of good over evil may be realized. "Thus if to protect himself a person uses more violence than is necessary, his action will be wrong, whereas if he resists his attacker in moderation, his defense will be licit."[65]

Other evidence, however, resists such a reading. Take the *Summa*'s treatment of suicide.[66] In answer to the question "whether it is lawful to kill oneself," Aquinas declares that it is altogether unlawful, for three reasons. First: "Suicide is contrary to the inclination of nature, and to charity whereby every man should love himself." Here no mention is made of life as a value. More important, no heed is paid to circumstances in which contrary evil or consequent good might tip the scales against life. The argument is as general as its conclusion. Second: "By killing himself he injures the community." Again, no consideration of conceivable cases, in which the community might benefit rather than suffer, complicates the reasoning. Still, these first two reasons might be viewed as hasty, one-sided value-balancing, in support of a preordained verdict, whereas the third reason abandons any semblance of value-maximization: "Whoever takes his own life, sins against God, even as he who kills another's slave, sins against that slave's master, and as he who usurps to himself judgment of a matter not entrusted to him. For it belongs to God alone to pronounce sentence of death and life, according to Deut. xxxii, 39, *I will kill and I will make to live.*" Other discussions, for instance of contraception and other "sins against nature,"[67] mix reasons similarly and create similar difficulty for a consistent VM reading of Aquinas's thought.

### OTHER POSSIBILITIES

"Following Augustine, Gregory, and Bernard," Gérard Gilleman notes, "from whom the early Middle Ages drew their inspiration, St. Thomas remains faithful to the traditional Catholic doctrine when he states that the substance and perfection of Christian life consists in charity."[68] "It is charity," writes Aquinas, "which directs the acts of all other virtues to the last end."[69] However, VM can claim to specify charity's requirements and thereby perform this service of direction. So can rival norms. Comparison with VM is not possible until agape's norm is spelled out.

More specific criteria, citing divine commands,[70] respect for persons,[71] inviolable goods,[72] or the proportion between act and end,[73] have been detected in Aquinas's writings, and will be considered in coming chapters, but not as readings of Aquinas. These readings fail as VM fails. No entirely general, nontautologous norm of objectively right conduct adequately captures Aquinas's thought.

This verdict may disappoint anyone who prizes such a supreme directive, imparting unity to the whole of ethics. However, St. Thomas may not have shared this dream. In his view, "Generalities about morals have a limited value because actions are so individual."[74]

Should it surprise us, then, if we discover in his writings no completely general principle that can usefully discriminate right from wrong? This final reading of Aquinas's position poses a more serious challenge to VM than do any of the specific formulas here scrutinized. It anticipates chapters 10 and 11, which question the validity and significance, not only of VM, but of any equally comprehensive norm.

# 5

# *Divine Commands: Adams*

Is right action right because it is commanded by God, or is it commanded by God because it is right? The voluntaristic doctrines of Scotus, Ockham, and subsequent thinkers give, or suggest, the former answer.[1] So do contemporary "divine-command" theories, whose recent vogue calls for fuller attention than *CMR* accorded them.[2]

"The basic idea behind a divine command theory of ethics," observes William Alston, "is that what I morally ought or ought not to do is determined by what God commands me to do or avoid. This, of course, gets spelled out in different ways by different theorists."[3] Indeed, it gets spelled out in different ways even by individual authors. Prominent in the literature is a series of articles by Robert Merrihew Adams, whose most recent position can furnish a focus for comparison and contrast with VM.[4]

## ADAMS'S THEORY

In "Divine Command Metaethics Modified Again," Adams proposes a modified version of a modified version of divine-command theory. The first theory in the sequence equates being morally wrong with violating God's commands; this, it says, is the meaning of the word *wrong*. The most obvious objection to this theory, Adams initially noted, "is that the word 'wrong' is used in ethical contexts by many people who cannot mean by it what the theory says they must mean, since they do not believe that there exists a God."[5] So the theory must be modified; it "cannot reasonably be offered except as a theory about what the word 'wrong' means as used by *some but not all* people in ethical contexts. Let us say that the theory offers an analysis of the meaning of 'wrong' in Judeo-Christian religious ethical discourse."[6] It indicates "what Judaeo-Christian believers mean by 'wrong.'"[7]

At first, Adams showed only slight recognition that, given the varying viewpoints of believers, even this modified claim faces similar difficulties.[8] Now, however, he characterizes his earlier theory "only as an analysis of the meaning of 'wrong' in the discourse of some Jewish and Christian believers," not of all.[9]

Such a thesis, semantic rather than ethical and restricted to certain unspecified believers, holds slight interest.[10] Adams presents his latest, further-modified theory as "a claim, not about the way in which some believers use the word 'wrong,' but about the wrongness that virtually everyone talks about."[11] As one cannot discover the nature of water by analyzing the concept *water*, so one cannot discover the nature of moral rightness and wrongness by analyzing the concepts *right* and *wrong*. To discover the nature of water one must undertake a chemical analysis; to discover the nature of rightness and wrongness, one must undertake an ethical analysis. The outcome in one case reveals what people talk about, whether they know it or not, when they talk about water; the outcome in the other case reveals what people talk about, whether they know it or not, when they talk about rightness or wrongness. Analysis identifies the essence.

For Adams, the moral status of an act is determined by the act's relation to the commands of a loving God. Not just to the will of God, or to the revealed will of God, for that might embrace matters of counsel as well as of precept. Nor just to the commands of any kind of God, but to those of a loving God; for a loving God would not prescribe, for example, that we torture infants for the fun of it. With this restriction added, Adams can allege: If X is wrong, then X is contrary to the commands of God; if X is obligatory, then X is required by the commands of God; if X is ethically permitted, then X is permitted by the commands of God.[12] The reverse also holds. Thus morality coincides with, indeed consists in, conformity with God's loving prescriptions. For convenience, I shall label this particular divine-command theory "DCT."

The theory has evident appeal. It sounds so simple, so sure, so transcendent, so evidently right in placing the divine pleasure at the heart of Christian ethics. Let us therefore consider its relation to VM. Is DCT a rival theory? Is it a better one?

## POSSIBLE CONVERGENCE

Adams counters the familiar charge of voluntaristic arbitrariness by stressing the goodness of God. "God is loving, and therefore does not and will not command such things as (e.g.) the practice of cruelty for its own sake."[13] Following the same logic, one would have to add further specifications: God's love is not merely attitudinal, but dispositional; not self-preferential, but generous; not parochial, but universal; not conditional, but unconditional; and so forth.[14] The rightness of God's commands is assured by the rightness of God's love. Adams, however, does not spell out what it means for God to be loving.

In this, his approach resembles Joseph Fletcher's. "There is only one thing," wrote Fletcher, "that is always good and right, intrinsically good regardless of the context, and that one thing is love."[15] This he could say with assurance because the love he had in mind was the good kind—the Christian, agapeic kind. Similarly, Adams can state that whatever a loving God ordains is right and good; for the love Adams has in mind is not just any kind: it is the perfect love of a perfect God. However, what is the nature of this perfect love? What does it prescribe?

When, in afterthought, Fletcher articulated the principle of agapeic love, his principle proved defective.[16] If Adams ventured a formulation of divine love, it might prove similarly unacceptable. Indeed, it might be identically flawed. Like Fletcher's ideal human agent, God might take account only of human, consequential values. Or his love might be more strictly utilitarian, focusing purely on human pleasure or human happiness.[17] As John Stuart Mill commented, "a utilitarian who believes in the perfect goodness and wisdom of *God* necessarily believes that whatever God has thought fit to reveal on the subject of morals must fulfill the requirements of utility in a supreme degree."[18] In the absence of further specification by Adams, this and many other possibilities remain open. God's love might take many forms.

Answers to the problem of evil, explaining permitted evil through greater intended good, suggest a value-maximizing Providence.[19] Nothing Adams says precludes this possibility. "I would not suggest," he writes, "that the descriptive force of 'good' as applied to God is exhausted by the notion of kindness. 'God is good' must be taken in many contexts as ascribing to God, rather generally, qualities of character which the believing speaker regards as virtues in human beings."[20]

It is clear, then, that both of these biconditionals may hold true: (1) an action is right if and only if it conforms with the commands of a loving God; (2) an action is right if and only if it conforms with VM. For all God's loving commands may conform with VM. Like Adams, most recent voluntaristic theorists leave room for this possibility; for most ground their biconditionals the same way he does.[21] The coincidence of the moral with the divinely commanded or divinely willed is assured by insisting that God is "the personification of goodness,"[22] "the perfectionist *par excellence*,"[23] "a morally perfect being,"[24] "wholly good,"[25] "loving and compassionate,"[26] "all-loving,"[27] "essentially loving,"[28] "perfect righteousness,"[29] "identical with perfect goodness itself."[30] In each instance the same questions may be asked: In what does moral perfection consist? What, therefore, does a morally perfect being desire or require? Only rarely do voluntaristic theorists sketch a brief response to these queries.[31]

Thus, the difference between VM and current voluntaristic theories is largely a matter of definiteness versus indefiniteness. There may be no conflict between them in practice. Clearly, however, theories that sound so unlike differ in more than definiteness. "Do good, avoid evil" may be an inchoate version of VM, but DCT is not. How else, then, do VM and DCT diverge? Where, perhaps, do they not only differ but disagree?

## CONFLICTING IDENTIFICATIONS

VM poses as a criterion of right and wrong, stating constitutive features, whereas Adams proposes conformity or nonconformity with God's loving commands as constitutive of morality. Can both answers be correct? If not, which one is preferable? How can we decide?

For a start, consider a simple comparison: What constitutes rain? A first response might be: "Drops of water falling from clouds." Not flakes or pellets, or drops of syrup, or drops of water running in streams. No: drops of water falling from clouds. For such is our use of the term *rain*. Believing that drops of water fell from clouds all day, we say, "The rain lasted all day." Believing that the drops were relatively sparse, we say, "The rain was light." However, we also say such things as, "Drenched with rain, his clothes clung close to his skin." Here the rain is not drops of water falling from clouds but drops of water that have fallen from clouds. The term's sense has shifted. It does not suffice, therefore, to consult usage when saying what constitutes rain; one must also consider the context and the corresponding sense of the word.

The like holds for moral terms. In deciding what constitutes rightness and wrongness, we should not only heed the language we are speaking and note the use of *right* and *wrong*; we should also attend to variations, noting shifts from person to person and setting to setting. Christian use differs somewhat from non-Christian use, and both are far from uniform. Thus some contexts require and impose a subjective sense, taking account of motive and intention, while others do not. Some contexts look backward, some forward, some in neither direction (see chap. 1).

In grounding and explaining VM, here and in *CMR*, I have attended explicitly to Christian linguistic usage and to context. Adams, like other divine-command theorists, attends somewhat to usage but not at all to context. He speaks of the "role" that moral concepts play, but takes no account of their varying roles in various settings. Thus his identification does not compare directly with mine. My equation of rightness with value-maximization holds only within a prospective, objective perspective. For other legitimate perspectives (e.g., agent-centered judgments of acts) it would be inaccurate. Adams, however, indicates no particular perspective for which his identification is supposed to hold true.

Nonetheless, his suggestion warrants scrutiny. Unlike some other rivals to VM, it entails no false moral verdicts, and reflects a familiar aspect of Christian moral deliberation. Specifically, within a prospective, objective perspective, Christians not only ask "What should I do?" or "What is for the best?" but also "What does God require of me? What do God's commands prescribe?"[32]

The question to be clarified is this: What is mere clue and what is defining criterion? Is being for the best a clue to being commanded by God or is being commanded by God a clue to being for the best? In what does the objective moral rightness of prospective acts *consist*?

In many contexts, such an identity-question is readily answered. Wet sidewalks, for example, are a clue to earlier rainfall but are not what raining consists in. Why not? One answer might be: Because sidewalks may be wet without its having rained, and rain may occur without sidewalks getting wet. What, then, of rightness and wrongness? Might there be rightness or wrongness without divine commands?

Adams replies in the negative. For him, moral terms are "rigid designators." In this, they resemble natural-kind words as analyzed by Donnellan, Kripke, and Putnam. As the actual analysis of water defines water for all possible worlds, so the actual analysis of moral rightness defines moral rightness for all possible worlds. In no possible world could water be anything other than $H_2O$. In no possible world could moral rightness be anything other than conformity with divine commands.

With many others, I question the doctrine of rigid designation, both with respect to proper names[33] and with respect to natural-kind terms.[34] Even if these expressions were rigid designators, it would not follow that ethical expressions are. The actual use of moral terms, by theists, atheists, and agnostics, gives no hint of rigidity. It is therefore incumbent on Adams to show that the doctrine of rigid designation can be extended to moral expressions. This he does not even attempt to do, nor do I think that he could succeed in the attempt.

However, let the matter pass. Before the advent of computers, chess did not consist necessarily in playing with people, but it did de facto. Similarly, even if morality does not consist necessarily in conformity with divine commands, it might de facto. Whether it does, remains to be decided. Given God's existence and moral legislation, does the prospective, objective morality of acts consist in their promising to maximize value or in their conformity with divine commands?

Adams argues his case as follows:

> Given typical Christian beliefs about God, it seems to me most plausible to identify wrongness with the property of being contrary to the commands of a loving God. (i) This is a property that actions have or lack objectively, regardless of whether we think they do. (I assume the theory can be filled out with a satisfactory account of what love consists in here.) (ii) The property of being contrary to the commands of a loving God is certainly believed by Christians to belong to all and only wrong actions. (iii) It also plays a causal role in our classification of actions as wrong, in so far as God has created our moral faculties to reflect his commands. (iv) Because of what is believed about God's actions, purposes, character, and power, he inspires such devotion and/or fear that contrariness to his commands is seen as a supremely weighty reason for opposing an action. Indeed, (v) God's commands constitute a law or standard that seems to believers to have a sanctity that is not possessed by any merely human will or institution. My new divine command theory of the nature of ethical wrongness, then, is that ethical wrongness *is* (i.e. is identical with) the property of being contrary to the commands of a loving God.[35]

Although (ii) looks problematic (some stretching of the term *command* may be needed to make the statement true), I shall not question Adams's premises. Nor shall I question the conclusion he draws from them—except for the assumption that it excludes other answers. VM too, I suggest, indicates a property which actions have or lack objectively; one which all and only wrong actions lack; one whose absence plays a causal role in our classification of actions as wrong, constitutes a reason weightier than any conflicting one for opposing an action, and stands above any merely human will or institution. Granted, "because of what is believed about God's actions, purposes, character, and power, he inspires such devotion and/or fear that contrariety to his commands is seen as a supremely weighty reason for opposing an action." But to fully understand this wrong-making reason it is necessary to examine "what is believed about God's actions, purposes, and character," and thereby to provide the missing account "of what love consists in here."

The morality of an action is comparable to the beauty of a sunset. As the features discerned in a sunset—its color, evanescence, form— are what make it beautiful, so the features discerned in an action are what make it right or wrong. They are not mere clues to something else.[36] If the action minimizes value, that, in itself, tells against the action. If the action maximizes value, that tells for the action. If it is wrong to torture children for the fun of it, as Adams acknowledges, the reason is not—at least not solely—that God forbids it. The action in itself is wrong. That is why Adams carefully precludes the possibility of God commanding any such thing.

Yet divine commands do affect an act's morality; so a more apt comparison is the following. "Tom," a mother calls, "come in and clean up the mess you've left in the living room." It is right for him to do so because it is a mess and because he made it; it is also right for him to do so because his mother has told him to. VM would recognize both reasons by saying: "Cleanliness is a value, and so is obedience; so obeying the command is doubly right." A parental-command theory would recognize both, more obliquely, by saying: "No, there is just one reason: the command of a mother who loves cleanliness." This analysis would obscure the intrinsic desirability of the act and its relation to the act's rightness. The same is true of DCT. As John Chandler has remarked: "If an action's being loving is a good (or compelling) reason for a loving God to command it, it must be an equally good reason for us to perform it insofar as we are loving in our limited way. That loving actions are commanded by God may be an additional reason for believers to perform them; but there is already sufficient (justificatory) reason."[37]

VM highlights what DCT leaves implicit: the intrinsic goodness and badness of acts, independent of divine commands. Likewise, DCT highlights what VM leaves implicit: the value of obedience to divine commands. So we may ask: Which formulation—VM's or DCT's—rings truer to Scripture? I suggest the following rough contrast: In DCT, emphasis falls on obedience, law, and divine transcendence, as in Old Testament morality; in VM, emphasis falls on immanence—on the inner goodness and rightness of charity, human and divine—as in New Testament morality. "Be perfect, therefore, as your heavenly Father is perfect" (Matt 5:48).[38] These words are a command, but what they urge is not obedience to commands. God is not the supremely, perfectly obedient One. "God is love, and those who abide in love abide in God, and God abides in them" (1 John 4:16).

## COMPARATIVE UTILITY

So much for theoretical merits and demerits. The chief difference between VM and DCT is practical. Adams does not claim practical utility for DCT, any more than I have for VM. So what follows should not be taken as criticism. DCT is not a method. It need not be useful to be valid. Nonetheless, the two theories can legitimately be compared with respect to their utility as well as their validity.

Defining criteria, such as these competing criteria of right and wrong, hold epistemological primacy relative to clues or mere symptoms. A symptom of $y$ is such through a regular connection with $y$ and therefore depends on the definition of $y$. Conceive $y$ differently, and the symptoms change.

Suppose, for example, that I am a utilitarian and judge morality by the criterion of human happiness. The evidence I will then consult, to determine right and wrong, will be attendance figures, say, indicating what forms of entertainment people most enjoy; standings within each category of entertainment; responses to questionnaires concerning marital felicity, contentment at work, satisfaction in one's calling, and the like. For the utilitarian such statistics, standings, and responses are all "symptoms": they do not constitute or define either happiness or morality, but they do suggest how to maximize happiness, and therefore what course to pursue: subsidies to the arts or to sports, a career in music or in science, an evening at the theater or at the arena. The significance of such clues to morality alters or entirely ceases, however, if the criteria of right and wrong change.[39]

Criteria fulfill their basic epistemological role better in proportion as they are more definite in themselves and related to clearer and more abundant symptoms or clues. In comparison with DCT, VM looks superior on both counts: it is more definite in itself and related to more sure clues.

Take killing. For VM, loss of human life is a sure clue, clearly related to value-maximization. For Adams's criterion, the fifth commandment furnishes more ambiguous evidence. Evidently, in the Old Testament the commandment cannot be taken to forbid all killing of human beings; and the New Testament provides no more refined, exceptionless version. Furthermore, even such explicit commandments as this are relatively rare in comparison with the moral questions that confront us. What has God said about abortion, genetic engineering, or nuclear disarmament?[40] What commands has God issued concerning open shop, in vitro fertilization, gambling, legalizing drugs, funding for UNESCO, the invasion of Panama, profit sharing, marrying, adopting a child, paying taxes, or placing Pop in a nursing home? Yet for these matters, too, pertinent values and disvalues are numerous and evident, even when the verdict is not.

At this point, Adams might wish to interject, with Peter Forrest: "Prohibition includes, but is not restricted to, a literal command (like God speaking to Moses and the people of Israel on Mount Sinai). God's prohibition is a disapproval manifested in some way which produces in us a tendency to avoid the prohibited act. This tendency could be due to the 'voice of conscience,' but it could be even more implicit."[41]

This suggestion introduces a second sort of vagueness in DCT: vagueness with regard to the ordinances' nature and etiology as well as their contents. Such implicit commands might take many forms—for example, the form of moral reflection leading to VM and to specific moral judgments based on VM. However, this possibility, left merely that, offers no guidance. To be sure, the voice of conscience, if inspired by grace, speaks infallibly; but what does it say, and how is one to know when it speaks? How is one to know that any given theory is divinely inspired?

VM, which may sometimes require us to compute present and future values, comprehensively, for alternative lines of action, hardly guarantees great clarity and sureness.[42] Nonetheless, it takes a major step beyond DCT toward greater definiteness. Adams's criterion is compatible with VM, with Fletcher's utilitarian principle, and with all the rival norms still be to considered, dictating different verdicts. Is a loving God an unrestricted proportionalist, a utilitarian, a Kantian, a restricted teleologist, a champion of inviolable goods, of irreducible rights, of "generic consistency"? If so, how does God communicate the divine will to us? No doubt in part by means of such inquiries as this one. So let us continue, and focus on theoretical differences that make a practical difference.

# 6

# *Respect for Persons: Donagan*

In *The Theory of Morality* Alan Donagan examined the Hebrew-Christian tradition and from it elicited the fundamental principle: "It is impermissible not to respect every human being, oneself or any other, as a rational creature."[1] He contrasted this norm principally with consequentialism, in particular with the utilitarianism of Mill and Sidgwick, and concluded: "The duty of beneficence in the Hebrew-Christian tradition is not the indiscriminate and unlimited maximizing of good imposed by utilitarianism. . . . Attempting to choose a moral system by its consequences is not only a mistake in moral theory but also futile."[2]

CMR, for its part, examined the Christian tradition and from it distilled VM. This norm appears more plausible than those Donagan considered and rejected, while his norm (which I shall term the principle of respect) looks more plausible than those I weighed and found wanting. So it seems desirable to provide what my book did not, and assess the respective merits of these alternative formulations—VM and the principle of respect. First I shall note similarities between them, then dissimilarities, and dwell on those that appear more significant for a possible verdict between the two principles.

## SIMILARITIES AND DISSIMILARITIES

Though importantly different in certain respects, the principle of respect and VM are both presented as general, Christian, substantive norms of objective morality. Of these characteristics the final three (their being *substantive* norms of *objective morality*) reveal the closest affinity, as follows.

**Substantive.** Neither the principle of respect nor VM is a merely formal principle. True, neither norm can render concrete verdicts by itself. Each has need of further specifications, concerning what is respectful (for the principle of respect) or what is valuable (for VM). For each this need is great, given their extreme generality. Still, when thus supplemented, both norms do yield verdicts—verdicts that conflict with those of rival norms.

*Objective.* Donagan distinguishes between two kinds of questions: "those about the rightness or wrongness of actions in themselves; and those about the culpability or inculpability of doers in doing them. Since answers to questions of the second kind presuppose answers to questions about the first, I describe them as 'first-order' and 'second-order' questions respectively."[3] The principle of respect figures as the fundamental principle of "first-order" morality; it concerns "the rightness or wrongness of actions in themselves."

Similarly, *CMR* stresses the difference between action-centered queries ("What shall I do?" "What action should I perform?") and agent-centered assessments of innocence or guilt,[4] argues the priority of the former,[5] then focuses on them. "Such, on the whole, is the perspective here adopted: 'concern with antecedent rather than consequent conscience, i.e., with prospective decision-making rather than with retrospective judgment-passing.'"[6] Within this chosen focus, VM answers the question: "By what consistent criterion are right and wrong to be assessed?"[7]

*Morality.* Donagan's principle specifies what is morally permissible and impermissible, mine what is morally right and wrong; neither specifies what is simply better or worse. This restriction might beget criticism, for abstraction is often taken for exclusion. Yet neither Donagan's principle nor mine can rightly be accused on this ground of minimalism. Both principles apply on both sides of the divide between counsel and precept. But "permissible" and "right" are not synonymous with "better" and "more perfect," and clarity is not served by supposing that they are (see chap. 1).

However, Donagan restricts the domain of the moral more than some critics and I would.[8] And even within that domain, VM is more broadly inclusive than the principle of respect. Here is a first significant difference between the two norms.

VM covers the whole of morality, whereas the principle of respect is doubly circumscribed. First, being conceived as "the fundamental principle of morality, with respect to the relations of rational creatures to themselves and to one another,"[9] it omits their relations to God, on the one hand, and to nonrational creatures on the other. (Thus cruelty to animals, for example, does not violate the principle of respect.)[10] Second, the principle is restricted to "that part of common morality according to the Hebrew-Christian tradition which does not depend on any theistic belief."[11] Of this secular morality, the principle of respect figures as the first, fundamental norm. From it, "common morality as a system" (in the doubly restricted sense just indicated)[12] is said to derive.[13]

The restrictions on Donagan's principle elicit various misgivings. It has been questioned, for instance, whether religious belief can be so neatly bracketed.[14] Further, regardless of their validity the restrictions beget unclarity concerning morality as a whole. What lies within the bounds of secular morality and what lies without? How do the two realms relate? Is the principle of respect always decisive? If not, when and how does it need to be completed in deciding concrete problems? Suppose duties to God or obligations to animals conflict with duties to humans: which take precedence, when, why? If, for instance, a biological researcher cites advantages to humans and a critic objects to the agony inflicted on animals, the principle of respect cannot adjudicate their disagreement, whereas VM can. Donagan does not address such issues, nor is it likely that he could do so effectively without employing some such norm as VM.

Doubtless, unclarity about the specifically religious or Christian part of morality is of more concern to believing readers than to nonbelieving. This is one indication of the audience Donagan had chiefly in view. Another is the manner of his derivation, which, unlike that in chapter 3, does not presuppose the basic soundness of Christian tradition. "For Donagan," notes Jeffrey Stout, "'the Hebrew-Christian moral tradition' is little more than a list of canonical texts drawn up with Kant in mind."[15] Thus Donagan provides scant historical evidence for supposing that Christians, if they wish to be true to their past, should embrace the principle of respect in preference to VM. I shall return to this point.

## FURTHER DISSIMILARITIES

I have suggested that the principle of respect and VM are comparable in five important respects. Both norms are proposed as objective, moral, substantive, general, and Christian. The first three similarities are close; the last two reveal significant differences. VM, I have noted, is both more general and more specifically Christian, at least in its derivation, than is Donagan's principle. And there are other differences.

## Definite Versus Indefinite Scope

VM is proposed as a criterion of right and wrong, in the sense already noted. Were Donagan to present respect for rational creatures as a rival criterion, defining the "permissible," it would be clear that all permissible actions must pass the same test: all must satisfy the principle of respect. However, abstracting as he does both from defining criteria and from religious beliefs, he leaves open various possibilities: (a) the principle of respect might apply to all actions and might decide all of them (though religious beliefs might sometimes have to determine what is truly respectful); (b) the principle might apply to all actions but might not be decisive for all, since religious considerations (e.g., the love of God) might sometimes take precedence; (c) the principle might apply to the majority of actions but not to all, and might be decisive for all it covered; (d) it might apply to the majority of actions but might not be decisive for all it covered, just for most; and so forth. The unclarity that thus enshrouds Christian ethics in *The Theory of Morality* infects its central principle as well. The reader is not told the precept's power and scope.

## Rich Versus Meager Historical Support

A criterial approach is not the only way to confront issues like these, but it does assure that they are faced. It has the further advantage of deepening and enriching the process of historical consultation. Sifting Christian tradition, *CMR* examines much more than the explicit moral principles that Christians cite in their moral reasoning. Explicit principles, like explicit definitions, are relatively rare. To see what people mean by their words—whether words like *time* and *true* or words like *right* and *wrong*—you must observe when, where, and why people employ them. Thus, among the evidence *CMR* weighs for and against the criterion of value-maximization, explicit norms as general as VM or the principle of respect rarely surface.

Indeed, no such norms appear in the varied moral reasoning surveyed in the first of the book's three historical chapters. Yet in each instance the mode of moral appraisal is similar:

(A) Jesus looked to the good of the handicapped man, recognized no comparable value in delay, and so argued the rightness of healing him on the Sabbath. (B) Similar weighing of advantages prompted Paul to recommend celibacy over marriage and to proscribe eating meat when a brother would be harmed. (C) Ignatius generalized the approach in his method of tabulations pro and con. (D) Thomas applied it to self-defense, comparing more- and less-violent modes of self-preservation and pronouncing against the former. (E) He recognized that similar balancing might sometimes tell against the general norm of restitution and saw this as typical. (F) Believers in precepts, like Ramsey and Mitchell, adduce the advantages of rules over no rules or of this rule over that. (G) They have sometimes pressed their reasons more strongly, not only in favor of specific rules but also against all exceptions. Value is best served by their exclusion. (H) Rahner countered similar rigidity in the practice of obedience by citing possible countervalues and insisting that they be taken seriously in assessing right action. (I) Similarly, Mackey noted the usual advantages and occasional disadvantages of conformity to church teaching and advised that these contrasting values guide decision. (J) With respect to political structures, Niebuhr advanced negative arguments, Maritain positive ones, in behalf of democracy. The right regime is the one that best promotes human welfare. (K) At a loftier level Teilhard's apologia evinced the same thrust. It would be wrong to pluck the cosmic fruit before it is mature. Value should be maximized.[16]

Had Donagan attended to such evidence as this he could hardly have passed over VM as he did. When in his brief review of sample norms he comes to Aquinas's "first principle in practical reason" that "good is to be done and pursued, and evil shunned," he does not mention the maximization of good over evil as a possible interpretation. Instead, he takes the principle's moral import to be: "Act so that the fundamental human goods, whether in your own person or in that of another, are promoted as may be possible, and under no circumstances violated."[17]

This norm he judges inferior to Kant's. "For while most acts of respecting human nature as an end in itself are also acts of respecting certain fundamental human goods as to be promoted and never violated, not all are. For example, respecting as an end in itself one human being who attacks the life of another, who is innocent, does not appear to exclude using deadly violence on him, if only so is the life or fundamental well-being of his innocent victim to be safeguarded."[18]

With this objection VM agrees. However, so did Thomas (e.g., *Summa theologica* 2–2, q.64,a.7). As Margart Farley notes: "Aquinas' first-order precepts regarding the protection and pursuit of human goods no more absolutize these goods than does Donagan's system. There is not one of the three basic inclinations which Aquinas lists in *Summa Theologiae* 1–2,94,3, which he is not willing at some point or other to subordinate to what may be a higher good."[19] The like may be said of Christian tradition as a whole. As a distillation of that long tradition, VM looks more plausible than does the principle, derived from Grisez, which Donagan considers and rejects.[20]

## Broad and Clear Versus Narrow or Misleading

Farley's comments suggest further points of comparison between the principle of respect and VM. As Thomas's applications of his principle often suggest VM, so do Donagan's applications of the principle of respect. Repeatedly, the respectful thing to do is the one that maximizes value; and where it is not, one may question, not the norm of respect, but Donagan's judgment of what is respectful. Thus, a principal question to consider in evaluating not only the Christian credentials of these two norms but also their respective moral merits is this: How genuinely do they differ? If suitably interpreted, would they perhaps yield identical verdicts?

Donagan's treatment of lying helps to focus the issue. "For benevolent purposes," he concedes, "it is sometimes permissible to dupe children, madmen, and those whose minds have been impaired by age or illness. Yet even with regard to them, the weight of Jewish and Christian opinion is on the side of veracity, except where it is beyond doubt that a truthful statement or evasion will cause unjustifiable harm."[21] Why unjustifiable? In virtue of what principle? Perhaps in virtue of a beneficent respect that desires the welfare of every human being, rational or irrational; but not, it would seem, by reason of respect such as Donagan's principle enjoins and such as he urges against lying to responsible adults: "The duty of veracity appears to be independent of the institution of contract and to rest simply on the fact that the respect due to another as a rational creature forbids misinforming him, not only for evil ends, but even for good ones. In duping another by lying to him, you deprive him of the opportunity of exercising his judgement on the best evidence available to him."[22]

Here Donagan's key value comes to view: autonomy.[23] Those who do not possess it cannot be deprived of it; those who do possess it should never be denied its exercise. However, a dominant value is not the same thing as a universal principle. So this comparison of cases serves to sharpen the following dilemma: either respect for others as rational beings is one value among many that determine right and wrong (in which case it fits within VM's larger perspective but cannot adequately ground the principle of respect's broad claims); or "respect" is made to embrace all values (in which case the labeling is unenlightening and misleading).

Some critics take Donagan's term "respect" at face-value and therefore complain of narrowness. Farley comments that "Donagan's theory . . . favors autonomy over well-being and the self as individual agent over the self in mutuality with others."[24] According to Jeffrey Stout, what we need "is a view of ourselves that is rich enough to sustain both a healthy respect for autonomy and a genuine regard for the positive dimensions of well-being."[25] "It is love-like attitudes," Roger Wertheimer notes, "that seek and take satisfaction in the well-being of their objects; respect does not take satisfaction at all, and does not aim at the good of its objects. Respect for truth may motivate honesty and candor, but not, as love of truth does, the quest for wisdom, certainty or scientific knowledge."[26]

Critiques like these are telling, however they are viewed. For the previous dilemma can be restated thus: either the principle of respect is indeed too narrow and the complaints are just, or the critics have been misled by a deceptively narrow formulation of a broader, more comprehensive viewpoint.

Why not call things by their names? When one tells untruths to the young, the senile, or the insane so as to shield them from harm or assure their welfare, one does as VM says: one seeks to maximize good and minimize evil. When one tells the truth to a responsible adult, despite the consequences, so as to allow the person to exercise his or her own judgment, one seeks a different good: autonomy.

There is no need to bundle all values under a single heading. Such terminological imperialism only generates confusion.

To illustrate the inadequacy of Donagan's formulation, consider Sartre's well-known student, who, fully aware that his mother lived only for him, had the choice of staying with her or leaving to join the Free French Forces, thereby plunging her into despair. According to Sartre, Kant's ethics can offer no solution to such a dilemma: if the student treated his mother as an end and stayed with her, he would risk treating the resistance forces as mere means; if, instead, he went to join them, he would treat them as an end but risk treating his mother as a means.[27] To this, Kant could reply that to show preference to one person, or group, over another when values conflict is not to treat the one party as an end and the other as a means. And Donagan might reply similarly were Sartre's objection couched in terms of respect for rational creatures. But such a response would not show the relevance of Kant's principle or Donagan's variant, in this or similar cases. Mere respect for persons does not indicate which person or persons to prefer. If the young man is moved by the millions who suffer under Hitler's heel and leaves to join the Free French, or is impressed by the sureness of the benefit to his mother and opts to stay with her, his decision is not based on greater respect for one party or the other but on the greater or surer good to be achieved. So again, why not call things by their names? Why hesitate to acknowledge the rule of value-maximization?

## REASONS FOR THE PRINCIPLE'S NARROWNESS

It appears that one of Donagan's reasons is Kantian[28] and agnostic. He is ready to specify the supreme value that should govern all conduct within the realm of "common morality," but thereafter disclaims any competence to judge what is best for others.

Aristotle's description of [happiness] has not been bettered: activity in accordance with human excellence (*arete*), in a complete life (*Eth. Nic.* 1098a16–20). That happiness in this sense presupposes the enjoyment of primary human goods, such as health, a certain amount of wealth, and a respected place in a free society, has been brought out by Rawls. There is no doubt at all that normal human beings naturally seek happiness. But they do not all in fact seek it; and when they do not, it may be presumed that they have reasons for not doing so which they consider of overriding importance. That is why Kant consistently held happiness to be the natural end of man but not an unconditional rational end. Action in pursuit of happiness is always intelligible in rational terms, but it is not imposed by reason.[29]

Donagan may be impressed by the reasons people have had for not pursuing happiness or the enjoyment of primary goods (and not by their reasons for denying respect to others), but Christian thought has not joined him in concluding that one person's value-judgments are as good as another's. In this it has arguably been more consistent than Donagan (see below). In any case, a principle based on such skepticism about all values save one hardly mirrors Hebrew-Christian thought through the centuries.

Donagan's remarks on beneficence suggest a second reason, in tension with the first, for the principle of respect's narrow focus: "If a man respects other men as rational creatures, not only will he not injure them, he will necessarily also take satisfaction in their achieving the well-being they seek, and will further their efforts as far as he prudently can. In short, he will observe the general precept: *It is impermissible not to promote the well-being of others by actions in themselves permissible, inasmuch as one can do so without disproportionate inconvenience.*"[30] Given this entailment, Donagan might say there is no need to mention other values; respect brings all values with it.

However, which values? The "well-being *they seek*," as in the first sentence, or "the well-being of others" (*tout court*, without subjective restriction), as in the second sentence? The first phrasing preserves autonomy. The second permits value judgments of one's own and admits other values than autonomy, hence implicitly calls for balancing of values when values conflict, as they regularly do.[31]

Understood in this second manner, the principle of respect differs from VM mainly in its wording, and its wording seems doubly deficient. For one thing, a term such as *love, care,* or *concern* more aptly indicates a beneficent attitude than does the word *respect.* For another, an effective norm of right conduct must do more than name an attitude. Donagan is rightly critical of those who "proclaim *agape* (as theologians like to call it) as the sole valid guide for action: and, as the sole and sufficient rule of conduct, 'Love, and do what you will!'"[32] However, "Respect, and do what you will!" succeeds no better. The works of respect, like those of love, require clearer specification, as in VM.

Donagan's critique of C. D. Broad's and W. D. Ross's "newer intuitionism" suggests a third likely reason for his unwillingness to broaden the principle of respect and give clear recognition to other ends besides autonomy. According to this intuitionist view, writes Donagan:

> A moral agent must . . . be familiar with all the more significant characteristics that count for or against doing the actions that have them. . . . Supposing that he is, and that he succeeds in reviewing all the morally significant characteristics of the various courses of action open to him, he may then proceed to the second stage: that of weighing the various considerations against one another, in order to judge what course of action is indicated by the greatest balance of favorable considerations over unfavorable ones.[33]

Against this position (and implicitly against VM), Donagan initially objects that "since the new intuitionist theory confers no definite weight on any consideration, every agent may assign to each of them whatever weight seems good to him."[34] In a sense this is obviously true, but also irrelevant. People may and do reach varied verdicts on any matter, whether theological, historical, scientific, or valuational. However, Donagan continues:

> Philosophically, the chief objection must be that it is fraudulent to describe what the new intuitionists take to be the process of moral deliberation as one of "weighing" or "balancing" considerations. For that metaphor to be appropriate, there must be a procedure for ascertaining the weight of each consideration, either comparatively or absolutely, a procedure analogous to that of putting objects on a balance or scale. It is an appropriate description, even a happy one, for deliberation in terms of a moral system in which different considerations are ordered serially; for in such deliberation, which consideration has priority over the others is determined by reflecting on their respective places in the series—a process unquestionably analogous to weighing different objects in order to find the heaviest. But by

> repudiating anything that might order the various considerations it acknowledges, and accepting as "weighing" or "balancing" any process whatever in which a man, hesitating before alternatives supported by different considerations, without conscious insincerity overcomes his hesitation, the new intuitionism deprives that description of any definite sense.[35]

In utilitarianism, the single factor "happiness" might perhaps order values as greater or less (according as they promised more or less happiness). However, once multiple, independent values are admitted, as by Broad and Ross (and VM), no verdict is possible. Considered by themselves, disparate values are not comparable.

When unpacked, this critique looks no more impressive than variants one encounters in Finnis, Grisez, and others (see chap. 2). With or without scales to check one's impressions, it is meaningful to speak of weighing objects in both hands and judging whether one is heavier than the other or both are roughly equal in weight. With or without thermal measures, it is meaningful to speak of feeling objects and judging whether one is warmer or colder than the other or both are roughly the same temperature. And none of Donagan's remarks reveals any reason to suppose that a similar procedure with regard to values is less meaningful or sound.

Donagan himself performs and enjoins much balancing of values with no other norm to guide him than the principle of respect. Yet as we have seen, the rule of respect cannot serve to order value considerations, and in fact does not. In *The Theory of Morality*, values determine respect more than respect determines values. Thus Donagan's practice conflicts with his theory. In instance after instance he applies the principle of respect by means of value-balancing.

Indeed, he grounds the principle of respect itself on comparative value considerations. "They are: first, that rational creatures are negatively free because they exhibit a kind of causality by virtue of which their actions are not determined to any end by their physical or biological nature; and second, that because of that causality, they are creatures of a *higher kind* than any others in nature. These characteristics, according to Kant, provide rational creatures with an end which their own reason must acknowledge: their own rational nature."[36] Donagan accepts these considerations as "rationally compelling," though not "intuitively self-evident," and proceeds to base his system on a piece of patent value-balancing, akin to that scrutinized in chapter 2.

In his treatment of particular precepts, his talk about respect veils much similar balancing; sometimes, however, the balancing protrudes unmistakably through the verbal camouflage. Comparisons of disparate values (e.g. justice, life, convenience, cost, community, self-respect, enjoyment) repeatedly determine what is "respectful" and therefore permissible. A few samples from among many:[37]

Respecting as an end in itself one human being who attacks the life of another, who is innocent, does not appear to exclude using deadly violence on him, if only so is the life or fundamental well-being of his innocent victim to be safeguarded.[38]

Inasmuch as the relief and enjoyment afforded by a drug compensate for any ill effects it may have, then it is permissible to use it. . . For anybody to place any kind of drug-induced enjoyment before the full use of his capacities as a rational creature, is a plain case of failure to respect himself as the kind of being he is. The objection is not to the enjoyment in itself but to the inordinate value set upon it.[39]

Nobody is morally obliged to promote the well-being of others at disproportionate inconvenience to himself. One does not fail to respect another as a rational creature by declining to procure a good for him, if that good can be procured only by relinquishing an equal or greater good for oneself.[40]

Solitude and civil anarchy are both human evils. Hence a man owes it to himself as a rational creature and to others, to obey even the defective laws of his civil society, while doing what he can to rectify defects and to prevent abuses. Only in extreme cases can direct disobedience, or general civil disobedience and rebellion, be justified.[41]

War is so horrible an evil that only a very clear and great cause can justify it.[42]

"Fervently desirous of preventing the abolition of Palestinian Jewry, [Judah ben Ilai] did draw the line where reprieve would be bought at the price of moral cohesion and self-respect." . . . There are minimum conditions for a life worthy of a human being, and . . . nobody may purchase anything—not even the lives of a whole community—by sacrificing these conditions.[43]

To avoid pain, or trouble, or even exertion is a perfectly good reason in itself for doing something; but not when there is adequate reason for putting up with it.[44]

I cite these passages as ad hominem evidence that value comparisons of the forbidden variety—judging more or less, without calibration or the mediation of any common measure other than value itself— are possible, legitimate, and decisive. The same and similar passages suggest the justice of Wertheimer's critique. "Donagan's tradition," he observes, "has never provided a facsimile of a philosophically adequate description of what this thing, respect, is that it directs us to have. Instead we are given assorted claims about an odd lot of behavioral expressions of respect."[45] The underlying rationale that makes sense of the preceding "odd lot" is VM, not the principle of respect.

In confirmation of this verdict, consider a case of apparent value-balancing which Donagan examines with special care, indeed with desperate ingenuity. The famous potholer caught in the rocks may, he concedes, be blown away so that those behind him will not drown. But the reason is not, he argues, that otherwise "many lives will be lost and far greater misery will obtain" (as Kai Nielsen contends[46]). Rather, the reason is that the potholers in question may have agreed, tacitly and legitimately, that if, "through nobody's fault, they should be confronted with a choice between either allowing certain of their number to be killed, or doing something that would, against everybody's will, cause the deaths of fewer of their number, the latter should be chosen."[47] In killing such a spelunker, his companions would be carrying out his own wishes, not sacrificing him for a greater good. Even in his death, autonomy would triumph.

But suppose there were no such tacit agreement? Well, "perhaps it would have force even if it were virtual; that is, even if all members of the group, were they to think about it, would agree that everybody in the group would think that so to conduct themselves was the only rational course."[48] Suppose, though, that there were no such tacit or virtual agreement: what then? And would they be right in thinking that "so to conduct themselves was the only rational course"? Would even the tacit agreement be permissible, as claimed? If so, why? Might they as legitimately agree to blast out anyone whose predicament threatened to delay their supper? I think it is clear that in Donagan's reasoning the balance of values is decisive and the judgment of what is respectful and permissible is derivative.

The passages quoted, and Wertheimer's summary verdict, suggest that a fourth reason for the narrowness of the principle of respect is no sounder than the preceding three. As a ground for preferring Kant's interpretation of the primary principle to that of Aquinas, Donagan cites its simplicity.[49] The structure of any system of morality based on the Principle of Respect is logically very simple, he explains, and,

> The structure of the fundamental principle is itself simple. It contains only one concept peculiar to moral thought, that of (moral) permissibility. And its sense is that no action which falls under the concept of not respecting some human being as a rational creature can fall under the concept of being permissible. The second concept it contains, that of (not) respecting some human being as a rational creature, is not peculiar to moral thinking. It has a place in descriptions of human conduct in anthropology and psychology, and of course in everyday descriptive discourse.[50]

Aquinas's principle, by contrast, speaks of good and evil rather than of respect, and therefore adds further concepts "peculiar to moral thought." So does VM.

Wertheimer's assessment suggests how illusory is this contrast. Bundle all manner of values under the single heading "respect" and the most varied disvalues under the single heading "disrespect," and one may create the impression of simplicity together with richness. But the simplicity will be purely verbal. And why stress simplicity, if the good we rightly strive for is a many-splendored thing? "Simplex sigillum veri," it has been said;[51] yet long experience suggests that the contrary has more often been the case: "Simplex sigillum falsi."

A series of illustrations in *CMR* (the limitation of intrinsic good to human good, to states of consciousness, to moral good, to virtue, to humans' final end, to the world to come, to the beatific vision, to God alone) documents the danger of undue simplification.[52] "As the mind's thirst for unity leads to repeated reductions in the speculative order (materialism, idealism, determinism, and so on), so the heart's kindred yearning reduces value after value to a servant of the one."[53] Donagan's yearning would seem to be more of the mind than of the heart, but his Kantian reduction leads to a similar outcome. As each of the cited reductions reveals inner incoherence,[54] so does his. The varied values he eliminates from the principle of respect play their inevitable roles. The comparisons he declares meaningless he nonetheless repeatedly performs. His practice, it seems, is sounder than his theory, and indicates the need to rethink and reformulate the theory.

# 7

# *Inviolable Goods: Grisez*

In contemporary Christian ethics, no other theory of ethical conduct has been so thoroughly, systematically developed and defended as that set forth in the writings of Germain Grisez, the leading representative of an influential school;[1] and no other volume has developed the theory as fully as Grisez's massive *Christian Moral Principles*. The whole work, notes its author, is "devoted to explicating this fundamental principle of a human life centered upon the Lord Jesus": "Precisely because we are called to share in his divine life, we ought to strive to realize the fullness of human life in ourselves and others."[2]

So formulated, the principle suggests a broad concern for value, comparable to VM's, and similar Christian inspiration. However, Grisez's exposition soon parts company with proportionalism. This favored target he characterizes sometimes as a "method of moral judgment,"[3] sometimes as a "theory of moral norms,"[4] and sometimes in both ways together, as "a mistaken theory of moral reasoning according to which one arrives at moral norms by comparing the proportion of good and bad in the alternatives for choice and judging that obligatory which seems to offer the greater good or lesser evil."[5] This fusion, or confusion, of the procedural and the normative complicates comparison with VM, which says nothing about moral reasoning; but it is clear that Grisez rejects both types of proportionalist theory—the normative as well as the procedural.

It could not be otherwise. If either type of theory is to stand, the values compared or maximized must be comparable. But Grisez denies their comparability (see chap. 2). Inevitably, then, his fully developed theory diverges from VM. Emphasis falls on individual values, taken individually, as in the claim already mentioned: according to Grisez, one may never act against a basic human good. Scrutiny of the thesis thus roughly stated reveals an underlying, fundamental challenge to VM.

## VALUE INVIOLABILITY

"The basic principle of morality," writes Grisez, "might best be formulated as follows: *In voluntarily acting for human goods and avoiding what is opposed to them, one ought to choose and otherwise will those and only those possibilities whose willing is compatible with a will toward integral human fulfillment.*"[6] Here, "'integral human fulfillment' does not refer to a definite goal to be pursued as a concrete objective of cooperative human effort,"[7] but instead refers, eschatologically, to "a single system in which all the goods of human persons would contribute to the fulfillment of the whole community of persons."[8]

This may seem a distant star by which to steer one's course, but as a first practical implication Grisez notes: "The guidance which the ideal of integral human fulfillment offers to choice is to avoid unnecessary limitation and so maintain openness to further goods."[9] Eight "modes of responsibility" add definiteness, yet remain more general than the specific moral norms to which the modes lead.[10] In particular, the eighth mode decrees:

> *One should not be moved by a stronger desire for one instance of an intelligible good to act for it by choosing to destroy, damage, or impede some other instance of an intelligible good.* This mode is violated by one who deliberately brings about something humanly bad, in order to prevent something else bad or to attain something humanly good. In such a case, one is moved to act according to the comparative strength of one's various desires. Thus one subordinates some possible elements of human fulfillment to others, even though there is no reasonable basis for doing so. In placing a nonrational limit on fulfillment, one proceeds in a way not consistent with a will toward integral human fulfillment.[11]

Violations of this eighth mode are to be found, for example, in the following: "To obtain a grant to continue his research, a scientist falsifies data to make the project's initial results appear more promising than they are. To obtain information which will save many lives, a military commander tortures children. To bring about what he considers a necessary change in moral teaching, a theologian encourages people to do something they believe wrong."[12]

Here a puzzle appears. These illustrations, and the second sentence in Grisez's account of the eighth mode, focus on evils used as means; they do not exclude evil side effects, such as Grisez countenances elsewhere. Yet the first, italicized sentence makes no distinction between permissible and impermissible evils; and other passages sound similarly broad in their condemnation of any choice "to destroy, damage, or impede some instance of a basic human good."[13]

Grisez provides an interpretive key when he writes: "What one does in the strict sense is what one chooses to do—that is, what is sought for its own sake and/or included as a means in the proposal one adopts."[14] Thus the reader's difficulties arise from a technical sense both for action verbs like *do* and for psychological verbs like *choose*. In ordinary parlance, a person who performs a therapeutic abortion, knowingly kills a fetus in the process of saving a life. With whatever regrets, that is what the therapist does and chooses to do. Not so, however, in Grisez's special terminology; for the person who licitly performs such an operation does not seek the fetus's death for its own sake nor employ it as a means to save the mother's life. That is achieved by removing the diseased organ.

It seems, therefore, that Grisez's eighth mode comes to this: One may never choose to destroy, damage, or impede a basic human good, save as an unsought side effect; one may not choose such an evil either as a means to some other good or as an end in itself.[15]

## AN IMPLICIT CHALLENGE

This norm is half objective, half subjective. The ban on evil means to good ends is objective; the ban on evils willed for themselves is subjective. Given this distinction, it might seem that I now have little more to do here. The objective norm has been considered in chapter 3, and the subjective norm causes no problem: of course we should not will any evils for themselves; of course we should not make them our ends. That can be taken for granted.

Yet a challenge lies implicit in Grisez's norm, a challenge not to VM alone but to any equally comprehensive criterion of objectively right conduct. According to a doctrine currently in vogue among Christian ethicians, "it is the whole action including circumstances and intention that constitutes the basis for ethical judgment."[16] Thus, a norm like VM is defective, since it does not "recognize both the objective and the subjective aspects of human behavior as indispensable to any genuine moral judgment."[17] Purely objective verdicts are either invalid or nonmoral.

Grisez shares this general viewpoint. Reading off intentions from objectively described acts and assessing the intentions thus ascertained, he sees no need for a strictly objective judgment of the acts. Any action that cannot voluntarily be performed without defect in the will is an immoral action. *CMR*, on the contrary, distinguishes between objective and subjective morality, and recognizes no way to infer one from the other, save to say that *if* a person performs an action which is objectively moral for the reasons which make it objectively moral, that person's will is in order; the act is subjectively as well as objectively moral. But *whether* a person performs the act for this or some other reason cannot be determined simply from the behavior the person freely chooses.

How basic this disagreement is can be grasped from Grisez's account of "the derivation of specific moral norms from modes of responsibility" (emphasis added):

> Its heart is a deduction which can be formulated in a categorical syllogism. In the simplest case, the normative premiss is a mode of responsibility, which excludes *a certain way of willing* in respect to the relevant goods. The other premiss is a description of *a type of action*, which is sufficient to make it clear that an action of this kind *cannot* be willed except in the excluded way. The conclusion is that doing an act of that kind is morally wrong.
>
> Actions not excluded by any mode are morally permissible; those whose omission would violate some mode are morally required.[18]

Theoretically, this disagreement with *CMR*, though basic, might occasion no conflict with VM. The verdicts Grisez deduced from behavior might reveal a regular pattern, permitting a behavioral description of right conduct; and this description might agree with VM. If, however, the verdicts revealed no such regularity, conflict with VM or any comparable norm would be inevitable. The objective norm would disapprove some conduct which the subjective verdicts approved, or would approve some conduct which the subjective verdicts disapproved; or both types of conflict might occur. There could be no general agreement between subjective and objective verdicts.

In Grisez's case, such appears to be the situation. For him, as for many others, intentions are tied with actions so tightly as to permit no independent judgment of the actions' objective morality, and so irregularly as to exclude any single, coherent norm of objective morality.

## AN ILLUSTRATION: CONTRACEPTION

Both the tightness and the irregularity appear, for example, in Grisez's treatment of contraception. He distinguishes three cases: (1) natural family planning (NFP); (2) artificial means employed in typical circumstances; (3) artificial means employed by a raped woman. In 2, no licit intention is possible (here is the tightness). In both 1 and 3, licit intention is possible, but for different reasons (here is the irregularity). Let us look more closely at this sampling.

Though Grisez's verdicts on 1, 2, and 3 have stayed constant, his reasons, as he notes, have not.[19] As of 1988, his argument runs as follows. New human life is a good. To block it requires some valid reason. However,

> To establish the rational preferability of the reason to choose to contracept, the two reasons must be rationally compared. To do this, one needs a standard by which to compare the two reasons precisely inasmuch as they are reasons for acting. But there is no such standard nor can there be. (We have argued this point at length elsewhere and will explain it only briefly here.) Therefore, the attempted justification inevitably fails, and so the choice to contracept is contrary to reason, and therefore is immoral.[20]

Natural family planning, which Grisez approves, poses an evident objection to this argument against contraception.

> How can NFP be chosen without contraceptive intent? Couples using NFP studiously abstain on the "baby days" and have intercourse only during the "safe" periods. It certainly seems that they do not *want* to have another baby and are doing what is necessary to avoid having one. Thus, the argument will go: Those who choose NFP must have exactly the same contralife will as those who choose to contracept. So, the argument will conclude, if contraception really is morally unacceptable, NFP is no less unacceptable.[21]

In reply, Grisez contends that NFP can be chosen without the contralife will that artificial contraception necessarily entails. For the intention of a couple practicing NFP may not include "the very not-being of the baby," but "only the burdens which having another baby would impose with respect to other goods, and/or the benefits which might flow from avoiding those burdens."[22] Thus there may be no weighing of one intended good against another intended good, in the manner deemed impossible. That such a focused intention is possible in the one case and not in the other he demonstrates as follows:

> When contraception is chosen, the choice is to impede the baby's coming to be, in order that the goods represented by [the agent's] reason be realized and/or the evils represented by it be avoided. When NFP is noncontraceptively chosen, the choice is to abstain from intercourse which would be likely to result in both the baby's coming to be and the loss of goods and/or occurrence of evils represented by that same reason, in order that the goods represented by that reason be realized or the evils represented by it be avoided.[23]

Of a raped woman, though, it might also be said (in the same not entirely happy fashion)[24] that "when contraception is chosen, the choice is to impede the baby's coming to be, in order that the goods represented by [the agent's] reason be realized and/or the evils represented by it be avoided." So a different rationale is required to justify her action. Such a woman, Grisez maintains, unlike a willing partner in intercourse, may take a contraceptive douche "without ever projecting and rejecting the baby who might be conceived."[25] Her sole concern may be her own protection. For, "the measures which are taken in this case are a defense of the woman's ovum (insofar as it is a part of her person) against the rapist's sperm (insofar as they are parts of his person)."[26] I shall say nothing for the moment about the merits of this reasoning, but shall just note that it differs from that which legitimizes NFP. There the fact of abstention is deemed psychologically decisive; here the alleged fact of self-defense permits a legitimate focus of the will.

Before assessing this reasoning, let us be clear about its implications. Conduct which necessarily contaminates the will cannot be legitimate. If, then, such contamination is common and the reasons for it vary, revealing no single objective pattern, there can be no single objective criterion of right conduct. A norm like VM is ruled out. Now, much Christian moral reasoning collectively conveys precisely this impression, of frequent contamination and irregularity. Hence the significance of the present sampling. It does not stand alone in Grisez's writings or in Christian ethics generally, but represents a mass of moral argumentation.

## ASSESSMENT

Since Grisez's argumentation focuses on the will, evaluation can be clarified and made more systematic by listing ways in which a person's will might be defective and by considering whether the will of those whom Grisez condemns must, in fact, be defective in any of these ways.

1. *A person might desire for itself the prevention, diminishment, or destruction of some good or the infliction of some evil.*

Various sayings of Grisez point in this direction. Of the couples he censures he writes:

They look ahead and think about the baby whose life they might initiate. Perhaps for some further good reason, perhaps not, they find the prospect repugnant: "We do not want that possible baby to begin to live." As the very definition of contraception makes clear, that will is contralife; it is a practical (though not necessarily an emotional) hatred of the possible baby they project and reject, just as the will to accept the coming to be of a baby is a practical love of that possible person.[27]

An earlier remark sounds similar: "To choose by our very action that the good not be realized is incompatible with fundamentally loving it, for such a choice is identically an unwillingness to permit the good to be."[28]

If type 1 ill will is intended,[29] such inferences are fallacious. Those who engage in contraception, natural or artificial, may not desire life-prevention for itself, but for a variety of reasons which they consider weighty. They may love their present children, and may regret that they cannot have more. Torn between alternatives, they may declare in all sincerity, "We wish we could have another child."

Grisez's argumentation suggests that people could not thus express their genuine desire, but only an emotional velleity. For they could not compare the good of the child with some other good and see that the other good outweighed it. Such comparisons, he claims, do not make sense.

I need not repeat chapter 2's critique of this contention. For present purposes it suffices to ask whether such comparisons make no sense to others besides Grisez. Do they make so little sense, so obviously, that any Jack or Jill who claims to have a positive will toward new life, in itself, yet chooses to prevent it, must be mistaken or be speaking insincerely? Must the person's pro-life will be not only weaker than it should be, but nonexistent? Must it be a mere sentiment, a mere emotion?[30] No, the alleged impossibility of comparison, if veridical, is not that evident; it is not akin to the impossibility of squaring a circle or adding two and two and getting five. Comparisons of the kind excluded are sanctioned and performed, validly or invalidly, by trained thinkers.

This fact is pertinent for a second possibility as well as the first:

2. *A person might will to act in a way the person thought was wrong.*

If trained thinkers are sincere in their claims, surely less trained and less reflective people may be sincere in theirs. They may employ artificial contraception, in typical circumstances, and believe that they are doing the right thing. For they may believe that they have good reasons. Grisez would apparently agree. He acknowledges that those who choose to contracept "may think that they are not choosing immorally, for they are likely to suppose that their reason to contracept somehow justifies choosing to do so."[31]

By implication, this admission snips the first kind of connection as well as the second: if people think they have good reason to contracept, their contraceptive intention need reflect no hatred for new life, in itself. This, too, Grisez appears to concede when he remarks that "a couple who otherwise would welcome another baby might . . . choose contraception with a view to preventing the consequences which the couple who choose NFP equally are trying to avoid."[32]

There remains a third possibility:

3. *A person might will to act in a way that was objectively wrong.*

If the condemned kind of contraception is objectively wrong, then those who will it, will something wrong. Their will is defective in this third sense. However, what grounds does Grisez have for asserting that such is the case? As we have seen, his objective-sounding norm cannot serve to show the objective wrongness of contraceptive behavior; for, if read objectively, the norm would condemn too much. And Grisez shuns the traditional argument from "unnaturalness." Instead, he relies on the badness of the will to show the badness of the act, and not vice versa. But our review of possibilities has revealed no way in which the badness of the will can be inferred from the mere willing of contraceptive behavior. The doer's bad faith cannot be inferred. Hatred of new life, in itself, cannot be inferred. What can?

Grisez might adduce a fourth possibility:

4. *A person might make a choice for which the person had no sound, valid reason.*

This response sidesteps the requirement of providing an objective norm by which to test the soundness of a person's reasons. Judgments can be reached case by case. With respect to contraception, once recourse to value-balancing is excluded, a justifying reason is excluded. "There can be no rational method by which to establish the rational preferability of the reason to contracept."[33]

A sufficient rejoinder is to deny, again, the alleged impossibility of cross-category value comparisons. However, a second response is worth pursuing: How can good reason be found for the kinds of contraception Grisez approves if it cannot be found for the kind he disapproves? "No couple," he writes, "can choose NFP without contraceptive intent unless they have a reason not to have another baby."[34] But those who choose artificial means may have the identical reason not to have another baby. What makes their reason unsound but not the others'? How can one comparison of values be valid and the other not, or one comparison be necessary if the other is not? How does the mere difference of means chosen to the same end entail such a radical difference in subjective possibilities?

Grisez perceives the problem of double standard but does not meet the objection as I have posed it. To justify his split verdict, he makes two points. First, one choice is a choice to do something, whereas the other is a choice not to do something ("namely, not to engage in possibly fertile sexual intercourse"). Second, in the latter choice, "the baby who might come into being need not be projected and rejected," whereas in the former choice it must.[35] This response fails in both its parts: the first assertion looks irrelevant to the problem I have posed; the second looks both irrelevant and untrue.

Let me start with the first point. Granted, we cannot be expected to have reasons for not doing all the countless things we might conceivably do but do not even contemplate. If, by sheer coincidence, a couple's intercourse fell into an infertile pattern, it would be unreasonable to demand their reason, good or bad, for adopting such a strategy. For them the pattern would not be a strategy. However, for NFP-users it is. Their method represents a deliberate choice, for which they have reasons. And the fact that the contraceptive means they adopt are active or inactive, natural or artificial, makes no evident difference with regard to the alleged impossibility of comparing the good avoided with the good sought. If the users of artificial means cannot make such a comparison, neither can the users of natural means. If the users of natural means do not need to make such a comparison,[36] but may simply focus on the good sought, so may the users of artificial means.

Grisez makes much of the distinction between *not wanting to have a baby*, which is common to users of both licit and illicit means, and *not wanting the baby one might have*, which he claims need not be present in users of NFP but must be in (typical) users of artificial means.[37] The latter must "project and reject" the child that might be. He does not explain or prove this necessity, or the basis for the alleged disparity between the two groups. Nor do I think he can. If users of NFP can carefully avoid conception without "not wanting the baby they might have," so can those who use artificial means. Thus the charge of irrationality fails. But with the other kinds of bad will excluded, there is nowhere else to turn. The argument reaches a dead end.

### THE LARGER LESSON

"Judge not," Scripture says (Matt 7:1, Luke 6:37; cf. Luke 18:11, Rom 2:1, James 4:11–12). "Do not pronounce judgment before the time, before the Lord comes, who will bring to light the things now hidden in darkness and will disclose the purposes of the heart" (1 Cor 4:5; cf. Rom 2:16). Yet Grisez professes to know the purposes of the heart. From outer conduct he would infer the inner disposition of the agent; from contraceptive behavior, for example, he would deduce a sinful will.

Reason, as well as Scripture, poses problems for this approach. Subjective immorality cannot, in general, be inferred from a description of the behavior chosen. As noted, this verdict is important for VM. However, it cannot be deduced from just the preceding sample criticism, or from this critique together with those to come in chapter 8, or from the failure of all such attempts that I have encountered, varied though they are. Inductive demonstration, running through all cases, is excluded; and an a priori demonstration, snipping all connection between behavior and subjective immorality, shows no brighter promise.

Such a demonstration would stress human fallibility. However strongly reasons tell for or against an action, some people may see things differently and choose wrongly in good faith. Yet could even the dullest persons honestly believe that torture, for example, is ever permissible? Yes, I think they could, in special circumstances. They might judge, for example, that torture of a captured soldier, to save a whole invasion force, might be legitimate, especially if slight torture sufficed. Lessen the benefits, however, and heighten the torture, and the likelihood of such approval alters proportionately. At the extreme, it looks uncertain whether even a sadist would see nothing wrong in severe, prolonged torture inflicted simply for the sake of the sadist's gratification.

These contrasting cases suggest a general pattern. The likeliest instances in which the will would be tightly bound, and objectively evil conduct would inescapably be recognized as evil, are ones where the value or disvalue is so heavily one-sided that no one could honestly suppose that the balance tipped the other way.[38] But in such instances as these, objective wrongness, as determined by VM, would entail subjective wrongness, and not the other way around. Besides, whichever way the entailment went, both verdicts—the objective and the subjective—would agree. Hence subjective wrongness could not be cited against VM, as by Grisez.

This, I suggest, is how the challenge implicit in his arguments can be met, not only for contraception but in general. The challenge comes, I said, from tight connections and irregular reasons: that is, from tight connections of subjective verdicts with sheer behavior, together with irregular reasons for the subjective verdicts. What I have now suggested is that, insofar as tight connections may be plausible in extreme cases, they reveal a constant pattern, and the pattern agrees with VM.

# 8

# *"Proportionate Reason": Knauer*

The contrast between VM and the views of Peter Knauer shows how problematic is the label "proportionalism." VM defines right and wrong by the proportion of value and disvalue in alternatives, and Knauer does not. Yet definitions of proportionalism based on popular versions often exclude VM, while many a discussion of proportionalism cites Knauer as a major representative.

This contrast structures the present chapter. First I consider the distinctive, nonproportionalist aspect of Knauer's thought; then I examine a tenet, often included in accounts of proportionalism, which he shares with many proportionalists but not with VM. The first part requires two sections, for Knauer's thinking has undergone important shifts, and it is therefore necessary to distinguish between a standard, more familiar version of his position (call it K1) and a recent, revised version (call it K2).

## THE STANDARD VERSION

According to K1, an action is right if and only if it has a "proportionate reason."[1] This phrase has misled many. "My reasoning," Knauer notes in correspondence, "has nothing to do with what generally is called proportionalism."[2] A reason is not made proportionate by the balance of good and evil;[3] rather, "the concept of 'proportionate reason' refers to a relation of appropriateness between the act and its reason."[4] Overall and in the long run, the act is not counter-productive;[5] it does not contradict its own end, as does, for example, excessive work or study, or whaling that depletes the whale supply.[6] "This valuation rests on the foundation that the value sought is commensurate when it is achieved in the highest possible measure for the whole."[7] "Moral good consists in the best possible realization of any particular value envisaged in its entirety."[8]

So stated, Knauer's criterion is more rigoristic than VM. However, the defect is easily remedied. So too is the reference to what an action *does* achieve rather than to what it *promises* to achieve (see chap. 1). Thus, Knauer might revise his norm to read: A prospective action is right if and only if it promises to achieve its end as well as, or nearly as well as, any alternative, incompatible action. However, what does Knauer mean by an action's "end"? What establishes a given value as an action's "reason"?

Although Knauer's formulas fluctuate,[9] with some passages suggesting an objective determination of the reason or end[10] and some a subjective determination, the latter predominate.[11] The value or end in question is the one "sought,"[12] the one "which is expressly sought,"[13] "the desired value,"[14] the one "recognized as present,"[15] the value "to which we aspire,"[16] "the chosen value,"[17] the one "by which the act is motivated at any given moment,"[18] the agent's "own end."[19] However, the end thus specified is not entirely subject to the agent's whim; it "must be universally formulated."[20] For example, a thief's purpose may be to enrich himself, and his action may not contradict that limited purpose, even in the long run; but it does contradict the generic value of wealth. Since the action undermines that value for society as a whole, it is immoral.[21]

Although this amplification of the end saves the theory from evident falsification, serious problems remain for the familiar version of Knauer's thought which I am now considering. Before reviewing these difficulties, let me say a word about the reasons that pointed him in this troublesome direction. Why, in K1, does he focus on a single good per act and eschew any form of proportionalism?

A first reason is familiar from previous chapters. For Knauer, as for others, disparate values are incommensurable.[22] In support of this claim he relies on supposedly evident examples rather than on arguments. How, he asks, could one rate the value of being a musician versus that of being a doctor;[23] or, "how could one declare the profession of musician objectively inferior, equal, or superior to that of lawyer, when there is question of choosing between them? Both are good and necessary, each in its way: they are simply different."[24]

As in chapter 2, I would reply that such disparate values are indeed incommensurable, just as abstract justice and truth are incommensurable—indeed with still more reason. Justice and truth are at least pure values, whereas being a lawyer or being a musician is not. As Knauer notes, in concrete choices like these, disvalue always accompanies value.[25] Furthermore, even if the options Knauer cites were free of all disvalue, they would still be too abstract for comparison. No general assessment is possible, for example, between being a musician and being a lawyer. Yet for a specific individual, with specific talents, inclinations, opportunities, and responsibilities, the verdict may be evident. For young Amadeus, the balance may tip clearly in favor of music rather than the law. Indeed, for him there might be no value in the law; pursuing a legal career might be a disvalue. Knauer omits all specifications of kind, extent, and probability that make comparison possible.

With still greater brevity, he alleges a second reason for rejecting value-maximization. "Does not such a conception lead to ethical rigorism? It would no longer be possible to do the good as well as the better, but whoever did not choose the better would act wrongly."[26] Some maximizing doctrines invite this objection,[27] but not all do. Recognizing that in standard usage *right* and *wrong* are not synonymous with *better* and *worse*, I have worded VM more cautiously: a prospective action is right if and only if it promises to maximize value as fully, *or nearly as fully*, as any alternative action.

As I have noted and Knauer has come to recognize, K1 has need of similar refinement to meet a similar objection.[28] However, this is just the first in a series of difficulties. The following considerations suggest how slow any teleologist should be to abandon value-commensurability and substitute a theory like K1.

***Faulty Foundation.*** For Knauer, the choice of one end rather than another is, in a sense, arbitrary. One incommensurable good is no better than another. One naturally wonders, therefore, why it should be obligatory to maximize a value which it is not obligatory to seek at all. Sanford Levy explains Knauer's rationale:

> To act without a commensurate reason in his sense is, he feels, to act in a self-contradictory manner. To explain this, he compares morality to prudence. If a student is so intent on learning that he neglects his health, he may learn a lot in the short run, but in the long run he will learn less. He therefore "contradicts his own purpose," and his actions are "unintelligent" and "self-contradictory." The same sort of thing, according to Knauer, happens in the moral case. If one seeks a kind of value but

accepts a short run gain at the expense of the long run, making it impossible to attain the maximum amount of the value, the action contradicts itself and is irrational. "Unintelligent and therefore immoral acts are in the last analysis self-contradictions."[29]

Levy notes problems with this argument. "First, even if there is a contradiction in these cases, and even if reason does reject contradictions, it is not clear that these rejections have moral significance. One is not generally wicked for failing to choose means best suited to one's good ends even though this means that, in a sense, one's chosen means contradict these ends."[30] If one chooses to go fishing, without being obliged to, and uses a weak line rather than a strong one, there is no sin in that. If one chooses to sleep away the day, without being obliged to, and curls up in an uncomfortable position, there is no sin in that. Maximum rest is not made mandatory by the fact that one chooses to rest.

"Second," Levy points out, "the view that acts lacking commensurate reason . . . are wrong because involving a self-contradiction, a contradiction between means and end, only works if the agent in fact has the end which the means contradict. . . . If the thief had as his end wealth in general, it is true that his act would be irrational; but his end is only his own wealth, and his means do not contradict that end."[31] Thus, Knauer's theory faces a dilemma. Take the "end" narrowly, and thieves may be saints (the more efficient, the more saintly). Take the "end" broadly, and all "self-contradiction" disappears, and with it any reason, in Knauer's incommensurabilist view, to insist on the fulfillment of the end chosen rather than of some other. Thus, the distinction between personal and universal ends that saves Knauer's principle from evident falsification deprives it of whatever rational justification it might appear to have.

*Single End.* Both objectively and subjectively, an action may have more than a single end, and often does. For example, President Bush's statements suggest that he had varied aims when he launched the war against Iraq, and he may have had others he did not mention. Which of these multiple ends determined the morality of his action? American prestige? Votes? Regional security? American access to oil? World access to oil? Kuwaiti independence? The rule of law in international affairs? A curb to nuclear proliferation? Freeing the Iraqi people from dictatorial rule? Countering the President's reputation as a "wimp"? If many or most acts have multiple ends,[32] how can a single-end criterion serve as a general guide to right action?

*One-Sided.* Objectively, the values ignored in Knauer's unilateral approach have as much claim to consideration as do the ones singled out. Procreation can be a value in intercourse, but so can union, love, and mutual support. Freedom had value in Kuwait, but so did life, property, and the environment. Any intrinsic value, as such, has a claim to consideration. It is something which, other things being equal, should be enhanced, preserved, or brought to be. Knauer himself speaks of the "obligation to realize in the best possible way all the values of creation."[33]

Consider St. Paul's advice to the Christians of Corinth about the eating of food offered to idols. According to Knauer's single-track criterion, if the diners desired simply to be nourished or to relish the tasty dish, prospective spiritual harm to the onlookers might be disregarded. The agent's end would be decisive for the act's morality. Since disparate ends such as pleasure, health, and spiritual or moral well-being are incommensurable, there is nothing to choose between them. Paul disagreed. "If food is a cause of their falling, I will never eat meat, so that I may not cause one of them to fall" (1 Cor 8:13). There is no need to consider whether eating the food would defeat the aim of the eating.

Scripture reveals other such instances. For example, King Herod, delighted by Salome's dance and thinking only of trinkets, pets, or pots of gold, promises to give her whatever she requests. To his chagrin, she asks for the head of John the Baptist. What to do? There is value in keeping promises and value in the life of an innocent, holy man. VM would permit the judgment that John's life is the greater value.[34] Knauer's single-track criterion would not. If Herod opts for keeping his word, then that value is decisive. Yet it is difficult to envisage a convincing account according to which, in thus favoring the good of promise keeping, Herod would compromise that same good in the long run. And even if one did manage a somewhat plausible account, it would not explain the immediate sureness of our judgment that Herod should not have had the Baptist beheaded. As in the case Paul cites, there is no need to engage in such complex calculations. John's life counts too, not just the value of keeping one's promises. The "standard-version" criterion is too narrow.[35]

*Impracticality.* In early reaction to the view he later adopted, McCormick noted a difficulty for Knauer's position:

> For Knauer, a reason is commensurate if the manner of the present achievement of a value will not undermine but support the value in the long run and in the whole picture. This is a sound description of proportionality. But who can confidently make such a judgment? An individual? Hardly. It seems to demand a clairvoyance not granted to many mortals and would paralyze decision in most cases. For example, what individual can say whether this present abortion will, in the long haul, undermine or promote the value of maternal and fetal life?[36]

The verdict thus arrived at may be nothing more than a "prudent bet."[37] Others have urged this objection still more strongly.[38]

Knauer acknowledges the difficulty of long-term calculations,[39] but may have felt reassured by the thought that any teleologist must consider both immediate and long-term consequences and that the latter are always difficult to estimate. Thus he may not have noticed what an epistemological revolution his single-track criterion entails. Repeatedly, what is most difficult to decipher becomes most crucial.

Consider the two examples just cited. The evil of the Baptist's death is sure; the long-term counterproductivity of Herod's keeping his promise is far less certain. The scandal to weak Christians looks likely enough, at least on some occasions, to elicit Paul's warning against eating food offered to idols; deleterious long-term effects on physical health or physical pleasure are a matter of mere conjecture, or wild surmise. Yet for Knauer's restricted criterion they alone are morally decisive if, as seems likely, nourishment or pleasure is the eater's goal.

*Overall Incoherence.* Knauer insists that the criterion of counterproductivity is not subjective or arbitrary; an action's overall, long-term prospects are not subjectively determined.[40] However, to judge from the evidence I have cited, for Knauer an action's end is subjectively determined, and the prospects for that end are what determine an action's morality. Hence an action's morality is, in this sense, subjectively determined. It can therefore be seen that Knauer's norm differs from VM in kind. VM is strictly objective, abstracting from motive or intention. K1 is mixed, looking somewhat to motive and somewhat to consequences, but to neither in the manner a strictly subjective or objective norm would require. A subjective judgment on action can and should abstract from long-term consequences, which a person may easily miscalculate. An objective judgment on morality can and should abstract from motive or other subjective determinations, which do not affect the objective rightness or wrongness of conduct.

The "Hanging Judge," I have heard, used to conclude his verdicts by saying: "And may God damn your soul to hell forever." Apocryphal or not, the words do suggest the possibility that a judge, in passing sentence, may wish that justice be done and society be served—and that the wretch suffer. In that case, the judge's action may be objectively moral and subjectively immoral. K1 permits no such distinction. Judged by one of the jurist's multiple motives, the action may be subjectively-objectively right; judged by another, it may be subjectively-objectively wrong. Which it is, there is no way to determine so long as Knauer's criterion speaks of only one reason or end.

*A Basic Ambiguity.* Suppose the judge's action were purely vindictive. It would then resemble many another act whose purpose is to harm. Are such actions made moral by their long-term effectiveness in achieving their end; that is, by their overall destructiveness? Knauer might suggest that the motive is the pleasure to be derived from harming, and not the harm itself. "One can only will some harm because of some connected good."[41] However, such is not the psychological reality in many instances. For example, the man whose affair had been terminated by a priest-confessor and who, enraged, stabbed a priest friend of mine twenty-one times was not motivated by a desire for pleasure, nor by a desire to go to jail, nor by a desire to recover his girl-friend, but by hatred. He wanted to hurt.

To free Knauer's theory from psychological error, one might have recourse to the conception cited earlier, according to which any object of the will is, ipso facto, a "good." "'Good,' in the widest sense in which it is applied to human actions and their principles, refers to anything a person can in any way desire."[42] However, this subjective reading of K1 is no more successful than the objective one. The act's genuine end—to harm—may now qualify as a "good," but it does not qualify as a justifying reason.

Thus, K1 faces a dilemma. On one hand, the subjective sense of *good* extends the theory to all actions, including malevolent ones, but deprives it of all credibility: a malevolent action, whose aim is to harm, is not made moral by its potential harmfulness, overall and in the long run. On the other hand, the objective sense of *good* makes the theory more plausible but restricts its coverage: on occasion, there may be no genuine good that the agent pursues, hence no way to judge the agent's act by its long-term implications for that good. As a comprehensive account of right action, K1 appears to rest on this subjective-objective ambiguity.

## THE REVISED VERSION

The position I have been considering deserves close scrutiny, because it is the view conveyed by Knauer's best-known writings (in no discussion of Knauer's views have I encountered the modifications I shall now describe) and is the view others have come to share as a result of those writings. Recently, however, in a revised edition of *Der Glaube kommt vom Hören* and in private correspondence, Knauer has importantly corrected the impression conveyed by his earlier writings. Whereas he at first envisioned only a single value sought in each action, by which its morality might be determined, he now recognizes the possibility of several such values. Whereas he previously required that the chosen end be maximized, he no longer imposes that requirement. Whereas he previously judged an action solely by the criterion of counterproductivity, he now adds a second test. "The fundamental moral norm runs as follows: So act that you do not, overall and in the long run, destroy the very value you are then seeking, *nor needlessly sacrifice other values.*"[43] Other values are needlessly sacrificed, he explains, if their surrender is not needed in order to save the value sought, overall and in the long run.[44]

This triply revised position is the one I have labeled K2. Though it resolves two of the difficulties I have cited against K1 (rigorism and single end), it only mitigates others, and leaves others in full force, while adding difficulties of its own.

Since the first clause of Knauer's new basic principle retains the norm of counterproductivity, and the second clause links with the first, much the same objections still obtain that I have made under the headings Faulty Foundation, One-Sided, and A Basic Ambiguity. Faulty Foundation: One still wonders why the fate of a value should be decisive for an act's morality when that value need not be sought at all rather than some alternative, supposedly incommensurable, value. One-Sided: Other values are still slighted, being accorded weight only in relation to the values that figure as motives. A Basic

Ambiguity: The "good" an agent seeks may still be such merely in the sense that it is in fact desired (the person may, for instance, seek revenge) or in a more objective sense that narrows the norm's coverage.

Difficulties also remain for the theory's overall coherence. K2 still gives the impression of answering two distinct questions, so answering neither properly. To the extent that it accords decisive importance to the agent's aim or purpose, the new theory looks like an answer to the question of subjective morality. To the extent that it revises the agent's (possibly multiple) end to make it universal, then accords decisive importance to objective counterproductivity and necessity, it looks like an answer to the question of objective morality.

Questions of these distinct kinds—subjective and objective—often arise. Many real-life settings call for judgments of one kind or the other, but none I can conceive calls for objective-subjective mixing as in K1 or K2. Some context might perhaps require comprehensive judgment, combining objective and subjective assessments; but in that case these assessments would first have to be accurately formulated, separately, before they were combined.

Like many ethicians, Knauer ignores contextual issues of this kind. But a theory devised for no specific real-life setting may be suitable for none. Such, I suggest, is the case for K2 as well as K1.

New difficulties also appear. Previously, considering a single value per act, Knauer saw no need to compare disparate values.[45] Now, however, with multiple end-values admitted, an action might conceivably be counterproductive for one end-value but not for another. VM-type comparisons would permit the judgment that value A is more important than value B, or vice versa; or that the long-term benefit to value A outweighs the long-term benefit to value B, or vice versa. But Knauer rejects such comparisons. How, then, can counterproductivity be judged for actions with multiple ends?

Similar unclarity infects the second clause of Knauer's new formula, proscribing unnecessary harm. In a proportionalist perspective, some disparate, proportionate benefit might legitimize a harm. But Knauer does not believe in disparate, proportionate benefits. The harm must somehow be required for the agent's end, whether single or multiple. However, if the end is multiple, must the harm be necessary for all the constituent ends, for a majority, or for at least one? If it is necessary for one but inimical to another, what then? By acknowledging multiple motives, Knauer appears to have entered a morass from which he can extricate himself only by abandoning the doctrine of value incommensurability: that is, only by becoming a proportionalist.

Even then, he might not accept VM; for a further aspect of his thinking allies him with many proportionalists but not with VM.

## THE MORAL/NONMORAL DICHOTOMY

In traditional precept ethics, the reasoning employed on behalf of various norms often smuggled moral values in before their time. Some argued, for example, that organ transplants entail "mutilation," hence employ an "evil" means, hence are unlawful. In reaction, others insisted that a means not be classified as morally evil before judgment is passed on the action as a whole. The evil of an organ donor's loss is physical, premoral; the morality of the transplant depends on the proportion between this premoral evil and the premoral good intended and achieved by the transfer. Unfortunately, this type of analysis, valid and enlightening in many cases, has been universalized. The result is an antithesis which seems as much in need of correction as the thesis it rejects.

VM, too, looks to the proportion of value and disvalue. However, as a species of unrestricted proportionalism, it envisages maximizing all values, moral as well as nonmoral. Many teleologists do not, but determine the morality of conduct by purely nonmoral considerations. This position, which I shall term the "moral/nonmoral dichotomy," is so widespread, at least in appearance, that it is often taken as a defining trait of proportionalism.

> To avoid approving the choice of moral evil, proportionalism requires that the goods which can be sacrificed for proportionate reasons not include moral specifications. Instead, the good is defined independently of moral considerations, and what is right and wrong is determined by benefits and harms in respect to the good thus defined. This way of defining the goods other than moral goodness itself is expressed in the language proportionalists use; the basic goods are often called "premoral," "nonmoral," "ontic," or "physical."[46]

VM, on the contrary, admits moral values among those to be maximized, and moral disvalues among those to be minimized, within its objective focus. This need entail no confusion. There need be no question-begging of the kind proportionalists and other teleologists rightly resist, provided that the final verdict is not sneaked in at the start or along the way. Moral aspects of an action may be weighed against other aspects, and moral effects may be weighed against other effects. And indeed they often are.

> For example, parents who desire their children's happiness risk overindulging them and thereby making them selfish and unappreciative; so they seek to strike a balance between present, nonmoral benefits (toys, ice cream, a trip to the zoo) and the children's long-term, moral welfare. Again, choosing between schools, they perhaps weigh the academic mediocrity of one against the low moral level of another, and its likely effect on their children's moral character and conduct. Or, concerned for their own virtue, they may have to decide between the financial advantages of their current work-place and the occasions of sin they recognize there. A moral theologian may have to balance the long-term benefits of truth against the unfortunate short-term effect which the truth, unassimilated, may have on the moral convictions of his audience.[47]

Such examples, of moral consequences balanced against nonmoral, could be multiplied at will.

Justice is an oft-cited illustration.[48] Suppose a legislator, reviewing a complex piece of proposed legislation, spots a clause that strikes him as unjust. That partial, perhaps minimal, injustice may not count decisively against the legislation; but it should be taken into account. It should be balanced against possible advantages in a search for the optimal practical solution. So, at any rate, VM would advise. Where does Knauer stand?

"It is a requirement of the scientific language of ethics," he writes, "always to distinguish between ontic evil and the morally bad."[49] Sometimes, as here, he speaks of "ontic" evil, sometimes of "physical," sometimes of "premoral." "A *moral* evil (the 'forbidden') can be defined in no other way than in connection with a harm. Here a 'harm' should be understood as a *premoral* reality. One could think of error, sickness, loss of property, and so forth."[50] Could one also think of evils commonly called moral—of injustice, hatred, selfishness, and so forth?

Repeated explanations invite an affirmative answer. For example: "Anything a person can strive for can, under this aspect, be formulated universally as a premoral good. Yet the fact of striving for a premoral good does not by itself suffice to render an action ethically right."[51] "By 'good' is here meant nothing other than the physical goodness of any reality whatsoever, that goodness by which something becomes desirable in any sense, according to the axiom *ens et bonum convertuntur*."[52] Material or premoral values "can be recognized simply by the fact that one can will them."[53] Since holiness, justice, and the like can be willed and striven for, it would seem that they too should qualify as "premoral" goods, and their absence or contraries as "premoral" evil.

Yet Knauer explicitly denies that moral good is a special sector of ontic good.[54] And he repeatedly contrasts moral and premoral values and disvalues, without hinting at the distinction that seems called for between moral values that help determine an action's rightness and that rightness itself,[55] and without including any such values in his sample listings of those that count as "ontic," "physical," or "premoral." In one sentence he cites sickness and error as ontic evils; in the very next sentence he asks: "But what is the relation between ontic evil and moral evil?"[56] Here there is no suggestion that "ontic" evils might include moral evils.

Thus, interpretation of Knauer's thought faces a triple dilemma. It is difficult to suppose that he simply overlooked the possibility of such moral determinants of right action. It is difficult to suppose that, considering the possibility, he rejected it, and, having thus parted company with Christian tradition, saw no need to justify or explain his position. It is equally difficult to suppose that, recognizing that there are such moral determinants, he called them "premoral" and, having so named them, offered no warning to his readers or justification for his odd labeling. What does seem clear is that the moral/nonmoral dichotomy, in Knauer and in others, is defective in one or the other of these three ways: oversight, false denial, or unfortunate terminology.[57]

In reply, Knauer has suggested that moral values are ultimately reducible to nonmoral.[58] I grant that moral values are related to nonmoral. A just distribution, for example, is usually a distribution of nonmoral goods. An objectively moral act is made so, at least partly, by its relation to nonmoral values and disvalues. A moral attitude, motive, or intention is made so, at least partly, by its relation to nonmoral values and disvalues. (For instance, one who loves others desires their nonmoral as well as their moral welfare.) However, none of these relationships is reductive. A just distribution is not the same thing as the goods thus distributed (e.g., the money, food, or health care). Being rightly motivated (e.g., wishing to alleviate suffering) is not the same thing as the motivating good (e.g., the relief of suffering). A person's loving attitude is not the same thing as the good desired for the beloved (e.g., health or happiness). Yet all of these—the just distribution, the right intention, the loving attitude—are themselves values to be aimed at.

Money, too, it might be said, is not identical with what it purchases. Yet its value is reducible to the value of what it can purchase; it has no value in itself. Is it so for moral values? Are they purely instrumental? Fair distribution is not, and neither is virtue. For virtue is not entirely dispositional (see chap. 11); and even if it were, its value would not be purely instrumental. There would still be inner value in a will so disposed. Love—Christian love, Jesus' love, the Father's love—is a splendid thing in itself, whereas money is not. Since, therefore, moral values are among those we can and should aim at in our conduct, objectively moral action cannot adequately be defined solely in terms of nonmoral value and disvalue. Moral value forms a distinct, irreducible category.[59]

## OVERVIEW

In Knauer's thought we have noted two kinds of narrowing, in conflict with VM. First, there is the narrowing entailed by the thesis of value incommensurability. Would-be teleologists, constrained by this thesis, may resort to various solutions. They may rely on a single, all-purpose value (such as Donagan's respect); or they may look to many, varied values but consider only one per act (as in Grisez's eighth mode or Knauer's single-track criterion). The moral/nonmoral dichotomy, which Knauer shares with many—perhaps most—proportionalists, effects a second narrowing and distances him still further from VM.

This chapter's critique has therefore served a double purpose. In behalf of proportionalism, it has suggested again, as in chapters 6 and 7, what difficulties the thesis of value incommensurability entails; neither K1 nor K2 offers a viable alternative to proportionalism. In behalf more specifically of VM, the chapter's critique has suggested what difficulties the moral/nonmoral dichotomy entails; an adequate proportionalism must embrace all values, moral as well as nonmoral.

# 9

# *Irreducible Rights: Thomson*

The preceding five chapters—on Aquinas, Adams, Donagan, Grisez, and Knauer—have considered Christian alternatives to VM. Other challenges come from ways of thinking that are not distinctively Christian, in their provenance or distribution, but which figure prominently in contemporary Christian ethics. Such, in particular, is the current insistence on rights.

As chapter 1 noted, VM makes place for moral values as well as nonmoral—for fairness and gratitude, say, as well as for life and health and truth. But rights may appear less readily assimilable. Of an article by Gustafson, McCormick writes:

> He proposes three contrasting options. (1) The rights of individuals are sacred and primary and therefore under no circumstances are they to be violated in favor of benefits to others. (2) Anticipated consequences judged in terms of the "good" that will be achieved or the "evil" avoided ought to determine policy and action regardless of the restrictions on individual rights that this might require. (3) Both 1 and 2 are one-sided. Decisions require consideration both of individual rights and of benefits to others.[1]

The first of these three options contrasts most sharply with VM; but the third option, as developed by Judith Thomson, mounts a more serious challenge to such a norm. "The varieties of utilitarianism," she writes in *The Realm of Rights*, "do not appeal to us primarily because of the various theories of value that their friends set before us— theories to the effect that it is only pleasure or happiness or welfare or what you will that *has* value; they appeal primarily because of what they all have in common, namely the underlying idea that value is what all morality reduces to. But it won't do. There is more to morality than value: there are also claims."[2]

*A HARD CASE*

Thomson makes her point by means of a series of cases, the first of which she labels "TRANSPLANT":

> Here is Bloggs, who is a transplant surgeon, an extraordinarily good one—he can transplant anything at all successfully. He has five patients who need parts and will soon die if they do not get them: two need one lung each, two need one kidney each, and one needs a heart. Here is a young man in excellent health; he has the right blood type and can be cut up to supply parts for the patients who need them. (Let us bypass a possible objection by supposing that none of the patients can be cut up to supply parts for the others.) The surgeon asks the young man whether he would like to volunteer his parts, but the young man says "I deeply sympathize, but no." If the surgeon proceeds despite the young man's refusal, he saves five lives at a cost of only one. Does this mean the surgeon ought to proceed? Surely not! It is not only false that he ought to proceed, it is false even that he *may* proceed.[3]

Strict consequentialism, weighing five lives against one, might have to disagree; but what of VM? Thomson acknowledges that a nonconsequentialist form of utilitarianism could make a better case.

> After all, consider the subparts of that complex act. One subpart is the surgeon's cutting the young man up and removing his parts. Since by hypothesis the young man did not consent to the surgeon's doing this, the surgeon's cutting the young man up and removing his parts is the surgeon's committing battery and theft. A very terrible battery and theft, since the battery is cutting up and the theft is of body parts. If any acts have negative value, this battery and theft has negative value, immense negative value.[4]

Indeed, one could plausibly say, "The negative value of the battery and theft is so very great as to outweigh the positive value of the transplanting." However, "this is not the end of the matter, for it can certainly be asked what is supposed to make the negative value of the first subpart of the surgeon's complex act be so great as to outweigh the positive value of the second subpart of the surgeon's complex act"[5]—the part that terminates in saving five human lives. Value-maximization appears inadequate to yield the requisite negative verdict.

Thomson's challenge merits a full, chapter-length reply because she focuses, as here, on what appear to be the hardest of hard cases for VM; because she discusses them with unusual thoroughness; because she explicitly targets any such norm as VM; and because, in doing so, she speaks for many. She, too, is a representative thinker.

A response to this first case, TRANSPLANT, might take one of three directions. It might: (1) accept Thomson's verdict but offer a different explanation, compatible with VM; (2) question or reject her verdict, for reasons compatible with VM; or (3) accept her verdict and her explanation, but show that they are compatible with VM. I shall consider each of these alternatives in turn.

## Different Explanations

Why ought the surgeon not proceed? Thomson notes a likely reply: "The surgeon will certainly kill the one young man if he proceeds, but there is no such certainty that he will save five by doing so."[6] VM, which attends to probabilities, would attach some weight to this consideration. However, "we may suppose," suggests Thomson, "that *this* particular operation is very likely to be successful (the surgeon we are imagining being so skillful)." And in any case, she adds, it can hardly be supposed that the more likely it is that the transplant would succeed, the more reasonable it is to think the surgeon may proceed.[7]

A second possible response would be to dismiss TRANSPLANT as a fantastic fabrication. Here is a superior surgeon, who not only can perform each of the five operations, individually, with sure success, but can perform them all, on successive days, with equal success—first a lung, then a kidney, then another lung, then another kidney, and finally the heart, with no harm to the organs in the meantime. Here, too, is a perfect match between the blood type of this one individual and these five people in need. Still less plausibly, no one else in the world, living or dead, can share the burden. Coincidence piles on coincidence. Granted, no laws of nature or human possibilities are contravened, at least not obviously. Yet how far-fetched the whole scenario appears. VM is meant for real-life situations, not for some never-never world.

There is something to this objection.[8] It has valid analogs, in ethics and elsewhere; and Thomson herself reasons similarly on occasion. However, TRANSPLANT's challenge might be urged more realistically, though less impressively, by means of real-life situations. Suppose a mother could save her child's life, without serious risk to her own, by donating a kidney. If she consents, the operation is legitimate; if she does not, it is not. Why not? Granted, there is a law against coercing her; but suppose there were no such law?

An alternative solution might invoke some form of rule-utilitarianism compatible with VM's broad injunction to maximize value. Wouldn't value be maximized if we accepted or followed, without fail, a rule which proscribed the killing of people for their body parts? No, not if value would be maximized by permitting exceptions like TRANSPLANT. Granted, the procedure would be known to the surgeon, the surgical team, those operated on, their relatives, and doubtless many others. To suppose the whole affair might remain secret appears far-fetched. Thus this single exception might grease a slippery slope toward abuse, and thereby threaten the fabric of society. But would the greasing be sufficient, and sufficiently certain, to warrant the sure loss of five lives?

There can be little doubt, though, that our judgment on TRANSPLANT is affected by social and legal considerations. The mere suggestion that the surgeon might be justified elicits alarming images of a society in which it is deemed permissible, and is legally allowed, to kill and cut up people for their body parts. What does not work as a rule-utilitarian justification, subject to analytic scrutiny, may work more effectively as psychological conditioning, triggering our strong reaction to any such suggestion as that in TRANSPLANT. If, therefore, the slippery-slope argument looks questionable, so too does this instinctive reaction of horror; and if that requires closer examination, so too does Thomson's negative verdict.

### A Different Verdict?

Why might we question her veto? Whether or not they warrant a firm denial, what reasons, compatible with VM, might at least call in question the validity of her verdict? A full response would be inappropriately long; I shall offer only a sketch. Thomson's verdict looks sure, I shall suggest, because she overweights the single person's claim and underweights the five persons' claims.

In fact, she denies that the five have any claim on the surgeon to save their lives. Her reasoning is simple. If they had such a claim, it would have to be weaker than the single person's claim. Otherwise it would be permissible to perform the operation, and that is out of the question. But why would their individual claims be weaker, asks Thomson, or their five claims be collectively weaker, if they had any claims at all?[9]

An equally good question would be: Why would they have no claims at all? If no convincing answer to this query can be given, other than the permissive verdict that would result, this constitutes a reason to reexamine the restrictive verdict. And it is not the sole reason. Not only do the five people's claims appear to have been underrated; the one person's claim appears to have been overrated. Left abstract, it looks maximally binding. Examined concretely, it looks less stringent.

The young man in TRANSPLANT says, "I deeply sympathize, but no." Suppose he went on to explain: "I wish I could help, I really do. I would willingly give my life for those five fine people— for Mr. Rawlins, the outstanding civic leader; for widow Delaney, with all her kids; for young Jimmy, so full of promise; for Sue, the only child of doting parents; for Bishop Giesling, a blessing to his flock. But I was taught in school that organ transplantation is mutilation and that mutilation is a sin. I'm caught between my desire to help and the dictates of my conscience, and I'm afraid I must follow my conscience." Poor man, he's deluded. A familiar fallacy blocks his altruistic preferences. So may we not act as he truly desires and disregard his erroneous conscience? Does his regretful, misguided "No" carry more weight than these five people's deaths, with all their ramifications?

Elsewhere, Thomson acknowledges that the motive for a person's refusal affects the strength of the person's claim.[10] So something needs to be said about the young man's reasons. Perhaps he simply wants to go on living. Perhaps he has religious scruples, or ethical reasons of the kind I have suggested. Thomson does not say. Remaining equally general, I propose a plausible correlation: the more egoistic the young man's refusal is, ignoring the needs of others, the less it merits our respect; the less egoistic his refusal is, the less his wishes are contravened by acting for the many. Either way, his claim to have his refusal honored looks less stringent than Thomson maintains.

Thomson believes that you injure people if you treat them contrary to their wishes—indeed that you may do them grievous harm
even by saving their lives if deep-seated convictions make them oppose your action. Consider this case, she suggests:

> Suppose a tree fell on David; his leg is crushed under the tree
> and he is unconscious. You are a doctor, and you can see that
> David will live if and only if you cut his leg off straightway. Is
> it permissible for you to proceed? I think we may feel inclined
> to say we can't tell until we hear more about David. If David is
> a Christian Scientist or Jehovah's Witness, then no. A man's
> deeply held religious or moral beliefs cut no ice when what is
> in question is operating on his child; when what is in question
> is operating on him, they surely settle the matter.[11]

How do they settle the matter? Not solely, Thomson replies, because
he would refuse permission, but principally because of what would
happen to him. "While the fact that David will live if and only if you
proceed means that it is in a measure good for him if you proceed,
the fact that David is a deeply committed Christian Scientist means
that your proceeding is bad for him, sufficiently bad to outweigh
the good of living, so that it is not on balance good for him if you
proceed."[12]

From this explanation, one can surmise why Thomson attaches
such importance to claims. One can also sense that she gives them
excessive weight. Perhaps there is some reason for letting David die,
but it surely is not the horrendous harm inflicted on him by saving
his life. Granted, we may not do whatever we wish to sleeping persons; their will carries some weight—often decisive weight—even
when they are unconscious. But David is no more violated in his
identity as a Christian Scientist by being operated on while unconscious than a Christian is violated in his identity as a Christian by
being martyred while conscious. When David comes to, he will be
none the worse as a person or as a Christian Scientist for having been
operated on. If serious damage is done by the operation on David, it
is done, not to him but to the one who performs it; and that remains
to be shown.

In other ways besides this critical one, Thomson unduly de-
presses the young man's side of the scales. For example, she repeatedly envisages his suddenly being grabbed off the street and being

promptly chopped up, without any chance to set his affairs in order.[13] How brutal! How reprehensible! Indeed—and how gratuitously supposed. Adopting a similar tactic, for the opposite effect, we could imagine the healthy young man to be waiting on death row, condemned for heinous crimes, and his refusing the gift of his organs through sheer malevolence. And if, even so, the laws of the land blocked the life-saving operation, we could imagine them out of existence without contradicting anything in Thomson's abstract sketch of the situation.

It is easy to intuit why, if left abstract, the young man's claim might appear maximally stringent. Comparison with lying suggests one reason. Lying is generally a bad thing, and society strongly discourages it. Hence Kant and others, so brought up, view lying with loathing regardless of the circumstances. Though the heavens should fall, one must never knowingly tell an untruth. Similarly, but still more decidedly, it is generally a bad thing to coerce people into serving as organ banks. In normal, real-life circumstances, laws forbid such behavior, and are wise to do so. Such being the background against which TRANSPLANT is viewed, the reaction appropriate to most cases readily transfers to Thomson's bizarre one.

History, too, helps to explain the weight now instinctively accorded the rights of individuals vis-à-vis the common good. This is not the place to chronicle the rise of rights to their present prominence. Multiple factors account for their ascent—some sound, some not; some Christian, some not. Unsound and unchristian influences, along with others, surface in Thomson's exposition.

I have noted unsound grounds for her stress on the young man's claim. An unchristian basis appears in her treatment of a kindred case where a single life vies with five. If preference is shown the five, the single person has "good reason to object," she writes, for the option is not to his advantage.[14] Other ethicians view matters similarly. Current thought has moved so far from the gospel perspective that one can read: "If being moral does not pay for individuals, it is difficult to see why they should bother with it."[15] "The only good reason for doing something is that it is in one's interests."[16] Others' interests do not matter.

"Owe no one anything," wrote Paul, "except to love one another" (Rom 13:8). Love the young man; love the five—each and every one of them. Yet love alone, without reference to rights, might occasion deep misgivings about the surgeon's intervention. Compare the Christian dialectic on peace. "How can you kill a man if you truly love him?" asks the Christian pacifist. "Because I love others too," comes the just-war response. "But does violence ever help in the long run?" retorts the pacifist. "Isn't war always counterproductive?" TRANSPLANT might elicit analogous doubts. If so, the resulting negative verdict would clearly not clash with VM. What of Thomson's reasons?

### Thomson's Solution

Why ought the surgeon not proceed? Thomson replies: "because the surgeon would thereby infringe some claims of the young man's, and it is not the case that sufficiently much more good would come of infringing them than would come of not infringing them."[17] Were it merely a matter of putting his health at risk, the saving of five lives might override his claim. However, "the worse the claim infringer would make things for the claim holder by infringing the claim, the larger the required increment of good."[18] And the worst thing one might do to the young man in TRANSPLANT is to take his life. Hence his claim is maximally stringent.[19] It cannot be overridden by five lives, or by five thousand.[20]

This analysis looks comparable to one in *CMR*. Most agree that a sheriff should not frame a prisoner he knows to be innocent so as to avert racial rioting and thereby save many lives. Why not?

> If we pick off an armed madman from his tower perch, from which he has already killed a dozen people, but would not shoot him down if he were killing stray dogs, the reason seems evident. We have balanced one human life against many human lives. If we reach a different verdict in the case of the prisoner, some other factor must be present. And from the words of those who condemn his punishment, it is clear what they take that factor to be. The lives or welfare of many are not weighed against just the life or welfare of the individual but against the *injustice* of his punishment. That is sensed as a higher, weightier consideration.[21]

Similarly, in Thomson's analysis the lives of five are not weighed against just the life of one but also against the infringement of his claim to life. That is sensed as a higher, weightier consideration. Thomson may accord it disproportionate weight, but that does not disturb the parallel between the two cases. If injustice can count as a competing disvalue, so can the infringement of a claim. And in that case no conflict with VM appears.

Thomson rejects any such assimilation. "It is not because a claim infringement has negative value," she argues, "that we ought not infringe claims. We ought not infringe claims—when we ought not infringe them—because of what a claim *is*."[22] This alleged contrast is perplexing. Claim infringement is what it is because of what a claim is, and given what both are, infringement of a claim is a disvalue. Quite generally, I suggest, whatever establishes a claim establishes infringement of the claim as a disvalue; if infringement were not a disvalue, there would be no claim.

Think of vows. Fidelity to one's marriage vows is a value, infidelity a disvalue, because of what vows are. This said, it is clear that, other things being equal, one should be faithful to one's marriage vows. Thomson might prefer to say that each partner has a claim on the other, because of what vows are. This said, it is equally clear that, other things being equal, one should be faithful to one's marriage vows. The second formulation, in terms of claims, does not conflict with the first, in terms of values; but it might conceivably give rise to an assertion like Thomson's. Overlooking the common reality that accounts for both formulations, one might insist that it is not because the claim infringement has negative value that we ought not infringe the claim, but because of what a claim is. However, given the underlying reality that grounds both formulations, it is clear that infringing the claim is a disvalue; for infringing the claim consists in being unfaithful to one's marriage vows, and being unfaithful to one's marriage vows is a disvalue.

As chapter 3 noted, all aspects of an action that count for it are values and all that count against it are disvalues. Thus if claim infringements count against an action, they are disvalues. If they count heavily against it, they are weighty disvalues. If they count decisively against it, they are decisive disvalues. Thomson may reject the term *value* or *disvalue*, but that is neither here nor there. Her analysis does not conflict with VM. There could be no question of weighing claim infringements against benefits, as in her discussion, unless the infringements and the benefits belonged on the same scales—the scales of value.

This rejoinder, like most of my comments on TRANSPLANT, applies equally to Thomson's variations on the same case. She may accord claim-infringement disproportionate weight; so her verdicts may not always be as sure and clear-cut as she supposes. However, sound or unsound, they do not clash with VM. Neither does the reasoning they rest on.

More interesting, therefore, than her variants on TRANSPLANT is the case Thomson cites as an objection to her position. Calling in question her verdicts and her grounds, it thereby calls further in question her challenge to VM.

## A COUNTERCASE

What should be said of the following scenario:

> TROLLEY: An out-of-control trolley is hurtling down a track. Straight ahead of it on the track are five men who will be killed if the trolley reaches them. Bloggs is a passerby, who happens at the moment to be standing by the track next to the switch; he can throw the switch, thereby turning the trolley onto a spur of track on the right. There is one man on that spur of track on the right; that man will be killed if Bloggs turns the trolley.[23]

Thomson comments:

> Most people would say it is permissible for Bloggs to turn the trolley. And wouldn't they be right to say this? If something— a trolley, an avalanche, an out-of-control satellite (does anyone remember Skylab?)—will kill five if nothing is done, and if also it can be deflected in such a way as to make it kill only one, surely it is permissible to deflect it. . . . But if it is permissible for Bloggs to turn the trolley, then we have been overlooking something important. For how exactly is TROLLEY supposed to differ from TRANSPLANT? In both cases, the agent saves five at a cost of only one.[24]

How explain the differing verdicts—positive in TROLLEY, negative in TRANSPLANT?

Thomson must do two things. First she must explain why it is permissible to save five lives by turning the trolley. Then she must show that the same explanation does not legitimize saving five lives by pilfering the young man's organs. I shall focus on the first part of her answer—the part that fails most notably.

She begins by stipulating more specific circumstances needed for her explanation to work. If the man on the right is a gardener tending an unused track and the five on the left are thrill-seekers who have disregarded a warning sign, it is not permissible to save their five lives at the expense of the gardener's single life.[25] If, however, "all six people on the tracks in TROLLEY are track workmen, out doing their job on the track, and if also their assignments to positions on the tracks for the day were made by lot, then it seems to be permissible for Bloggs to turn the trolley."[26]

Why? It may occur to us, writes Thomson, that all six men would have given their consent if they had been asked in advance, that is, in advance of being assigned to positions on the track for the day. However, this by itself is not enough. The decisive fact is that then, in the morning, it would be to the advantage of all to consent.[27] Thus the crucial move, to explain at least this very special case (TROLLEY thus refined), consists in passing from the premise:

> **(2′)** At early morning, it is to the advantage of all that Bloggs turn the trolley if and when the situation in TROLLEY arises, even though it will not then be to the advantage of the one then on the spur of track on the right (whoever he may be) that Bloggs turn it,[28]

to the conclusion:

> **(3′)** It is permissible for Bloggs to turn the trolley if and when the situation in TROLLEY arises even though it will not then be to the advantage of the one then on the spur of track on the right (whoever he may be) that Bloggs turn it.[29]

Of 3′ Thomson states: "*That* cannot be made false at 3:00 by the fact that it is no longer to the advantage of the one by then on the spur of track that Bloggs turn it." To be sure, it cannot. But how can 3′ be derived from 2′? And why take 2′ as premise? Without negating Thomson's premise, we might start instead with

> **(4)** At *noon*, it is not to the advantage of all that Bloggs turn the trolley if and when the situation in TROLLEY arises,

and reach the opposite conclusion:

(5) It is impermissible for Bloggs to turn the trolley if and when the situation in TROLLEY arises.

The game, it seems, might be played either way—this way or Thomson's. Why choose 2' over 4, or 4 over 2'? How deduce 3' from 2', or 5 from 4?

In both inferences, the present tense in the permission or in its denial links with the present-tense statement of fact in the premise, thereby obscuring the crucial leap from the momentary situation to the enduring moral verdict. In both cases, the moral verdict extends beyond the moment described to subsequent moments, without regard for possible changes in circumstances (e.g., the way the lots fall in the morning, new assignments after noon, or a trolley on the tracks). Not surprisingly, the two conclusions thus faultily inferred contradict each another: "it is permissible," "it is not permissible."

This objection is decisive by itself,[30] and there are others. Suppose that the men's locations were not decided by lot. There might be, instead, a class of track workmen who are always sent out to work alone on the tracks, and others who are always sent out to work in groups of five. In that case, Thomson notes, we can no longer suppose that all would consent in the morning to Bloggs's diverting the trolley should the occasion arise, or that it would be to the advantage of all, at that time, for him to do so. So her permission is revoked. Bloggs may not lift a finger to save the five workmen on the track.[31] We may now ask, again: why is early morning decisive; why not go back to some moment before the two groups were constituted? Thomson's choice of time looks arbitrary. In any case, though, her veto looks clearly counterintuitive. If such is the verdict required by her explanation, then so much the worse for the explanation.

VM would say that one not only may but should divert the trolley, whereas, even in the circumstances Thomson imagines, with the men all positioned by lot, she concedes nothing more than the permission.

The bystander Bloggs may turn the trolley. *Ought* he turn it? There is nothing in the proposal I make that issues in the conclusion that he ought to. And isn't that as it should be? For mightn't Bloggs himself think these things should be left to chance (or Fate or God)? Alternatively, mightn't Bloggs think these things should not be left to chance, but all the same feel incapable of killing a person, even to save five others?[32]

To be sure. And Bloggs might deny the existence of rights, might reject all Thomson's explanations, might be a crass utilitarian, or anything you please. But his moral convictions have no relevance for the objective issue Thomson is presumably addressing. As her denial of obligation is not disproved by Bloggs's being a utilitarian, so VM's assertion of obligation is not disproved by any of the possible beliefs Thomson cites.

How account for so evident a conflation of objective and subjective perspectives? Thomson tips her hand when she adds: "The view that morality requires Bloggs to turn the trolley seems to me to be merely a morally insensitive descendant of the Central Utilitarian Idea"[33]—that is, of the idea "that one ought to do a thing, whatever it may be, if and only if more good (even just a little more good) would come of doing it than would come of not doing it."[34] Thomson's target and motivation are clear. It is not clear, however, why a view which shows concern for human lives may be taxed with insensitivity; the charge can more plausibly be urged against a view for which it makes no moral difference whether one dies or five die—indeed, whether ten thousand die in a like situation.

## THE CASES COMPARED

A veto on transplanting the young man's organs looks plausible; a veto on turning the trolley does not. How account for this difference? In both instances, the imagined circumstances are highly improbable. In both, there is the same imbalance of one life versus five. In both, the agent would actively bring about the single person's demise and not merely permit it. In both, the contemplated victim is innocent of any wrongdoing. In both, the victim has not consented to the saving stratagem (transplanting the organs, diverting the trolley). In neither case can we assume the victim's consent; hence the young man's explicit "No" in TRANSPLANT and not in TROLLEY hardly warrants a split verdict. What might?

This query has been dubbed "The Trolley Problem." As we have seen, Thomson's solution in *The Realm of Rights* proves no more satisfactory than her earlier ones; and others' attempts have proved equally unsuccessful.[35] This general failure lends support to a recent argument of John Martin Fischer, which does not solve the Trolley Problem but dissolves it.

Fischer argues that TROLLEY and TRANSPLANT are morally equivalent: "it is permissible to save the five in one case if and only if it is permissible to save the five in the other."[36] He establishes this conclusion by constructing intermediary examples between the two cases. One such demonstration inserts FAT MAN, then RAMP. In FAT MAN:

> You are standing on a bridge watching a trolley hurtling down the tracks toward five innocent persons. The brakes have failed, and the only way in which you can stop the train is by impeding its progress by throwing a heavy object in its path. There is a fat man standing on the bridge next to you, and you could push him over the railing and onto the tracks below. If you do so, the fat man will die but the five will be saved.[37]

Shoving the fat man looks as objectionable as cutting up the young man. However, consider RAMP:

> "Ramp" is in many respects quite similar to "Fat Man": there is a trolley hurtling down a track toward five innocent persons, and an innocent fat man standing on a bridge above the tracks. Let us suppose that the bridge is a railroad bridge (*i.e.*, with railroad tracks on it). And let us imagine that you could push a button and thus cause a ramp to go up underneath the trolley. Further, if you were to push the button and thus cause the ramp to go up, you would thereby cause the trolley to jump up to the tracks on the bridge and to continue along those tracks. If you were to push the button, you would save the five, but, regrettably, the trolley would run over the fat man. In "Fat Man" the only way in which you could save the five would be by shoving the fat man onto the trolley. In "Ramp" the only way in which you could save the five would be by "shoving the trolley onto the fat man." In all other respects the cases are the same, and I have a strong inclination to say that "Fat Man" and "Ramp" are morally on a par.[38]

But RAMP, in turn, is morally on a par with TROLLEY. Shunt the trolley upwards or shunt it sideways—what moral difference does that make? Hence, if the action in TROLLEY is permissible, so is the action in RAMP. But if the action in RAMP is permissible, so is the action in FAT MAN; and if the action in FAT MAN is permissible, so is the action in TRANSPLANT. It follows, by transitivity, that if the action in TROLLEY is permissible, as it clearly seems to be, the action in TRANSPLANT is also permissible. The surgeon may proceed.

So construed, the argument would remove any threat to VM from examples such as FAT MAN and TRANSPLANT. However, as Fischer notes, to fully establish this favorable conclusion, one would need to indicate why the inference should go from TROLLEY to TRANSPLANT rather than from TRANSPLANT to TROLLEY. Fischer "feels some sympathy" for the former direction but does not know how to argue for it.[39] Neither do I. But neither do I see how one might justify proceeding in the opposite direction, and deducing a negative verdict in TROLLEY from the negative verdict in TRANSPLANT.

Here, then, is a further obstacle which Thomson must surmount if she wishes to urge her case against proportionalism. Fischer's argument, with its intermediate steps, aggravates the problem with which she has grappled for years: "How exactly is TROLLEY supposed to differ from TRANSPLANT?"

# 10

# A Single Supreme Norm?

Only two of the preceding thinkers—Adams and Knauer—proposed norms as general as VM, defining right action. The rest—Aquinas, Donagan, Grisez, Thomson—did not. In this, they resemble a great many other ethicians.

The notion of a single supreme norm of morality meets widespread resistance. Edmund Pincoffs insists, for example, "that there are mutually irreducible types of moral consideration, that there is no hierarchy—with the king consideration at ease on the apex—no one-principle system that incorporates all of the moral rules."[1] Such systems "are more threats to moral sanity and balance than instruments for their attainment. They have these malign characteristics principally because they are, by nature, reductive."[2] Others concur.[3] They, too, oppose any "completely general account of what should be done,"[4] any "reductive unification of ethics."[5] Moral philosophy's "prevailing fault, in all its styles, is to impose on ethical life some immensely simple model, whether it be of the concepts that we actually use or of moral rules by which we should be guided."[6]

It is evident how utilitarianism might give rise to such objections. Hedonistic utilitarianism reduces all intrinsic value to pleasure. Eudaemonistic utilitarianism reduces all intrinsic value to happiness. Utilitarianism like Moore's, disregarding nonhuman experience and the objects of human experience, accords inner worth only to human experience. And any utilitarianism that merits the name filters out acts and attends only to their consequences. VM, however, is not reductive in these or any of the other ways we have seen (Fletcher's, Donagan's, Knauer's). So how to explain the chorus of naysayers to any supreme norm? Have the objectors confused norm and method? Or have they simply overlooked the possibility of a single comprehensive, nonreductive norm? Such often seems to be the case. Of special illustrative interest is the much-cited viewpoint of W. D. Ross, more recently revived by H. J. McCloskey.

## ROSS AND MCCLOSKEY

Late in his *Meta-Ethics and Normative Ethics* McCloskey writes:

> The two foregoing chapters have prepared the way for our posi-
> tive contention that there are many irreducible principles of obli-
> gation which are not principles of absolute obligation. . . . They
> dispose of rival theories, and in so doing, they suggest that a
> theory of the kind outlined by Richard Price in *A Review of the
> Principal Questions in Morals*, and, in this century, by W. D.
> Ross in *The Right and the Good and Foundations of Ethics* might
> satisfactorily explain why we have the duties we have. That is
> to say, negative arguments against the theories of Aquinas, Kant
> and the utilitarians create a strong positive presumption in favour
> of such a theory.[7]

McCloskey's insistence on multiple, irreducible principles echoes
Ross's:

> I would contend that in principle there is no reason to anticipate
> that every act that is our duty is so for one and the same reason.
> Why should two sets of circumstances, or one set of circum-
> stances, *not* possess different characteristics, any one of which
> makes a certain act our *prima facie* duty? When I ask what it is
> that makes me in certain cases sure that I have a *prima facie* duty
> to do so and so, I find that it lies in the fact that I have made a
> promise; when I ask the same question in another case, I find
> the answer lies in the fact that I have done a wrong. And if on
> reflection I find (as I think I do) that neither of these reasons is
> reducible to the other, I must not on any *a priori* ground assume
> that such a reduction is possible.[8]

The only sort of unifying principle Ross here envisages is one that
would reduce doing a wrong to breaking a promise or breaking a
promise to doing a wrong; he does not contemplate the possibility of
a still higher principle than these two, that would unify them without
reducing one to the other. He does not envision an all-encompassing
norm such as VM. Yet his analysis points in that direction.

> Any act that we do contains various elements in virtue of which
> it falls under various categories. In virtue of being the breaking

of a promise, for instance, it tends to be wrong; in virtue of being an instance of relieving distress it tends to be right. Tendency to be one's duty may be called a parti-resultant attribute, i.e. one which belongs to an act in virtue of some one component in its nature. *Being* one's duty is a toti-resultant attribute, one which belongs to an act in virtue of its whole nature and of nothing less than this.[9]

Label these "various elements" values and disvalues, and at least partial convergence with VM becomes evident. For VM, too, each such element counts for or against an action, but not alone; duty or rightness is, in Ross's words, a "toti-resultant attribute, one which belongs to an act in virtue of its whole nature and of nothing less than this." In what sense, though, is duty a "resultant" attribute? Ross's explanation takes a further step toward VM:

Every act therefore, viewed in some aspects, will be *prima facie* right, and viewed in others, *prima facie* wrong, and right acts can be distinguished from wrong acts only as being those which, of all those possible for the agent in the circumstances, have the greatest balance of *prima facie* rightness, in those respects in which they are *prima facie* right, over their *prima facie* wrongness, in those respects in which they are *prima facie* wrong—*prima facie* rightness and wrongness being understood in the sense previously explained. For the estimation of the comparative stringency of these *prima facie* obligations no general rules can, so far as I can see, be laid down.[10]

Perhaps not, but a general rule of rightness and wrongness, in terms of comparative stringency, can be laid down. Implicit in Ross's account is a norm like VM.

Consider Ross's illustrations. In various ways and to varying degrees, the importance of promises and of keeping them varies from instance to instance. So does the distress to be relieved on different occasions and the importance of a given agent's relieving it, in a given manner. Thus, rules cannot be stated in advance to decide between keeping a promise, in general, and relieving distress, in general. But it is possible to prescribe that, however the concrete estimates fall out, value be maximized.

McCloskey's exposition resembles Ross's, explicitly denying a single supreme norm while implicitly affirming one. On one hand he

writes: "An examination of the activities which are *prima facie* obligatory completes our case for claiming that there are a number of principles of obligation which are ultimate and such as do not admit of
being reduced to some one single principle whatever it may be."[11]
On the other hand he thus sums up his position:

> If we reflect on how we determine our absolute duties in concrete
> moral situations, and on the nature of the various kinds of activi-
> ties which we apprehend to be morally significant in their own
> right, and to be grounds of our obligations, we find that there
> are four general, irreducible grounds of obligations—promotion
> of good, justice, respect for persons, and honesty. These are
> grounds of *prima facie* obligations in the sense that an action's
> being of one or other kind—of promoting good, justice, respect
> for persons, or of honesty—does not ensure that it will be the
> action he ought to do. It ensures that it is the action he is *prima
> facie* obliged to do, and which, if there are no conflicting *prima
> facie* obligations, he is absolutely obliged to perform. Where there
> are conflicting *prima facie* duties the determination of our absolute
> duty involves weighing these various *prima facie* duties, and any
> derivative duties to which they give rise, against one another,
> estimating their stringencies and the stringencies of the various
> derivative duties which might arise if one or other of the *prima
> facie* duties is not done.[12]

McCloskey has four basic grounds or values; others have more. Whatever their number, to each a prima facie obligation corresponds. And
when the grounds and corresponding obligations conflict, as they
frequently do, value should be maximized. VM lies implicit in McCloskey's account as it does in Ross's.

Nonetheless, McCloskey does not contradict himself. He does
not explicitly deny that there is *any* supreme norm, of any kind, while
implicitly affirming one. He denies that his four principles of obligation
can be reduced to one another or to any similar principle. And this
may be true. They can, however, be nonreductively subsumed under
a single, broader principle. They can all fit under VM's capacious
umbrella. This McCloskey, like Ross and many others,[13] apparently
did not notice. Thus he, as they, stopped where the present inquiry
begins.

Denials like Ross's and McCloskey's show the need of what they
appear to deny. They appear to deny any single, supreme norm

of objective morality. Yet the multiple grounds, elements, aspects, principles, and obligations they cite constantly conflict; and if these varied determinants were not subject to some higher rationale there would be no way of resolving the conflicts. Without a norm like VM, Ross and McCloskey's whole system would collapse in incoherence. As preceding chapters attest, this underlying norm cannot be taken for granted. It cannot simply be applied, unreflectively. It needs to be formulated, clarified, and assessed.

Once articulated as a norm, not a method, VM permits a reply to objections aimed at "the neointuitionist theory of W. D. Ross, C. D. Broad, and their numerous followers."[14] Donagan finds it difficult to accept "that reaching conclusions about what one is morally obliged to do is not a matter of reasoning—that, as Davidson has satirically put it, the sum of our moral wisdom concerning what to do in a given situation has the form: there is something to be said for doing so and so, and something to be said against—and also for and against not doing it."[15] As methodological guidelines—in comparison, say, with subsequent debates about rule-utilitarianism versus act-utilitarianism—the neointuitionists' remarks do appear jejune. As implicit indications of an underlying, unifying norm, they look more satisfactory.

## GEWIRTH'S GENERAL CLAIM

Alan Gewirth argues that the function "of resolving conflicts among particular moral judgments and rules" requires that there be a supreme principle of morality and that there be only one. He rejects the idea that, provided they are consistent, "a plurality of principles, none of which is derivable from the others, can . . . serve to resolve conflicts." "This coherence view . . . does not deal adequately with conflicts among the principles themselves. There are occasions when the requirements of one principle may clash with the requirements of another." "The coherence test provides no answer here."[16]

"This claim goes unsupported," objects Marcus Singer, "perhaps because Gewirth does not sufficiently develop an example of a 'coherence view' to examine. No doubt some such views would be in the predicament, if predicament it is, that Gewirth describes. But this is not true necessarily or of all. A set of principles so ordered as to form a coherent system—and I mean *coherent*, not merely consistent— would contain provisions for dealing with conflict; if it did not, it would not be a coherent system."[17] "There is no inherent reason why a one-principle theory is better able to adjudicate such conflicts than a coherent battery or system of principles."[18] Thus, according to Singer, there may be no need of a single supreme norm, whether Gewirth's or mine.

Singer does not spell out his suggestion or explain how a "coherent battery or system of principles" might satisfactorily adjudicate conflicts. John Rawls is more explicit, noting "two obvious and simple ways of dealing constructively with the priority problem: namely, either by a single overall principle, or by a plurality of principles in lexical order."[19]

> This is an order which requires us to satisfy the first principle in the ordering before we can move on to the second, the second before we consider the third, and so on. A principle does not come into play until those previous to it are either fully met or do not apply. A serial ordering avoids, then, having to balance principles at all; those earlier in the ordering have an absolute weight, so to speak, with respect to later ones, and hold without exception.[20]

Thus in a system composed of four separate principles—A, B, C, and D—dictating action-rules and specific obligations, there might be a further principle stating that in case of conflict between one principle and any one later in the series (e.g., between A and B), the earlier principle prevails.

This might not suffice. If more than one later principle could compete with an earlier one (e.g., B and C with A), or if an earlier principle could combine with a later principle in competition with the others (e.g., A and D with B and C), further preference-rules would be required. The more such stipulations multiplied, the less plausible this hypothetical system would appear, and the less it would resemble any system that has actually been proposed. However, whether the rules were many or few, how might they be justified?

Only, I would say, by the values the ordered principles represented. If the principles spoke for no values, directly or indirectly, they would have no claim to recognition. If the values they spoke for were equal or incommensurable, the principles would have no claim to preference, one over the other. Thus of his own system Rawls remarks: "The serial ordering of principles expresses an underlying preference among primary social goods. When this preference is rational so likewise is the choice of these principles in this order."[21]

Its abstract generality might make problems for such ordering.[22] Here too, however, as for Ross and McCloskey, the supreme principle implicitly at work, if only imperfectly, would be VM. When there was no conflict, VM would say to follow the pertinent subprinciples. When there was conflict, VM would say to follow the subprinciples backed by more value. Value-maximization would furnish the common rationale.

### GEWIRTH'S SOLUTION

Gewirth answers differently. He, too, believes that where principles or parts of principles yield conflicting verdicts, resolution must be sought in a single justificatory ground. But his ground is not value, and his supreme principle is not VM. "My main thesis," he explains, "is that every agent, by the fact of engaging in action, is logically committed to the acceptance of certain evaluative and deontic judgments and ultimately of a supreme moral principle, the Principle of Generic Consistency [PGC], which requires that he respect his recipients' necessary conditions of action"[23]—namely their freedom and well-being.[24] This principle resolves conflicts

> by considerations derived from its justificatory ground. This ground consists in the necessary conditions of human action: the main requirement of the principle is that, as a matter of right, every prospective agent have the conditions and abilities needed both for the very possibility of action and for success in general in achieving the purposes of his action. Hence, in cases of conflicting rights those rights take priority that are more necessary for action. . . . This is why, for example, the right not to be lied to is overridden by the right to life, in cases of conflict.[25]

Despite its different focus, Gewirth's PGC does not differ greatly from VM in its scope or its requirements. It covers duties as well as rights, duties to oneself as well as to others,[26] conduct toward animals as well as toward humans.[27] And VM might agree, for its own reasons, that the right to life overrides the right not to be lied to. More generally, it might agree that "the necessary conditions of action take precedence, within the whole sphere of practice, over all other practical goods, since, by definition, without these conditions no other such goods can be attained by action."[28]

The PGC differs chiefly from VM in its mode of derivation and consequent status. Whereas I have argued for VM's validity or truth, Gewirth does not argue that the PGC is true, but only that any agent who wishes to be rational must accept it.[29] "If the agent heeds the canons of deductive logic," he contends, "as these are applied to the analysis of what it is to be an agent who wants to achieve his purposes, he will recognize that in order to avoid self-contradiction he must act in accord with the generic rights of his recipients as well as of himself."[30]

Faced, then, with two supreme moral norms, the first established assertorically (VM) and the second dialectically (PGC), one naturally wonders: may the conclusions of assertoric and dialectical arguments diverge and the arguments still be valid? If they may, which conclusion should we go by? If they may not, how can we adjudicate between verdicts so differently derived? Within this chapter's focus—"A Single Supreme Norm?"—these are all pertinent questions.

In answer, I shall make three observations. First: an argument like that in chapter 3, if successful, leaves no doubt about the truth of its conclusion. If it is sound, VM is sound. Second: if VM is sound, there must be a flaw in any argument which claims that no agent can coherently embrace the norm. Third: regardless of VM's truth, it seems a priori unlikely that any argument starting from the mere fact of rational agency could validly deduce the impossibility of coherently embracing such a norm.

Granted, agents who see some value in their purposes must see some value in the conditions which permit the pursuit of those purposes. But this inference need yield no more than a set of prima facie rights and corresponding obligations. And the same rights, if itemized, summarized, or universalized, would not cease to be prima facie.[31] Thus a principle which stated these rights comprehensively would no more conflict with VM than does the viewpoint of Ross and McCloskey, and would need to be completed by VM. When right conflicts with right, or one person's welfare with another's, value should be maximized.

## LEWIS'S ALTERNATIVE

For C. I. Lewis, the "definitive dictate of the moral" is, "Do unto others as you would that others should do unto you."[32] Whether formulated as the Golden Rule, as Kant's categorical imperative, or some other way, this principle discriminates the moral not only from the nonmoral but also from the immoral.

> We may back up the moral law, or spell it out, by supplementary and subordinate rules, beaten out in the course of experience, and accepted as representing what will be in accord with this basic principle in particular kinds of cases. (The frequently quoted moral dictates, such as "Tell no lies" and "Keep your promises," are such subordinate rules of thumb for moral guidance.) But there is no other and final test of what is morally right than this basic principle; and no test having different import could be final.[33]

VM does have different import; so the challenge to its supremacy looks clear.

The challenge holds special interest, since I too accept the principle of impartial universality. It is made still more intriguing by the fact that Lewis himself accepts a maximizing norm which, like VM, appears to conflict with the claim just quoted. For Lewis, "an act is objectively right if and only if, on the available evidence, it is genuinely probable that its consequences will be good, or better than those of any alternative."[34] This, too, sounds like a "final test of what is morally right." It, too, passes judgment on subordinate rules such as "Tell no lies" and "Keep your promises."[35] Yet it is hardly identical with the Golden Rule or Kant's categorical imperative. So in Lewis's thought two norms appear to vie for supremacy: this consequentialist norm and the principle of universality.

His claim that the latter is *the* final test might be made good by distinguishing a four-level hierarchy, with the principle of universality at the summit, the consequentialist norm subject to this supreme principle, subsidiary rules such as those about lying and promises subject to the consequentialist norm, and individual acts subject to these subsidiary rules, under the norm's supervision. In this scheme, both the principle of universality and the consequentialist norm would, in a sense, reign supreme. The principle would be the only final test, but a weak one, stating just a necessary condition: it would not decide between Lewis's norm and Mill's, Gewirth's, mine, or many another. For its part, the consequentialist norm, though not final, would be strong: it alone would provide a defining criterion—sufficient as well as necessary—discriminating right from wrong.

Does the like hold for VM? Is such its status relative to the principle of universality? Yes and no. It is one thing for pronouncements to exemplify a general, more comprehensive formal principle, another for them to depend on it logically or epistemologically. VM exemplifies the principle of universality, but does not depend on it either logically or epistemologically. It does not depend on the principle logically, because it would not be falsified by the principle's falsity. It does not depend on the principle epistemologically, because it is not derived from the principle but from the theological and philosophical grounds set forth in chapter 3.

Stating both a sufficient and a necessary condition of objectively right conduct, VM automatically assures universality. Thus the formal principle of universality is superfluous—as superfluous as the principle of noncontradiction. If my eyes inform me that an object is white, I have no need of the principle of noncontradiction to assure me that the object is not simultaneously nonwhite: the whiteness does that. Similarly, if VM informs me that an action is wrong for one person, I have no need of the principle of universality to assure me that the same action is, other things being equal, wrong for all persons: the wrongness of the identical value-configuration does that. If wrong for one, then wrong for all; if not wrong for one, then wrong for none—such are VM's clear implications.

If anything, the dependence goes the other way: VM does not need the Kantian principle, but the principle needs VM. Consider this comparison. If no satisfactory analysis of water were ever forthcoming, we might doubt whether it had one; that is, we might doubt whether there was such a chemical substance as water. Similarly, if no satisfactory analysis of right and wrong were ever forthcoming, we might doubt whether it had one; that is, we might doubt whether there was any such thing as impartial right and wrong. Thus VM, if valid, functions much as does $H_2O$: it validates the general conception underlying attempted analyses of right action, including that aspect—universality—captured in Kant's imperative.

We may further query, with Lewis, "what constitutes the *categorical* character" of the Kantian principle. "What is the *imperativeness* of it and what does it rest upon?"[36] Kant would say it rests on the very nature or concept of law. However, from a mere nature or concept no moral obligation follows, much less a categorical one. Logical or conceptual necessity should not be confused with moral necessity. The imperativeness and categoricalness of moral obligation are grounded as moral obligation is grounded: not only in divine commands (see chap. 5) but in value. Imperativeness derives from the demand of value to be realized, categoricalness from the collective verdict of all values, comprehensively considered.

## THE FINAL QUESTION

In ways and senses now suggested, VM may furnish a "final test." Yet how strongly it functions as a test remains to be seen. The Kantian principle may be a mere figurehead sovereign; but does VM rule in its stead, or do particular judgments depend no more on VM than it depends on the principle of universality?

This query signals a shift of perspective. The present chapter, like those that precede it, has helped to situate VM in the moral landscape. It has indicated important differences from principles targeted by Ross, McCloskey, Taylor, Williams, Nagel, and others, and from the norm proposed by Gewirth. It has suggested why VM is not open to similar objections, hence is preferable to these alternatives. Therewith, it has completed the task of previous chapters. VM is valid—more valid than its rivals. However, does the norm matter? Does it make a difference? This is the issue still to be confronted.

The strength of the case for VM may also be its weakness. It meets objections by absorbing them. All becomes "value" or "disvalue," hence grist for this single mill. There may be no abuse in thus employing the terms *value* and *disvalue*; they are, after all, very general. But the resulting theory may be so accommodating that it lacks theoretical or practical significance. When all is said and done—when Scripture, tradition, and reason have been cited in support, and rival theories have been shown to be deficient—what has been achieved? What is the interest of a norm so broadly understood and so broadly grounded? As Richard Mouw observes: "A general theory of moral justification should be expected to show that the important insights of other proposed theories are capable of being absorbed into its own account. But in attempting to demonstrate this capability theorists also run the real risk of stretching their own concepts beyond the point where they are interesting and useful."[37] The next chapter will inquire—honestly—whether such is the case for VM.

# 11

# *The Norm's Significance*

In 1978 James Gustafson described the fundamental goal of Christian moral theory:

> Protestant theological ethics and Catholic moral theology currently share a serious quest, namely, for a philosophical foundation for Christian ethical thought and Christian moral activity which takes the Christian tradition seriously, which provides a common ground with nonreligious persons and communities and with other religions, and which has openness to historic changes and to personalistic values without becoming utterly relativistic.[1]

I view VM as an answer to this quest. Firmly grounded in Christian tradition, strongly linking Christian and non-Christian ethics,[2] open to historical developments and every kind of value without becoming relativistic, it provides a foundation for Christian ethical thought and Christian moral activity. Not everyone, however, takes such a sanguine view.

Many Christian ethicians cast a tacit or explicit vote of no confidence in the attempt to formulate a single supreme norm of morality. Some, like Rudolf Bultmann and Karl Barth, oppose any ethics.[3] ("What the serpent has in mind is the establishment of ethics."[4] "For one who stands in love, an 'ethic' is no longer necessary."[5]) Others oppose systematic ethics. ("*Any* ethical system is unchristian or at least sub-Christian, whatever might be its claim to theological orthodoxy."[6]) For such thinkers, the present inquiry and the norm it proposes may appear symptomatic of "an 'intellectualist fallacy' rampant in contemporary ethical deliberation, an analytical and rationalistic approach that assumes that morality becomes intelligible in the same way that mathematics and logic do."[7]

Philosophers voice similar misgivings. Charles Taylor has warned against the "drive towards unification" that has characterized modern moral philosophy.[8] Richard Rorty has spoken for contemporary pragmatists who "doubt that there is much to be said about the common feature shared by such morally praiseworthy actions as Susan leaving her husband, America joining the war against the Nazis, America pulling out of Vietnam, Socrates not escaping from jail, Roger picking up litter from the trail, and the suicide of the Jews at Masada. They see certain acts as good ones to perform, under the circumstances, but doubt that there is anything general and useful to say about what makes them all good."[9]

"Anything general and useful"—there is the dilemma. Utility, it seems, requires specificity, whereas system and unity call for greater generality. Consider Donagan's principle of respect (chap. 6). If interpreted solely in terms of autonomy, the principle makes a difference, but is too narrow. If interpreted broadly and vaguely enough to avoid the charge of reductionistic falsity, the principle no longer offers clear guidance. Thus the Scylla and Charybdis between which a norm as general as VM must navigate are falsity on one side and futility on the other. I have argued till now that the norm steers clear of falsity. Does it thereby founder in futility?

It can hardly be doubted that VM, if valid, has considerable significance. Indeed, despite notable limitations which I shall indicate, one might ask: Is there any single question more momentous for Christian ethics than the one VM answers? An adequate response requires that a noncomparative examination precede the comparative. Before assessing VM's contribution in comparison with others, it will be necessary to estimate its own contribution.

## VM'S THEORETICAL AND PRACTICAL SIGNIFICANCE

C. I. Lewis states a case for the importance of a norm as broad as VM when he writes:

> *Whatever* it is that it is right to do, what makes it so? What constitutes the rightness of it? How can one tell whether a way of acting or a particular precept of action is genuinely right or not? What is the ground on which such a question of right principles can be settled? And unless there is some manner in which we can so distinguish between precepts it is genuinely

imperative to adhere to and spurious ones which may be put forward, then it becomes utterly obscure how any difference of conviction regarding right and wrong could possibly be resolved. There must be some criterion for distinguishing between valid dictates of the right and baseless claims that may be made upon our conduct: otherwise the distinction between right and wrong is itself illusory.[10]

VM serves this discriminating function. In a sense, being so abstract, it "gives no answers." However, as Onora O'Neill has remarked, "if ethical principles are to be relevant to a wide range of situations or of agents, they surely not merely *may* but *must* be abstract."[11] VM, being maximally abstract, has maximally comprehensive relevance. Its divergence from rival supreme principles makes a difference at all levels: at the next level of generality (that, for example, of the ban on evil means), at the level of particular precepts (for example, the prohibition of organ transplants), and at the level of particular actions (for example, the gift of this mother's kidney to her child).

The preceding chapters furnish numerous illustrations of the difference VM makes, to which others can be added. Thus VM counters:

- natural-law thinking banning contraception, shaving, false speech, etc., as "unnatural";
- divine-dominion arguments, for instance with regard to suicide;
- claims of inevitable sin, when values and corresponding prima facie duties conflict;
- the question-begging use of loaded terms (e.g., *murder, mutilation*);
- similar employment of the veto on "evil means";
- non-question-begging prohibition of nonmorally evil means, in general or in individual cases;
- reasoning that treats the life of an innocent person as an absolute value, without regard for the lives of other, equally innocent people;
- the doctrine of inviolable goods propounded by Grisez and others;
- single-track teleological arguments like Knauer's, focusing on the "end" alone;

- Kantian reasoning resulting in such verdicts as the exceptionless condemnation of all verbal falsehood;
- moral verdicts (e.g., for or against abortion) based on the implicit redefinition of terms (e.g., *person, human being*);
- act-intention linkage of the kind critiqued in chapters 7 and 8;
- use of the "principle of totality" against organ transplants;
- the doctrine of "purely penal law," as often propounded or applied;
- the proliferation of absolute or near-absolute rights;
- life-termination judgments citing "ordinary" or "extraordinary" means, understood statistically not teleologically;
- treatment of some important moral questions as matters of mere "counsel";
- arguments based on some single key consideration pro or con (as in single-issue voting);
- the restriction of the realm of morality to decisions that affect other people;
- conflations of the moral and juridical orders, as in Viktor Cathrein's argument for marital indissolubility and Paul Ramsey's exclusion of any exception to the norm of informed consent;[12]
- varied, idiosyncratic reasonings such as Donagan's appeal to implicit consent (in the case of the trapped spelunkers); Arthur Vermeersch's contention that artificial contraception violates the spouses' obligations as "representatives of the human species";[13] Janet Smith's alternative arguments (as summarized by Edward Vacek) that "it is wrong (1) to impede the procreative power of sexual actions, (2) to impede actions that assist God in God's creative act, and (3) to destroy the power of sexual acts to represent total self-giving";[14] L. Bender's objection that "excising an organ so as to insert it in another's body, is to treat a human being (another or oneself) as something useful, as something subordinated to the good or utility of other creatures";[15] the traditional argument for marital indissolubility based on the symbolism of the union of Christ with the church; invoking "mental reservation" to justify false statements; various arguments adduced, by Aquinas and others, in favor of self-preference;[16] and *Donum vitae*'s arguments against homologous in vitro fertilization.[17]

This list, which could be continued, looks impressive; yet what, precisely, is its genuine relevance?

Remarks of Lewis evoke a familiar perspective: "Any conclusion as to the rightness of doing in a concrete case calls for premises of two sorts. First, it requires some presumption as to rightness itself or the specific kind of rightness which is in question. It is such a premise which introduces the norm. And second, it requires some further premise or premises which introduce particularities of the case to be decided and relate it to the norm or rule of right doing."[18] If the normative premise is specific, it stands in need of similar validation, by means of a still more general normative premise, and so on, up to the supreme moral norm that serves as the basic premise of all such demonstrations—that is (I would say), up to VM.

Such a perspective can be challenged. Suppose a child has severe appendicitis. Should the doctor operate? Of course the doctor should, to save the child's life. That is evident. To reach such a conclusion, we have no need of a major premise enjoining that value be maximized. Both epistemologically and logically, priority belongs to the concrete balance of values. Epistemologically, the specific desirability of saving the child's life may be more evident than the principle that value should always be maximized. Logically, whereas a single exception (e.g., in the child's case) would invalidate the general norm, the norm's falsehood would not invalidate the single verdict. VM might be false for any of various reasons, and it still might be true that in this particular instance value should be maximized by saving the child's life.

In reply, it might be noted that people have in fact contested even so apparently evident a moral verdict as the one that favors an appendectomy to save a child's life. Indeed, people have died as a result of such opposition. So VM does make a difference; it is not an empty truism.

This response can in turn be contested. Christian Scientists who oppose appendectomies do so, not because they oppose value-maximization, but because they conceive both the facts and the values of this individual case differently than do most people. Christian Scientists believe that spiritual means are preferable and more powerful than physical means. For such beliefs, VM offers no remedy.

This instance stands for many. Viewing a fetus as a person, some see a great value at stake in abortion; viewing a fetus as an appendage of a woman's body, others see much less at stake. Regarding war as always counterproductive, some are pacifists; regarding war as sometimes the lesser of two evils, others are not pacifists. Assessing the pertinent values and disvalues one way, some oppose a given war—Vietnam, Panama, Desert Storm—while others support it. Looking to long-term consequences, some favor the principle of triage in succoring the needy peoples of the world; looking to the sure immediate need, others reject the principle. Believing in its deterrent effect, some favor capital punishment; doubting its deterrent effect, others oppose capital punishment. And so forth. Time and again, VM would make no difference; teleology vies with teleology, not teleology with deontology.

Frequently, however, it is otherwise. As my long list of counter-cases makes clear, conflicting verdicts repeatedly arise, not from differing teleology but from the acceptance or rejection of a teleological criterion. Notable examples, past and present, are the exceptionless exclusion of false speech, artificial contraception, divorce and remarriage, artificial insemination, *in vitro* fertilization, sterilization, extramarital sex, suicide, euthanasia, interest on loans, homosexual relations, organ transplants, masturbation (e.g., for the procurement of semen). Disagreement in such cases might be teleological, and sometimes is; but often it is not. The exclusions either appeal to Scripture and tradition, in absolutist fashion (see chap. 3), or are based on reasoning of the kinds just cataloged. Hence there is truth in McCormick's observation: "This discussion of the meaning of moral norms may seem to many an abstract, academic affair. Actually it is at the heart of many polarizations between men of good will inside and outside the Catholic community. It is the core of contemporary discussions on abortion, sterilization, contraception, capital punishment, warfare, etc."[19]

This alternating dialectic, pro and con VM's significance, might continue, and does. On one hand, "it is the framework of argument which . . . is critically important, for it determines the answers to such questions as 'Which considerations are relevant?', 'How does one begin to evaluate morally conflicting considerations?', 'Under what moral categories should this behavior be classified and thereby assessed?' . . . ."[20] On the other hand, "checklists and wooden schemes of analysis cannot attend to the subtle nuances that are involved in refined discriminations; they seem to stress the more universal elements found in all objects of a given class, rather than the particularities to be appreciated in a single representative of what might be a class."[21] On one hand, "as a glance at history will show us, such doctrines have actually molded the life of nations by their all-powerful influence on developing moral feeling."[22] On the other hand, as a bumblebee has no need of physics to fly, so a Mother Teresa has no need of ethical theory to lead a life of loving service. On one hand, theory has its own intrinsic worth, apart from its practicality: "We do not merely want to have true moral beliefs; we want to know what makes them true."[23] On the other hand, there are alternative ways of achieving understanding. Moral seeing and hearing, it has been said, depend more on metaphor and vision than on rules and principles.

It may be, too, that focusing on actions, as VM does, is not the best way to illuminate Christian morality. It is difficult enough within that limited focus to strike a just balance between "all-important" and "unimportant" and accurately estimate VM's utility.[24] However, so confined, the preceding evaluation takes only the first step toward an overall assessment of the norm's significance.

## VM'S COMPARATIVE SIGNIFICANCE

Whether greater or less, practical benefit is sure to result, as well as intellectual satisfaction, whenever a vast, complex, much-travelled terrain is more clearly, accurately mapped than heretofore. This I have attempted for the domain of objectively right conduct. However, a larger area remains to be reconnoitered. Where does VM figure on a comprehensive map of morality? Are answers to other moral questions perhaps still more significant than this one? What other perspectives vie for primacy? Let us consider some leading candidates.

### Method versus Criterion

"Most of the polemics in Christian ethics," writes Gustafson, "have been about *how Christians ought to make judgments.* They ought to use rules in a highly rational way, or they ought to exercise their graced imaginations, or they ought to obey the tradition of the Church, or they ought to respond to the situation of which they are a part."[25] This judgment appears to focus just on methods and procedures and not on norms and criteria, hence is questionable. Much debate has centered on what makes actions right or wrong. Much has confused the two kinds of question—the criterial and the methodological.

Once the two are distinguished, a notable difference appears: whereas numerous ethicians have proposed a single supreme norm of morality, few if any have proposed a single, supreme procedure. Consider Gustafson's sampling. Who has argued that Christians should rely only on rules or only on their graced imaginations or only on church tradition or only on the dictates of the situation? Emphases differ; that is all. This is a first reason for doubting that any single methodological answer possesses the significance of VM's single criterial answer.

True, in the dispute between act-utilitarianism and rule-utilitarianism, one sometimes receives the impression that a single answer, for or against rules, is to be generalized to all actions and all situations. Thus William Frankena could write: "Act-utilitarians hold that *in general* or at least where it is practicable, one is to tell what is right or obligatory by appealing directly to the principle of utility. . . . [Rule-utilitarianism] emphasizes the centrality of rules in morality and insists that we are generally, if not always, to tell what to do in particular situations by appeal to a rule like that of truth-telling rather than by asking what particular action will have the best consequences in the situation in question."[26] On both sides, the more moderate positions, differing only in emphasis ("where it is practicable," "not always"), are the more plausible ones. Thus understood, neither method— neither rule-following nor case-by-case evaluation—compares in universality with VM.

Besides, whereas moral methods do not validate moral criteria, moral criteria do validate moral methods (see chap. 1). VM, together with specific value data, determines which procedures are acceptable, which should be emphasized, when to use one rather than another, and how to employ the one applied. For example, it determines whether rules should be followed, which rules should be followed, when they should be followed, and how. It backs rules in general because some rules tend to maximize value. It backs the rule of truth-telling in particular because that rule tends to maximize value. It backs exceptions to the rule when telling the truth would not maximize value. It opposes the blind, exceptionless application of the rule, a la Kant, because such application does not maximize value. To this single illustration, countless others could be added.

Here too, however, with respect to VM's methodological importance, exaggeration must be avoided. A good antidote is McCormick's

list of "contemporary failings in moral discourse": confusion of pare-
netic discourse with normative discourse; rhetoric as normative argument; straightforward *petitio principii*; doubling the middle term; con-
fusing authority for argument; various forms of the "genetic fallacy";
misplaced or misnamed pairs; *post hoc ergo propter hoc*; attributing and
attacking positions no one holds.[27] These aberrations all sin against
VM, but we do not need VM in order to discern their error. McCormick
opposes them, yet does not accept VM.

Nevertheless, given the diversity of acceptable procedures and
VM's importance for them all, it seems clear that no single methodological determination surpasses or equals the importance of this single norm. What might?

## A System of Values

"We expect consequentialists to begin," writes L. W. Sumner, "by
giving us an inventory of ultimate or intrinsic values: those states of
affairs which are valuable for their own sake and not for the sake of
any further states which they produce or promote."[28] Here, I have
not attempted any such listing, nor have I seen any need to—whether
for theoretical or for practical purposes. (Must an economist begin by
cataloging currencies? Must a banker know all currencies in order to
change dollars for yen?) I have just insisted on values' variety and
multiplicity.

Given this variety and multiplicity, it has been suggested that
"the goal of practical morals is, then, to put things in their right order;
its fundamental task is to determine the true relative values of things.
It is in the achievement of this goal and in the prosecution of this task
that ethical theory plays its chief role."[29] Various orderings have in
fact been proposed. In the classical hierarchy of goods, "first come
the supernatural, then the natural goods of the soul, the intrinsic
goods of the body, and finally all external goods."[30] More simply, for
Maurizio Flick and Zoltan Alszeghy, "holiness is worth more than
purely human perfection, and harmoniously perfected humanity is
worth more than the possession of external goods."[31] David Ross
ranks virtue over knowledge and knowledge over pleasure.[32] Max
Scheler's ascending values—the useful, agreeable, vital, spiritual,
holy—form an ordered series, each value "founded" in the next.[33]

Such listings face a dilemma. On one hand, a hierarchical ordering might be understood to signify that one class of values is—generally, typically, on the average, or as a group—higher than another

class of values, and that class higher than another, and so forth. Such a claim might be plausible, but would make no connection with concrete action-verdicts. In order to judge between rival values and adjudicate action, we would have to know the values' probability, extent, and more specific kind—this and nothing more; and the abstract value-ordering would furnish no such information.[34]

In order, then, to have implications for action, a listing would have to be strictly serial, with any higher value, no matter how slight or unsure, taking precedence over any lower value, however massive and certain. Thereupon, whenever a higher value conflicted with a lower, the higher would win out. Whenever a higher value conflicted with several lower values, of whatever level, the higher would win out. Whenever a higher value conflicted with a lower value that affected the higher value, one would need only to compare the direct and indirect benefit to the higher: if the direct benefit was greater, it would win out. Such an ordering, though abstract, would indeed make a difference.

The trouble is, the ordering would no longer be valid. It cannot plausibly be maintained that every particular value of a higher general class, no matter how low its specific rank, slight its extent, and minimal its probability, has greater weight than every lower value, or sum of lower values, no matter how massive their extent or certain their occurrence.[35]

In response, it has been suggested that the proposed hierarchy be understood as follows: *other things*—both extent and probability—*being equal*, any value of a higher class takes precedence over any value of a lower class. With this modification, the ordering looks both more plausible and more useful. Nonetheless, problems remain.

For one thing, the saving condition—"other things being equal"—does not make evident sense. It makes sense to say that one person's life is equal in number with one sparrow's life; it does not make sense to say that a given friendship is equal in degree with a given pleasure, that a given pain is equal in degree with a given sorrow, or the like. Yet degree as well as number must be taken into consideration.

A second difficulty concerns the possibility of achieving clear, comprehensive coverage by means of a few general terms. Let me illustrate. Discussing this project with a proponent, I cited social and aesthetic values, and asked which rated higher. He said aesthetic values did. When, taking friendship for a social value, I asked whether a friendship automatically rates lower than a work of art, he replied that for him friendship is a personal value, not social, and that personal values rate higher than aesthetic. Evidently, then, general terms like *social* and *personal* need to be clarified, by means of still other general terms or, ultimately, by listing all or most examples. Otherwise, classes may overlap, or fail to cover all specific values, or may order some values incorrectly.

The more closely one scrutinizes this undertaking, the more dubious and daunting it appears. And what is its genuine utility? The ordering of value classes (e.g., personal values versus aesthetic) is derivative from and far less evident than the ordering of specific values (e.g., nourishing this friendship versus working on that fresco).

It might be otherwise if uniform essences could be compared with uniform essences (e.g., the essence of personal value with the essence of aesthetic value). But if we look beneath the broad labels required for a system of values—e.g., "personal," "aesthetic," "social," "intellectual," "religious,"—we discover no corresponding essences as invariant as the labels. And careful explication by means of other general terms would not generate invariant essences—not if the terms employed did not denote such essences, as most terms do not. For these reasons, the vision of a guiding value hierarchy looks chimerical.

## Ways of Life

Of VM, too, and the ordering of values, Charles Taylor might critically observe: "Articulating them would be indispensable if our aim were to get clearer on the contours of the good life, but that is not a task which this theory recognizes as relevant. All we need are action-descriptions, plus a criterion for picking out the obligatory ones."[36] Focusing on individual actions, VM may appear myopic. To be realistic, ethics must be holistic; to be holistic, it may need to map values.

Such is Mortimer Adler's approach in *The Time of Our Lives*. Do you understand, he asks,

> that the problem of making a whole human life that is really good—good in each of its parts, and good in a way that results from each part's contributing what it ought to contribute to the whole—exists for you precisely because, at every stage of your life, in every day of your existence, you are faced with the basic

moral alternative of choosing between a good time today and a good life as a whole—a choice between what is only useful, expedient, or pleasant in the short run, and what will contribute, in the long run, to making your whole life good?[37]

The latter choice may satisfy VM, in the sense that it maximizes value; but VM's abstract formula does not furnish what is needed. "In the light of the fact that making a good life as a whole necessarily entails long-range considerations, does it not now seem evident that you cannot make a good life for yourself by choice rather than by chance unless you have some kind of plan for your life as a whole—a plan for the use of its time in the present, in the years immediately ahead, and in the long run?"[38]

This project is not private or purely personal; it is a task for ethics.

A plan of that character consists of a small number of prescriptions about the goods to be sought and the manner and order of seeking them. These prescriptions, formulated with a universality that makes them applicable to all men without regard to their individual differences or the special circumstances of their individual lives, constitute what little wisdom it is possible for the moral philosopher to attain with reasonable certitude, and that little is nothing but a distillation of the wisdom of common sense.[39]

Adler's common sense recognizes five components of a good human life, which he identifies, broadly but suggestively, as *idling, sleeping, working, playing,* and *leisuring.* "With the five parts of life—the five basic forms of human activity—fully described and seen in relation to one another, we should be able to put them in some order. We should be able to construct a scale of values governing the use of our time which would be a rough plan of life."[40]

Evidently, what Adler envisages, by means of this listing and ordering, is a strategy for maximizing value, not merely for this or that person but for people generally, and not merely in this or that action but in life as a whole. Such a project does not clash with VM; yet, if realized, it might furnish something more valuable than VM. What, then, are its prospects? How might an abstract ordering of the basic forms of human activity help order a person's life in detail?

Well, let us consider a specific life and a specific problem. Father Hesburgh, the long-time head of the University of Notre Dame, recounts at one point in his autobiography: "I was in the middle of my first term as president, which I assumed might be my last, and I was working very long days far into the nights trying to cram in all my work."[41] People told him he looked haggard. He knew he was not getting much sleep. Was he getting too little? Could Adler's hierarchy tell him whether he was? Could it do so more surely or clearly than VM?

VM would require Hesburgh to consider, as doubtless he did, the importance and urgency of his immediate work, the likelihood of his being reappointed president, and the immediate and long-term effects of his getting less sleep. Was the reduction likely to be counterproductive in the long run? Was it proving counterproductive even in the short run? These are the questions VM would have him ask. Would Adler's scheme suggest different, better questions, or help with these questions?

In Hesburgh's situation, work—a combination of what Adler terms "subsistence-work" and "leisure-work"—vied with sleep. Concerning such a conflict, Adler notes that "a certain amount of time *must* be spent in sleeping, as anyone knows."[42] However, "we ought to subordinate all other activities to leisure-work," since "the goods of leisure are the highest goods in the scale of partial goods."[43] Accordingly, sleep should be kept to a "reasonable minimum."[44] Regarding what constitutes a reasonable minimum, Adler wisely declines to become more explicit.

> When the man of common sense says that in the overall economy of our life's time, sleep and play should be kept to reasonable minimums, his common sense leads him to acknowledge that the standard of a reasonable minimum varies with differences in individual make-up, with differences in external circumstances, and above all with differences in age. There can be no hard and fixed rules about the proportion of one's time to be devoted to sleep and play. To say this is not to say that anything goes— that any and every use of one's time is equally reasonable. It is only to say that the standard of a reasonable minimum must be applied by individual judgment in the individual case.[45]

That is, by individual judgment seeking to maximize value. This is the master norm, implicit in such references to reasonable minimums.

It makes a similar, veiled appearance when Adler advises that "nothing we do should *unnecessarily* consume the time left for the pursuits of leisure,"[46] that within the limits imposed by other needs "one should leisure *as much as possible.*"[47] This sampling illustrates a general paradox: Adler's guidelines are more detailed than VM; yet VM provides more detailed guidance. VM is the ultimate, operative norm—the one that dots the i's.

Dotting them for each option, it dots them for a whole life. This does not signify that there can be no general plan, goal, purpose, or pattern for one's life as a whole.[48] However, the gap between such a plan and VM's guidance for individual "actions" is not as great as it may appear. Action-options, too, may be very general. One may choose to marry or remain single, to be a doctor or priest or painter, to make a career in politics or devote one's life to cancer research—all in the light of VM. As chapter 1 notes, concerning all such matters one may ask, "What should I do?"

The more general the determination, the more decisive it is likely to be, if adhered to. One takes this course in chemistry because one has chosen a premedical program; one has chosen a premedical program because one has chosen to be a doctor; one has chosen to be a doctor because one ambitions to be a medical missionary; one ambitions to be a medical missionary because one wishes to bring healing, health, and spiritual life to those in need, and thereby maximize value. VM provides the broadest, most decisive framework of all: the one within which, for this person, being a medical missionary fits, whereas many other life-options do not.

There may be something still more decisive, though, than even this most comprehensive option.

## Motivation

VM may furnish the framework for life's choices—provided a person adopts and applies such a norm. However, many people do not. Thus a further possibility must be considered: whatever motivates the norm's adoption may have greater importance than the norm; for the norm says nothing about its own motivation. In reply, I suggest that though VM does not speak of motivation, it does furnish motivation.

Of late there has been much discussion of Plato's query: "Why be moral?" Some, like Plato, suggest that being moral is in one's own best interests. Even in its Christian version, citing the hereafter, this reply is neither theologically nor philosophically satisfactory. If, however, VM aptly characterizes right action, the answer is obvious: we should be moral because morality maximizes value; and we should maximize value because it is valuable. Why else? Thus the answer to the question "Why be moral?" ceases to be puzzling once one accurately specifies what being moral consists in.

To Kurt Baier, the very question "Why be moral?" seems perplexing. In *The Moral Point of View*, he cites "a powerful argument," one to which he has seen no satisfactory reply:

> Even if "Why should I be moral?" is a request for a justification and not for an explanation, it is still illegitimate. For how could there be such a justification? It cannot be a justification in terms of self-interest, for it must be admitted that morality does not necessarily pay. Nor can it be in terms of moral reasons, for we are now talking *about*, not *within*, morality. "Why should I be moral?" cannot mean "Does being moral pay?" or "Is there a moral reason for being moral?" But it cannot mean anything else either, for there are no other types of reason. Hence it is an illegitimate question.[49]

Baier has overlooked a possibility. Values of every variety—moral, religious, social, aesthetic, cognitive, and other—are reasons for being moral if, as I propose, objective morality consists in maximizing value. However, the term *moral* is not so defined for English-speakers generally (see chap. 1). Hence "Why be moral?" does not *mean* "Why maximize value?" and it makes good sense to reply: "Because being moral maximizes value."

Most answers take a different tack.

> Writers like Baier, Rawls, Richards, Gert, Warnock, Singer, Brandt, and Gewirth are agreed that moral principles are properly derived by a method that involves rational choice under conditions of impartiality. On this shared account, moral principles are generated by a single procedure according to which a rational individual is asked to pursue his advantage while deprived of knowledge that is likely to particularize his judgment. By virtue of this procedure, moral principles evidence their characteristics of universality, publicity, and their supremacy over merely private volitions. As for the procedure itself, it is variously justified in terms of some very basic moral axioms—Rawls and

Scriven perhaps exemplify this tendency—or more properly and more basically, . . . its rationale is traced to the very conditions of rational justification itself.[50]

In the end, though, one may still ask, "Why should I seek consistency or avoid contradiction?" "Why should I step behind the veil of ignorance or accept any verdict so arrived at?" "Why should I be 'rational' in the manner prescribed?"[51] VM elicits no such puzzlement.

It is true, however, that mere acceptance of the norm will not make it operative in our lives. A person may perceive the better and not choose it (recall chap. 2), or may perceive it in a vague and abstract way that exerts little tug on the will. To perceive the need to maximize value concretely, we must recognize values concretely. To love our neighbors as ourselves, we must recognize their full human resemblance to ourselves. ("If you prick us, do we not bleed?") To wish to promote religion, education, or the arts, we must have an appreciation of religion, education, or the arts. To wish to save forests, whales, or dolphins, "we must learn what we are destroying, and then it will not be so easy to destroy."[52] "You cannot wantonly kill what you come to know and love."[53] Such realization of value comes through experience and imagination, plus particularized reflection (on God, truth, technology, deforestation, or the like), not through the answer to any single abstract question. Thus, for motivation there may be something more important than VM, but that something is not the answer to a still more significant query concerning motivation.

Paul Ramsey writes: "In numerous works of philosophical ethics today after 'the moral point of view' has been fully set forth, there is yet another chapter called for, one usually entitled 'Why Be Moral?' Given the univocity of the authorizing and the exciting reasons in religious ethics, no such chapter is needed."[54] For reasons just indicated, I agree. Value both elicits and authorizes. However, it is not solely value which motivates loving action, but love of God or neighbor; and love is not a norm. We thus come to the principal perspective which vies with VM's for primacy.

### Virtue

"The moral goodness of the person," writes Bernard Hoose, "is, of course, the chief concern of moral theology. Proportionalism, however, is concerned only with the secondary aspect, which is, of course, intimately linked to the primary one, but not to be confused with it."[55] In this era of resurgent virtue-ethics, many agree. "Duty, obligation, and rightness are only one part—indeed, only a small part, a dry and minimal part—of ethics."[56] "Moral goodness is primarily a perfection of persons, not of acts."[57] "Christian ethics is best understood as an ethics of character since the Christian moral life is fundamentally an orientation of the self."[58] "The moral-spiritual life is primarily and properly a manner of being (good-bad, to use the language used earlier) and only by analogy taken up with rightness-wrongness of action."[59] "Precepts or obligations are subordinate to the virtues."[60]

In this current emphasis, there is much unclarity about the intimate linkage Hoose concedes between the goodness of persons and the rightness of acts, and about the alleged primacy of the former. The primacy might be *causal, evaluative, conceptual,* or *epistemological.* Indeed, all four sorts of primacy have been asserted. Let us consider each in turn.

*Causally,* connections go both ways: "The person forms his or her character or virtue through specific deeds. The deed affects the character, and the character affects the deed."[61] However, in both directions the influence is only partial. On the one hand, virtuous actions result from more than virtuous persons; for various reasons, good persons sometimes do objectively bad deeds and bad persons sometimes do objectively good deeds. On the other hand, virtuous persons result from more than virtuous deeds; "the formation of our dispositions stems in part from our loyalties to particular persons and communities, and from our conscious commitments to particular values and ways of life."[62] Thus, no clear causal primacy appears, one way or the other.

*Evaluatively,* strong claims have been made in both directions. According to Iris Murdoch, "a genuine sense of mortality enables us to see virtue as the only thing of worth."[63] From this perspective, "theistic morality is concerned with the realization of a certain sort of character and attitude rather than with external observance of moral rules, or even with the obedience to moral rules for their own sake. It is concerned with what a man must become in himself rather than with what specific acts he must do."[64] For others, on the contrary, "virtues have no other value and purpose than to make us apt for their corresponding acts, and for acts ever more perfect."[65] Doubtless truth lies somewhere between these two extremes, but where?

It is easy to exaggerate the value of character relative to conduct. One may note the intrinsic value of persons and their perfections but not note that these perfections are intrinsic to the goodness of good actions, which have as their principal outcome the perfecting of persons. One may view the human values realized by action not only as extrinsic to actions (which they need not be) and to the goodness of actions (which they are not) but also as extrinsic to the goodness of the actions' agents, statically, atomically conceived. "We do form for ourselves an ideal of human conduct," Milton Gonsalves remarks, "and an ideal of personhood." However, "these are not two ideals, for a person's conduct is that person's life."[66]

It is also easy to err in the opposite direction, and exaggerate the value of conduct relative to character. "The end of virtue," we are told, "since it is an operative habit, is operation."[67] "By its very notion virtue is a means and not an end."[68] Yet, even if virtue were nothing but a disposition to right action, it would not follow that right action, in itself, is more precious than virtue, in itself. And virtue is something more than dynamic inclination. How much more it is depends on how it is defined, and how it is defined brings us to the question of *conceptual* primacy.

Here, too, viewpoints differ sharply. For some, "moral rightness stands unequivocally at the beginning."[69] "One cannot conceive of traits of character except as dispositions and tendencies to act in certain ways in certain circumstances."[70] Thus "a habit is not called good or bad, save in so far as it induces to a good or bad act."[71] In contrast stands the thesis "that all act-appraisals are explicable in terms of more basic appraisals of persons or of traits—that the moral status of acts depends entirely on whether they would be performed by morally good persons or are manifestations of virtue."[72] Thus, "actions are good only in relation to the goodness of persons."[73] "We say that an action, which is objectively (in truth) capable of incarnating our good disposition, is morally right, whereas we qualify as morally wrong an action which is inappropriate for that purpose."[74]

I side with those who take a more balanced view.[75] We readily judge the objective rightness of an individual act without regard for the subjective goodness of the agent, and the subjective goodness of the agent without regard for the objective rightness of the act. More broadly, however, we cannot and do not judge persons' character without regard for their dispositions to action, and we cannot and do not judge the objective rightness of conduct without regard for its effect on persons' character. True, some aspects of character can be judged good or bad independently of the conduct to which they incline ("For example, someone with a settled inclination to view situations from the standpoints of others involved in those situations evidently possesses a morally good character trait"[76]); but so can some aspects of conduct be judged good or bad independently of the conduct's effects on character. Thus, again, the two sides balance out. Neither subjective nor objective morality enjoys clear conceptual primacy.

What of *epistemological* primacy? Here too, given the dependence of knowledge on causal and conceptual connections, something can be said on both sides. On one hand, the rightness of people's actions reveals much about the goodness of their characters ("By their fruits you will know them"). On the other hand, being a good person assists greatly in judging the rightness of actions.[77] There is, however, an epistemological perspective which may finally end all this back-and-forth balancing: Which kind of understanding—act-centered or agent-centered—is more urgently needed? Where has unclarity been greatest?

For Christian ethics, especially, I think the answer is evident. Christian virtue-ethicians have been chiefly concerned to stress the primacy, or at least desirability, of virtue ethics. They have not engaged in any debate comparable to that reflected in the present study, concerning the objective morality of acts. This contrast suggests a sense in which the latter type of understanding enjoys epistemological primacy, at least in Christian ethics. A norm like VM answers a more pressing need.

Reflection suggests not only that this is so but also why it is so. Consider agape, the central Christian virtue.

> In what does this special Christian love consist? Pieper notes three features: (1) In all love the fundamental element is benevolent approval—"it's good that you exist." . . . In the Christian virtue of love this same affirmation is made, but from a different perspective and with a new awareness. . . . (2) Not only is our affirmation of others made from a new perspective, it is also made with a "more intensive force of approval." . . . . (3) Finally, to love another from this new perspective and with this more intensive force of approval means ultimately "to love another as the possible companion of future beatitude."[78]

Concerning these three characterizations—this benevolent approval, this intensive force, this eschatological perspective—no dispute has agitated Christian ethics. It is the deeds of love that have occasioned controversy.

Within the confines of the mind, all values cohabit irenically. Our benevolent approval may extend to all—to God and God's creation, to oneself and others, to humans and nonhumans, to nearest and neediest, to present and future generations—without conflict. Viewed in their subjective purity, without behavioral implications, kindly thoughts and feelings may clash with unkindly thoughts and feelings, but not with other kindly thoughts and feelings. It is when the thoughts and feelings are related to action that problems arise. For there, in action, the interests of humans may compete with those of nonhumans, or one's own interests with others', or the interests of one's nearest and dearest with those of the neediest, or the interests of present generations with those of future generations, and so forth. Action is the arena where Christian values—and theories—clash.

VM, proposing a general standard for adjudicating conflict, illumines this area, whereas virtue ethics does not.[79] According to VM, all competing values count; they can and should be compared; and options that maximize value should be preferred. Various rival theories contest these claims, denying that all values should be considered, or that they can be compared, or that value should always be maximized. Here, controversy swirls. In Christian virtue ethics, no comparable solutions are needed or proposed; relative harmony reigns.

So perhaps a reply can finally be given to this chapter's opening query. Is there any single question, I asked, more momentous for Christian ethics generally than the one VM answers? It is now possible, in the sense and for the reason indicated, to venture a negative reply. True, we have noted many limitations—causal, evaluative, conceptual, epistemological, and other—on VM's significance. There is far more to Christian ethics than this single question, and far more to Christian living than Christian moral theory. Nonetheless, in the realm of theory, the question VM answers looks more momentous for Christian ethics than any other I can think of, because it is the question that most urgently needs to be clarified. The debate continued and mirrored by the present discussion—by the objections countered in chapter 2, the alternative positions reviewed in subsequent chapters, and the contrary modes of reasoning inventoried at the start of this chapter—testifies to the need.

Still, the norm is only a norm. However valid and important VM may be, it is but an abstract, theoretical reflection of its impressive, paradigmatic inspiration:

Jesus exhibited the wholeness that is the Father's will for His children by the way he acted on behalf of men in his saving acts. He cursed the fig tree because it did not produce figs, and he repudiated the man with the one talent for burying it. Where there was paralysis he released it, where there was withering of limbs he restored them; blindness became seeing; hunger was fed with bread; life returned where it had been lost. All of which is to say that every motion of the Spirit of Christ will be known by the fact that, like Jesus' own acts, it will bring wholeness to the human order, not diminishment.[80]

# Notes

## Chapter 1: A Christian Criterion of Right and Wrong

1. In philosophical circles, the term *consequentialism* is often stretched, misleadingly, to cover all forms of proportionalism, including this one.

2. *CMR*, 45.

3. *CMR*, 224.

4. Gula, *Reason Informed by Faith*, 275; Janssens, "Norms and Priorities," 213; McKinney, "Quest," 69–72; O'Connell, *Principles for a Catholic Morality*, 152–53; Schüller, "Zur Problematik," 3–4; Vacek, "Proportionalism," 61, and review of *CMR*, 187.

5. This account is rough. For instance, it ignores two different senses of "constitutive of X": what constitutes the referent alone (e.g., falling drops of water) and what satisfies the definition (e.g., drops of water falling from clouds). For further refinements, see chapter 4.

6. See Hallett, *Language and Truth*, 160–61, and *Reason and Right*, 104–10.

7. See Hallett, *Logic for the Labyrinth*, 123–26.

8. *CMR*, 39.

9. See *CMR*, ch. 9.

10. Walter, "Foundation," 129, 132; Levy, "Richard McCormick," 259.

11. Grisez, *Christian Moral Principles*, 154.

12. Compare ibid., 141 ("Proportionalism is a theory of moral norms"), with ibid., 159 ("Proportionalism begins by claiming to be a reasonable method of moral judgment").

13. E.g., Stocker, "Schizophrenia," 40–41. See *CMR*, 171–72.

14. Ratzinger, "Dissent and Proportionalism," 668. In like vein, see Carney, "On McCormick and Teleological Morality," 90, and Nagel, who in *Mortal Questions* conflates "a single general theory of how to decide the right thing to do" (135) with "a completely general account of what should be done" (136), "a general and complete theory of right and wrong" (137).

15. This "challenging" criticism is reported by Vacek ("Proportionalism," 72). Cf. Gula, *Reason Informed by Faith*, 278.

16. Finnis, *Fundamentals of Ethics*, 88.

17. According to Sumner, "the basic principles of most moral frameworks, perhaps of all, take this omniscient, after-the-fact, as-things-turn-out point of view" (*Moral Foundation of Rights*, 179).

**18.** *CMR*, 163–65. Tense does not automatically determine perspective and sense. Of a contemplated action one may ask whether it promises to maximize value; of a past action one may ask not only whether it did maximize value but also whether it promised to do so. The prospective perspective is not confined to the present, nor is VM. Actions already performed as well as those presently contemplated may be judged prospectively.

**19.** Black, *Language and Philosophy*, 69.

**20.** Lewis, *Values and Imperatives*, 36–37. Cf. ibid., 35, 42. I prescind here from the consequentialist cast of Lewis's definition.

**21.** Swinburne, "Duty and the Will of God," 289.

**22.** Finnis, Boyle, and Grisez, *Nuclear Deterrence, Morality and Realism*, 277.

**23.** *CMR*, 207–8.

**24.** Nagel, "Limits of Objectivity," 102.

**25.** For fuller discussion, see *CMR*, 160–63. Interests, desires, and evaluations may themselves be evaluated objectively, in which case the interests, desires, and evaluations abstracted from are not, of course, the ones evaluated, but any directed to them. Is it a good thing for the Corinthians to be interested in their salvation? Yes. Is it a good thing because Paul wants them to be interested in their salvation? No.

**26.** *CMR*, 21–23, 24–26. For similar distinctions, see Schüller, "Neuere Beiträge," 156–57. Some distinguish intention (motive, goal, aim) from intent—"that which an agent wills actually to be doing at the moment" (Quay, "Disvalue of Ontic Evil," 269). Both fall outside prospective moral deliberation, coherently conducted.

**27.** Schüller, "Double Effect," 190.

**28.** Milhaven, "Towards an Epistemology of Ethics," 238. On this paragraph's exclusions, see *CMR*, ch. 2.

**29.** On this common extension of *action* to "forbearances," cf., e.g., Bergström, *Alternatives*, 24–25.

**30.** Hallett, "Place of Moral Values," 133–34; Sinnott-Armstrong, *Moral Dilemmas*, 16.

**31.** *CMR*, 169–70.

**32.** *CMR*, 99–101.

**33.** Hallett, "Place of Moral Values," 132–40.

**34.** Bergström, *Alternatives*, 29.

**35.** Ibid., 30.

**36.** Hallett, *Reason and Right*, 44–47.

**37.** The impression of more serious conflict may arise from the troublesome distinction already noted, between the conditional and unconditional senses of moral terms.

**38.** Grisez and Boyle, *Life and Death*, 346.

## Chapter 2: A Major Objection

**1.** For a set of objections and replies in defense of a kindred position, see Feldman, *Doing the Best We Can*, chapter 3. In reply to the familiar objection, which Feldman does not address, that total, long-term consequences cannot accurately be assessed, I briefly comment as follows. First, since VM is a criterion of right conduct and not a methodological prescription (see chap. 1), it is not directly impugned by such a practical difficulty. Second, given the importance of consequences—their great value and disvalue—no moral theory may disregard them (see chap. 3); hence no moral theory can entirely escape the same practical limitation. Third, the upshot, of course, is that we may often be uncertain, and often mistaken, about what we should do. But that should come as no surprise. "No other problems, in any single science, are as difficult as the issues we must often face in ethics" (Hallett, *Reason and Right*, 41; see 40–43).

2. I have stated this dilemma cleanly, without the dubious semantics ("same sense," "different sense," "analogous sense," etc.) in which it is often wrapped; such expressions are notoriously vague and permit no conclusions concerning the referential homogeneity or heterogeneity of the terms whose sense is thus described.

3. Grisez, "Against Consequentialism," 43. Cf. idem, "Choice and Consequentialism," 149, and *Christian Moral Principles*, 160; Finnis, Boyle, and Grisez, *Nuclear Deterrence, Morality and Realism*, 254, 263; Finnis, *Moral Absolutes*, 51–54. Both horns of the same dilemma appear in Knauer, "Fundamentalethik," 328–32, explaining his restricted, nonproportionalist teleology.

4. Grisez, *Abortion*, 310–11; idem, "Christian Moral Theology and Consequentialism," 298; idem, *Life and Death*, 350–51; Finnis, Boyle, and Grisez, *Nuclear Deterrence, Morality and Realism*, 254–58; Finnis, *Fundamentals of Ethics*, 89–90; May, *Moral Absolutes*, 53–54. On Bentham's and Frank Ramsey's similar view, see Charlton, *Weakness of Will*, 3. This charge explains others: the claim that consequentialism "implicitly involves a principle alien to faith" ("The proof is that Christian faith is clearly incompatible with the thesis, implicit in consequentialism, that there can be morally significant choices that are not free choices") and the claim that consequentialism has "devastating effects": "The first point is that consequentialist reflection upon past action tends to create the illusion that we could not have done otherwise than we did. . . . Second, if we cannot consistently consider choices regulated by consequentialist reasoning to be free, we cannot consistently consider mortal sin to be a possibility in matters of such choices" (Grisez, "Christian Moral Theology and Consequentialism," 317–18, 313–14).

5. Some readers may recognize the basis of this account; since some plausible details are additions of mine, I have not named names.

6. For signs of such conflation, which chapter 8 further critiques, see, e.g., Finnis, *Fundamentals of Ethics*, 89; Finnis, Boyle, and Grisez, *Nuclear Deterrence, Morality and Realism*, 254–55; Grisez, *Abortion*, 311; idem, "Against Consequentialism," 42; idem, *Life and Death*, 351: "By the common standard one possibility would be found to have all the good, all the appeal, of any alternative possibility, and then some."

7. Cf. McKim and Simpson, "Alleged Incoherence," 350–51.

8. Hallett, *Christian Neighbor-Love*, 7.

**9.** Grisez, "Against Consequentialism," 45.

**10.** Ibid., 46.

**11.** Cf. Grisez, Boyle, and Finnis, "Practical Principles," 131: "In carrying out such morally good choices, other aspects of the personality will gradually be drawn into line, errors in moral thinking corrected, and facility in carrying out right choices gained. In this way, virtues are acquired."

**12.** Lewis, *Analysis*, 368.

**13.** "As a matter of psychology, pleasure, though rated lowest, attracts strongly, indeed perhaps more powerfully than any higher type of value. It is this disparity between rating and force, I suspect, which accounts above all for the distrust of Christian ethicians and their tendency to remove pleasure from the catalog of legitimate considerations" (*CMR*, 129).

**14.** Cf. Davidson, *Essays on Actions and Events*, 42 ("in the case of incontinence, the attempt to read reason into behaviour is necessarily subject to a degree of frustration").

**15.** Cf. Gowans, *Moral Dilemmas*, 29: "The concept of incommensurability is a familiar if troublesome concept from recent discussions in the philosophy of science. What gives it plausibility in the moral realm is our sense of bafflement in the face of questions such as whether the good of friendship is more or less worthwhile than the good of justice, or whether the good of integrity is better or worse than the good of some worthy objective."

**16.** Grisez, "Against Consequentialism," 39. Cf. ibid., 27–31; Finnis, *Fundamentals of Ethics*, 86–90; May, *Moral Absolutes*, 49.

**17.** See Hallett, "'Incommensurability of Values,'" 382–83 (nos. 3 and 4), 384–85 (no. 8), and *CMR*, 139–40. For discussion of a refinement not considered there, see chapter 11 ("A System of Values"). It is often suggested that a "basic" value like life takes priority over values for which it is required. However, in the concrete there is no conflict between such a value and the values that depend on it, thus no question of the former taking precedence over the latter; and in the abstract it is not true, for example, that any risk (however slight) to life (however minimal) outweighs any risk (however great) to other values (however numerous or maximal) of kinds that (in general) depend on life.

**18.** In critics of commensurability, it is difficult to identify precisely what kinds of values are supposed to be incommensurable, and why. The target shifts. Up to this point, judging from examples given (e.g., justice and truth), reasons often alleged (e.g., lack of univocity, of a common denominator), and the obvious comparability of like values (e.g., of pains with pains), I have described the supposedly incomparable values as disparate ones.

**19.** Finnis, Boyle, and Grisez, *Nuclear Deterrence, Morality and Realism*, 261. Cf. ibid., 255 ("to the upright person the morally right is always a greater good than non-moral good, and any non-moral evil is always a lesser evil than any moral evil whatsoever"), 261–63, and Hughes's comments ("Philosophical Debate on Nuclear Disarmament," 227–28); Donagan, *Theory of Morality*, 237; Grisez, "Structures of Practical Reason," 283: "Moral goods such as practical reasonableness and justice are morally superior to the substantive goods such as truth and life. Moreover, among the moral goods, religion (harmony with the more-than-human source of meaning and value, i.e., with the good itself in which all human goods participate) is superior to the rest."

20. Finnis, Boyle, and Grisez, *Nuclear Deterrence, Morality and Realism*, 262. Cf. Finnis, *Moral Absolutes*, 53.

21. Kagan, *Limits of Morality*, 16.

22. Rescher, *Ethical Idealism*, 70.

23. Ibid., 67.

24. Cf. Nagel, *Mortal Questions*, 134–35.

25. Hallett, "'Incommensurability' of Values."

26. For instance, Finnis, responding to my "The 'Incommensurability' of Values," argues that disparate goods are good in analogous, not univocal, senses of *good*, and that this variation of sense precludes comparative evaluation (*Moral Absolutes*, 53). The gospel paradigms—people and sparrows, people and sheep—suggest how necessary it would be to demonstrate these two points and not simply assert them. Given their diversity, are sparrows and humans "valuable" in different, analogous senses, and does this difference of sense preclude comparison? What are the two senses in question? Why does their difference preclude comparison? It is not generally true that every difference in reference entails a difference in sense, or that every difference in sense precludes rational comparison.

27. Cf. Schüller, "Neuere Beiträge," 162: "Ersparte Mühen sind als Wert qualitativ verschieden vom Wert vertiefter philosophischer Einsicht. Trotzdem tragen wir keinerlei Bedenken, das Urteil zu fällen, für eine tiefere Einsicht in dieses oder jenes philosophische Problem lohne es sich, die Mühen langen Nachdenkens und Meditierens auf sich zu nehmen." For further biblical illustrations, see chapter 8. Concerning disparate instances of similar values, whose comparability has also been denied, cf. Baier, *Moral Point of View*, 65: "that Plato was a greater philosopher than Joad, that cars are now better than they were fifty years ago, that *Hamlet* is a greater play than *A Streetcar Named Desire*, that Gandhi was a better man than Stalin, are not matters of opinion, but are quite indubitably true. Anyone who maintained the opposite would have to be said not to know what he was talking about."

## Chapter 3: The Positive Case for VM

1. Attfield, *Theory of Value and Obligation*, 95. Compare Janssens, "Norms and Priorities," 213; Veatch, "Are There Non-Moral Goods?," 471; Schüller, "Die Bedeutung des natürlichen Sittgensetzes," 126–27; Lewis, *Values and Imperatives*, 25: "If there were no such fact as good and bad in the experience of life, there would also be no such fact as right and wrong in what is done. Nobody would have any reason to care."

2. Nagel, "Limits of Objectivity," 104.

3. Ibid., 105.

4. Lewis, *Analysis*, 373. Cf. ibid., 366.

5. See also, e.g., Attfield, *Theory of Value and Obligation*, chap. 2; Bergman, "Experience of Value"; Lewis, *Analysis*, chap. 12; Nagel, "Limits of Objectivity," 97–118.

**6.** Von Hildebrand, *Fundamental Moral Attitudes*, 4–5; Knauer, "Fundamentalethik," 338, 354; Janssens, "Ontic Good and Evil," 81; Hallett, *Reason and Right*, 105–6.

**7.** Attfield, *Theory of Value and Obligation*, 25–26.

**8.** Gonsalves, *Fagothey's Right and Reason*, 72. Such a claim, morally understood, requires a stronger sense of *value* than Gonsalves indicates: "Value or worth is a term used for anything that appeals to us in any way" (ibid., 79).

**9.** Foot, *Theories of Ethics*, 7.

**10.** Veatch, "Are There Non-Moral Goods?," 471.

**11.** *CMR*, 76–77.

**12.** Gustafson, "Moral Discernment," 35.

**13.** Ramsey, "Biblical Norm of Righteousness," 422.

**14.** Cf. Dodd, "Ethics of the New Testament," 551: "The *agape* of God as exhibited in the character and action of Christ is an energy of unqualified good will, which sets a value even upon its unworthy objects (see Romans 5:6–8) and stops at nothing to secure their highest good. It is the imitation, or reproduction, of this divine *agape* that is the norm of Christian ethical action (compare John 3:16 with John 13:34, 1 John 4:10–11, 19)." Here is the truth in a claim like Rudolf Hofmann's: "Im Begriff der Nachfolge Jesu wird Wesen und Eigenart der christlichen Sittlichkeit so umfassend und so zutreffend aus ihrem Quellpunkt erhoben, wie dies keine andere Sichtweise ermöglicht. Das ist für die Moraltheologie Grund, in ihm den zentralen Gesichtspunkt ihrer Erkenntnis zu finden" (*Moraltheologische Erkenntnis- und Methodenlehre*, 246). Following Christ does not mean duplicating his specific deeds, but living by his mind, revealed in and by his deeds.

**15.** *CMR*, 128.

**16.** Grelot, *Problèmes de morale fondamentale*, 79.

**17.** Schnackenburg, *John*, 360.

**18.** Morris, *Gospel According to John*, 83.

**19.** Schnackenburg, *John*, 352.

**20.** Meier, *Matthew*, 304.

**21.** Cope, "Matthew XXV:31–46," 44.

**22.** Donahue, "Parable," 30.

**23.** *Decree on the Apostolate of the Laity*, 8.

**24.** Fitzmyer, *Gospel According to Luke*, 884.

**25.** Cf. Blank, "Zum Problem ethischer Normen," 182; Weber, "Historisches zum Utilitarismus," 231–34 (on utility, broadly understood, as a ground of morality in the New Testament).

**26.** "A formulation reminiscent of the rabbinic distinction between heavy and light commandments" (Gardner, *Matthew*, 104). "A distinction was drawn between 'heavy' or serious commandments like honoring one's parents (Deut 5:16) and 'light' commandments like the law of the bird's nest (Deut 22:6–7)" (Harrington, *Gospel of Matthew*, 316). (Here and in the other notes for this paragraph, the comments I quote are such as to suggest the possible pertinence of the quoted comparisons.)

**27.** "The perspective is that of judgment which makes even physical integrity a matter of second rank" (Luz, *Matthew 1–7*, 297). "Better to go limping into heaven than leaping into hell" (Bruner, *Matthew*, vol. 1, 186).

**28.** "The implied argument is *a minori ad maius*, . . . Will not God, having given the greater thing (hē psychē), supply the lesser things such as food and clothing?" (Davies and Allison, *Matthew*, vol. 1, 648). "Put this way, even the poorest must agree that, important as are food and clothing, they are not the most important things of all" (Morris, *Matthew*, 157).

**29.** "The 'greater' is a matter of dispute: Is it Jesus, or the kingdom of God inaugurated by Jesus, or the community around Jesus? All three aspects are probably present, with the idea of Jesus' community being most prominent" (Harrington, *Matthew*, 172). "Although some have thought of the kingdom, others of love, Jesus' interpretation of the law, or the community of disciples, the reference must be to Jesus . . . As Gundry writes, 'the neuter gender . . . stresses the quality of superior greatness rather than Jesus' personal identity' (*Commentary*, 223)" (Davies and Allison, *Matthew*, vol. 2, 314). "What God was doing in the sending of Jesus far surpassed what he did in setting up the temple worship" (Morris, *Gospel according to Matthew*, 303).

**30.** "We might have expected the masculine 'someone greater,' but the neuter points to God's whole work in Jesus . . ." (ibid., 327).

**31.** "Solomon was proverbial for wisdom, but his wisdom was not to be compared to what had happened with the coming of Jesus" (ibid.). "Three times in this chapter we have heard Jesus say 'and more than such-and-such is here' (vv. 6, 41, 42). He has claimed to be more than the temple (in the law), more than Jonah (in the prophets), and more than Solomon (in the poetic and wisdom literature), in other words, to be more than the entire revelation of Hebrew Scripture" (Bruner, *Matthew*, vol. 1, 469).

**32.** "When Jesus says that it would be better to be drowned with this stone around the neck than to trip up even one little one, he means that it would be a blessing if a person died this awful death *before* misleading a little one by false-teaching or false-living and so suffer eternal damnation (Schl., *Der*, 548; Bertram, *TDNT* 3:916f; cf. 1 Cor 5), for 'the only thing more terrible than being drowned with a millstone about one's neck is damnation at the Last Judgment (Staehlin, *TDNT* 7:351)" (Bruner, *Matthew*, vol. 2, 638; cf. Fenton, *Gospel of St Matthew*, 293; Meier, *Matthew*, 203).

**33.** Cf. note 26.

**34.** "The Pharisees overlooked the fact that *the altar that sanctifies the gift* is surely greater than *the gift* it has sanctified" (Morris, *Gospel according to Matthew*, 581). "Their priorities are topsy-turvy" (Meier, *Matthew*, 270).

**35.** "El remedio que propone el Evangelio contra el abuso de descuidar lo principal no consiste en descuidar lo secundario, ni tampoco en allanar todos los valores con un mismo rasero, sino en integrarlos dentro de una razonable escala de 'gravedad' o importancia" (Civit, *El Evangelio segun San Mateo*, 443).

**36.** "The radical demand that the hand or foot should be hacked off or the eye plucked out if they expose a man to the danger of final rejection juxtaposes the relative value of physical life with the absolute value of that authentic, imperishable life which is bestowed by God alone" (Lane, *Gospel According to Mark*, 348).

37. "There is no doubt what Christ would have preferred—he would have preferred Martha's fellowship to her service—nor what he in fact regarded as more necessary for Martha" (Gooding, *According to Luke*, 216). "Here the 'many things' are set in contrast to the one thing needful: hearing the word of Jesus, which provides a very different kind of nourishment" (Schweizer, *Good News*, 189). "What feeds the soul is more important than what feeds the body" (Stein, *Luke*, 321). "Wenn Jesus in einem Hause als Gast einkehrt, sollen die Hausbewohner das Hören Seiner Worte als das Höchste und Wichtigste ansehen" (Rienecker, *Das Evangelium des Lukas*, 276).

38. "Disciples are not to be anxiously concerned about food and clothing. These are of less importance than the person himself" (Marshall, *Gospel of Luke*, 525). "We shall, if we are not careful, allow our quest for food and clothes to become the major pre-occupation of our lives to the neglect, or even the complete exclusion, of far more important things" (Gooding, *According to Luke*, 241–42). "What may be implied is that anxious concern about means leads to a preoccupation with them as ends (cf. v. 30); but in the gospels there is no analysis of human life in itself, and apart from its relation to God" (Evans, *Saint Luke*, 527).

39. "The judgment of God ('something worse') would fall heavily on him" (Kirk and Obach, *John*, 84).

40. "[Paul] takes it for granted that there is nothing morally wrong either with marriage or with sexual relations within marriage" (Murphy-O'Connor, *1 Corinthians*, 59). However, "there can be little doubt that Paul was convinced that his way of life was better than the married state" (ibid.).

41. "1 Cor 13:1–13 is an aretalogy of love . . . that falls into an *aba'* pattern: (*a*) the superiority of love (vv. 1–3); (*b*) the characterization of love (vv. 4–7); and (*a'*) the superiority of love (vv. 8–13)" (Talbert, *Reading Corinthians*, 86).

42. "Death for the Christian is never pictured in the Bible as a gain over the worst in this life. *It is portrayed as an improvement on the best.* Certainly it is in this sense that Paul intends his words to the Philippians" (Boice, *Philippians*, 94).

43. "The believer, who has had the opportunity to learn the deeper meaning of love in his associations with the Savior, places himself on a level beneath that of the unprivileged unbeliever if he fails to practice this fundamental demand of love" (Moellering, *1 Timothy*, 102).

44. "The comparative adjective 'better' is used thirteen times in Hebrews to contrast Christ and his new order with what went before him. Here his superiority to the angels is asserted" (Bruce, *Epistle to the Hebrews*, 51).

45. "In view of the positive tone of chap. 11 as a whole, the contrast must be between good and better, not, as in 6:9, between good and bad" (Ellingworth, *Epistle to the Hebrews*, 636). "The reference to God's final action is deliberately vague so as to suggest in an inclusive fashion the results of

Christ's sacrifice" (Attridge, *Epistle to the Hebrews*, 352). "The 'better plan' which God had made embraces the better hope, the better promises, the better covenant, the better sacrifices, the better and abiding possession, and the better resurrection which is their heritage, and ours" (Bruce, *Epistle to the Hebrews*, 330).

**46.** "The testing of the faith is said to be many times more precious than gold, for the latter is perishable, although tested by fire as the Christians are by persecution" (Reicke, *Epistles*, 80).

**47.** "Pleiōn seems here to be used as meaning greater in quality, better" (Charles, *Revelation*, 69).

**48.** Finnis, *Moral Absolutes*, 60–61. In a similar vein, see Grisez, *Christian Moral Principles*, 168, n. 32. Cf. Collins, *Christian Morality*, 238–39 (and his critique).

**49.** Finnis, *Moral Absolutes*, 62.

**50.** John Paul II, *Veritatis splendor* 75.

**51.** Ibid., 81.

**52.** Deidun, "Exceptionless Norms," 166. Cf. 203 of the same volume (where, in a follow-up discussion, Deidun expands on these remarks); Blank, "Zum Problem ethischer Normen," 175–80; Furger, "Zur Begründung eines christlichen Ethos," 39–42; Kerber, "Grenzen der biblischen Moral," 117–22; McNamara, "Use of the Bible," 104–5.

**53.** For further illustrations, see *CMR*, chap. 4; Schüller, "Neuere Beiträge," 122–27; Weber, "Historisches zum Utilitarismus," 234–39. On past appeals to utility, Weber comments: "Dass es sich um bedenkliche Gedankengänge handeln könnte, scheint man nur selten einmal bemerkt zu haben. Im allgemeinen zeigt sich eine unbefangene Einstellung. Es scheint, dass die im Raum der katholischen Theologie heute feststellbare Reserve ein Resultat der vor allem von Kant ausgelösten und weithin bestimmten Kontroverse ist. Dabei dürfte für das Einschwenken der Moraltheologie auf eine kritische Distanz ausschlaggebend gewesen sein, dass der englische Utilitarismus von seinen Anfängen an einen säkularistischen und z. T. materialistisch-hedonistischen Anstrich hatte" (ibid., 239).

**54.** To see that this is so, it suffices to pass these positions quickly in review. Either likely reading of Aquinas's first principle might claim historical backing, but neither reading challenges VM. The broader reading of Donagan's principle of respect coincides with VM, whereas the narrower reading, stressing autonomy over value-maximization, has slight support in Christian tradition. Historical linking of conduct and intention evinces no more consistency than does Grisez's. Knauer's single-track criterion requires reasoning of a kind seldom encountered even today; it does not speak for Christian teleology in general, much less for the whole of Christian tradition. Thomson's emphasis on rights, as opposed to beneficence, reflects a recent trend, stronger in philosophical than in theological ethics.

**55.** Implicit in this and the preceding paragraphs is a response to Vacek's objection (review of *CMR*, 189): "It would be hard to demonstrate, without counting noses, H.'s claim that the value-maximalization approach has been more often used than any other single approach." There is no need to count noses; one can identify major rivals and note how comparatively weak is their historical representation.

56. Augustine, *Contra mendacium* vii, 18.

57. Mercken, *Greek Commentaries*, 239 (translation from Finnis, *Moral Absolutes*, 35, of Grosseteste's insertion).

58. Aquinas, *De malo*, q.15.a.1.arg. 5.

59. *CMR*, 112.

60. Concerning "intended pain of the child whom we spank pedagogically," Finnis remarks: "Pain is not itself an intelligible evil; indeed, it is itself an intelligible good, as one can understand by considering the difficult, usually short lives of those born with no sense of pain. Pain is experienced as a sensory evil; the horror it arouses in us is essential to its intelligible function" (*Moral Absolutes*, 79). Pain just feels bad; it isn't really bad, in itself: such is the apparent implication of Finnis's remarks. However, tagging the evil "sensory" rather than "intelligible" does not make it disappear, or eliminate it from the category of nonmoral evils. The same holds for mental distress—e.g., the unpleasantness of prison, the unhappiness caused by a salutary scolding.

61. E.g., Finnis, *Moral Absolutes*, 78–79.

62. Augustine, *Contra mendacium* vii.18.

63. John Paul II, *Veritatis splendor* 80, quoting the Apostolic Exhortation *Reconciliatio et paenitentia* (2 December 1984), 17: *AAS* 77 (1985), 221.

64. John Paul II, *Veritatis splendor* 77.

65. Ibid., 75.

66. Ibid., 74.

67. Grisez, "Against Consequentialism," 28.

68. Grisez, "Are There Exceptionless Moral Norms?", 117–20.

69. Donahue, "Divorce: New Testament Perspectives," 117–18.

70. Ibid., 116: "While the details of my historical reconstruction would doubtless be debated by New Testament scholars, virtually all would admit that Matthew represents some kind of exception to an absolute prohibition of divorce." See, e.g., Schierse, "Das Scheidungsverbot Jesu," 35–38.

71. Mackin, *Divorce and Remarriage*, 184 (on adultery as permitting or requiring dissolution).

72. Ibid., 372–74 ("All the Eastern Churches permitted divorce and remarriage . . . The adultery warranting dismissal and dissolution was understood to be not the only cause, but to be only a sample and a point of departure for other and equivalent causes. It was taken as self-evident that other crimes are possible to spouses that injure their marriages with equal or greater severity. Abortion and attempted murder of the spouse were only two of these").

73. Hallett, "'Whatever You Loose,'" 188. Cf. Kelleher, *Divorce and Remarriage for Catholics?*, 51.

74. Hallett, "'Whatever You Loose,'" 188–89.

75. Donahue, "Divorce: New Testament Perspectives," 117.

**76.** Pius XI, *On Christian Marriage*, 16.
**77.** Ibid.
**78.** Ibid., 15–16.
**79.** *CMR*, 56–61.

## Chapter 4: Natural Law: Aquinas

**1.** O'Connor, *Aquinas and Natural Law*, 57.

**2.** Clearly the best known and most influential theory of natural law, O'Connor judges Aquinas's account to be also "the most systematic, careful and subtle attempt to do justice to the idea" (ibid., 82).

**3.** Aquinas, *Summa theologica* 1–2, q.3.a.5.c.

**4.** Aquinas, *Contra gentiles*, bk. 3, chap. 63.

**5.** Ibid., chap. 130.

**6.** "Nec homo nec aliqua creatura potest consequi beatitudinem ultimam per sua naturalia" (*Summa theologica* 1–2, q.5.a.5.c).

**7.** Cf. Grisez, "First Principle," 183 ("Hence the end transcends morality and provides an extrinsic foundation for it"); Hofmann, *Moraltheologische Erkenntnis- und Methodenlehre*, 223–25.

**8.** See Gallagher, *Time Past, Time Future*, 76–78. "The consistent understanding of the neo-Thomist manualists was that 'the ultimate end of man is God himself so that in all his action man must direct himself to God'" (ibid., 54, with references).

**9.** Lottin, "L'ordre moral," 364.

**10.** McHugh and Callan, *Moral Theology*, vol. 1, 22.

**11.** Aquinas, *Summa theologica* 1–2, q.18.a.5.c. Cf. ibid., ad2; a.8.c; q.71.a.6.c. Sometimes the word *ratio* designates a faculty, sometimes the faculty's dictates (Lehu, *La raison*, 6–7); but what dictates the dictates?

**12.** Aquinas, *Summa theologica* 1–2, q.64.a.3.c.; Elter, "Norma honestatis," 339–40, 342.

**13.** "There were two distinct positions taken by the neo-Thomist manualists with regard to the natural law. The one emphasized natural law as right reason; the second associated the natural law with human nature as endowed with reason and natural inclinations" (Gallagher, *Time Past, Time Future*, 87).

**14.** Aquinas, *Summa theologica* 1–2, q.94.a.2.c. See ibid., q.21.a.1.

**15.** O'Connor, *Aquinas and Natural Law*, 28–30; McGrath, "Natural Law and Moral Argument," 65–66.

**16.** O'Connor, *Aquinas and Natural Law*, 72. Cf. Finnis, *Natural Law and Natural Rights*, 66; Bujo, *Moralautonomie und Normenfindung*, 240.

**17.** Aquinas, *Summa theologica* 1–2, q.100.a.5.ad4.

**18.** McGrath, "Natural Law and Moral Argument," 66. McGrath's list of three is not complete, but his point is valid. Cf. Battaglia, *Basis of Morals*, 55–56.

**19.** Aquinas, *Summa theologica* 1–2, q.94.a.2.c (English Dominican translation).

20. For specially full discussion of the passage and the article, see Schuster, "Von den ethischen Prinzipien"; Murray, *Problems in Ethics*, 220–35; and Grisez, "First Principle."

21. Grisez, "First Principle," 189.

22. Ibid., 188. Cf. Battaglia, *Basis of Morals*, chap. 3 (in agreement), and Porter, *Recovery of Virtue*, 86–87 (ambiguous).

23. Lottin, *Psychologie et morale*, 103–349.

24. E.g., Bourke, "Is Thomas," 57, and "El principio de la Sindéresis," 621; D'Arcy, *Conscience*, 50–52; Korff, *Norm und Sittlichkeit*, 51; Mahoney, *Making of Moral Theology*, 80; McInerny, *Ethica Thomistica*, 43; Schuster, "Von den ethischen Prinzipien," 58–59; Simon, *Fonder la morale*, 108.

25. Cf., e.g., Aquinas, *In 2 Sent.* d.24.q.2.aa.3 and 4; *De veritate*, q.16.aa. 1–3; *Summa theologica* 1–2, q.18.a.2.c. and a.4.ad 1; q.19.a.3.ad2; q.58.a.4.c, and a.5.c; q.65.a.2.c; q.91.a.3.ad1; q.94.a.1.ad2; q.100.a.1.c; 2–2, q.79.a.1; Bourke, "El Pincipio de la Sindéresis," 616–21. Both Grisez's argument for a nonmoral interpretation (*Christian Moral Principles*, 179) and J. A. Aertsen's rebuttal ("Natural Law," 105–6) look weak.

26. Grisez ("First Principle," 181–86) is a notable exception to the rule, at least with respect to "good" and "evil" (he too readily supposes a nonmoral sense for the gerundive), whereas Schuster ("Von den ethischen Prinzipien," 54–55) only comes close. Although often there is no telling which of the two readings an author prefers, unhesitating reference to the norm as "formal" or "tautologous," which is common, suggests Reading 1 (cf. reason 7 in the list for that reading). Proponents of Reading 1 include D'Arcy, *Conscience*, 50–52, and Simon, *Fonder la morale*, 108. Proponents of Reading 2 include: Mahoney, *Making of Moral Theology*, 80; McInerny, *Ethica Thomistica*, 43, 47; Murray, *Problems in Ethics*, 231, 232; Seidl, "Natürliche Sittlichkeit," 101. Bourke's formulations suggest now Reading 1 ("Is Thomas," 57), now Reading 2 ("Synderesis Rule," 73).

27. St. Albert, *Summa de creaturis, pars secunda (De homine)*, q.71.a.1.c. See Lottin, *Psychologie et morale*, 213–14, 217, 221.

28. Aquinas, *In 2 Sent.*, d.24.q.2.a.4.

29. Murray, *Problems in Ethics*, 224.

30. *In 3 Sent.*, d.38.a.3.ad6; *Quodlibeta* 8.a.14; *Summa theologica* 2–2, q.110.a.3; Dedek, "Intrinsically Evil Acts," 406–8.

31. *Summa theologica* 1–2, q.108.a.4; 2–2, q.184.a.3; *Contra gentiles*, bk. 3, chap. 130; *Quodlibeta* 5.a.19.

32. Noonan, *Contraception*, 293–95.

33. Lottin, *Le droit naturel*, 98 (see also 27).

34. Dedek, "Intrinsically Evil Acts," 387–88.

35. Aquinas, *Summa theologica* 1–2, q.94.a.2.c.

36. Ibid.

37. Hallett, *Reason and Right*, 105–6. Compare Stevens, "Relations of Law and Obligation," 198–99; Murray, *Problems in Ethics*, 230–31.

38. Aquinas, *Summa theologica* 1–2, q.94.a.2.c.

39. Ibid., q.8.a.1.

40. Aquinas, *Contra gentiles*, bk. 3, chap. 3.

**41.** E.g., "obiectum autem voluntatis est finis et bonum" (*Summa theologica* 1–2, q.1.a.1; see *Contra gentiles*, bk. 3, chap. 1); "unicuique autem est bonum id quod est sibi connaturale et proportionatum" (*Summa theologica* 1–2, q.27.a.1); "objectum autem voluntatis, quae est appetitus humanus, est universale bonum" (ibid., q.2.a.8.c).

**42.** Armstrong, *Primary and Secondary Precepts*, 40–41.

**43.** Aquinas, *In 2 Sent.*, d.24.q.2.a.3.

**44.** Aquinas, *Summa theologica* 1–2, q.100.a.3.ad1.

**45.** Ibid.

**46.** Ibid., a.3.c.

**47.** See McInerny, "On Knowing Natural Law," 136–37.

**48.** Aristotle, *Nichomachean Ethics*, VI.5.1140b 20–21. Cf. ibid., 1140a.25–28.

**49.** See Wolter, *Duns Scotus*, 25 (citing *PL* 176, 268).

**50.** Lottin, *Le droit naturel*, 27, 98.

**51.** In Lottin, *Psychologie et morale*, see, e.g., 141 (Philip the Chancellor: "Sensualitas et synderesis dicuntur opposite quantum ad suas inclinationes, ut sicut sensualitas inclinat rationem in bona mutabilia consequenda et mala hiis opposita fugienda, ita synderesis inclinat rationem in bona simpliciter et retrahit rationem aut liberum arbitrium a malis simpliciter"), 148 (idem: "Dico quod synderesis mouet liberum arbitrium dictando bonum et cohibendo a malo, et mouet in bonum commune quod inuenitur in isto bono aut in illo. Non ergo est in bonum particulare secundum se, sed in commune inuentum in eo"), 178 (Alexander of Hales: "'. . . et optimum concupiscunt, scilicet esse, uiuere et intelligere que sunt existentia.' Ergo in illis synderesis non est ex toto extincta").

**52.** Cf. Aquinas, *Summa theologica* 1–2, q.1.a.6.c; q.13.a.4.c; q.65.a.2.c.

**53.** Cf. Grisez, "First Principle," 181.

**54.** See also Weber, "Historisches zum Utilitarismus," 236–37.

**55.** Aquinas, *Contra gentiles*, bk. 3, chap. 24. See idem, *Summa theologica* 1–2, q.19.a.10.c.

**56.** E.g., Aquinas, *Summa theologica* 1–2, qq.90–97; q.100.a.8.

**57.** E.g., ibid., q.105.a.2.ad1.

**58.** Ibid., 2–2, q.53.a.5; *De veritate*, q.5.a.4.ad4; *2 Cor.* 12, lect. 3 (beginning).

**59.** Aquinas, *Contra gentiles*, bk. 3, chap. 122.

**60.** For a closely similar ambiguity, or alternation of perspectives, see *In Psalm.* 36:19.

**61.** Aquinas, *Summa theologica* 1–2, q.94.a.2.ad1.

**62.** Cf. Grisez, *Contraception and the Natural Law*, 66–67.

**63.** *CMR*, 114.

**64.** Aquinas, *Summa theologica* 2–2, q.53.a.5.

**65.** Ibid., q.64.a.7. Compare, e.g., *Summa theologica* 1–2, q.97.a.2.c; q.100.a.8.c.

**66.** Ibid., 2–2, q.64.a.5 (English Dominican translation). See ibid., q.59.a.3.ad2; q.124.a.1.ad2; 3, q.47.a.6.ad3.

**67.** Noonan, *Contraception*, 238–41, 293–95; *CMR*, 82–85.

**68.** Gilleman, *Primacy of Charity*, xxvii–xxviii.

**69.** Aquinas, *Summa theologica* 2–2, q.23.a.8. See idem, *De perfectione vitae spiritualis*, chap. 1; *Summa theologica* 2–2, q.184.a.1.ad2.

**70.** Quinn, "Recent Revival," 357–59.

**71.** Donagan, "Scholastic Theory," 337.

**72.** Donagan, *Theory of Morality*, 61–63.

**73.** Knauer, "Hermeneutic Function," 4. Cf. Aquinas, *Summa theologica* 1–2, q.102.a.1.c; 2–2, q.64.a.7.c.

**74.** Aquinas, Foreword to *Summa theologica* 2–2. See ibid., 1–2, q.77.a.2.ad1.

## Chapter 5: *Divine Commands: Adams*

**1.** Idziak, "Divine Command Morality," 3–7.

**2.** Quinn, "Recent Revival."

**3.** Alston, "Some Suggestions," 303.

**4.** Besides the sources indicated, all the articles of Adams I shall cite can be found in Adams, *The Virtue of Faith*. Numerous authors—e.g., Quinn, "Recent Revival," 347; Wierenga, *Nature of God*, 213; Alston, "Some Suggestions," 303; Mouw, *God Who Commands*, 28—attest to the articles' importance. For an alternative critique of Adams's most recent theory, see Davis, "Ethical Properties and Divine Commands."

**5.** Adams, "Modified Divine Command Theory," 84.

**6.** Ibid.

**7.** Ibid., 108.

**8.** Ibid., 85–86.

**9.** Adams, "Divine Command Metaethics Modified Again," 67.

**10.** Cf. Davis, "Ethical Properties and Divine Commands," 280–81.

**11.** Adams, "Divine Command Metaethics Modified Again," 66.

**12.** Ibid., 67.

**13.** Ibid.

**14.** Cf. Chandler, "Divine Command Theories," 237–38.

**15.** Fletcher, *Situation Ethics*, 60.

**16.** Ibid., 95: "It becomes plain that as the love ethic searches seriously for a social policy it must form a coalition with utilitarianism. It takes over from Bentham and Mill the strategic principle of 'the greatest good of the greatest number.'"

**17.** "One should keep in mind the British divine command moralists William Paley and John Gay, both of whom regarded utilitarianism as a way of knowing what God commands" (Idziak, "Divine Command Morality," 14).

**18.** Mill, *Utilitarianism*, 21.

**19.** *CMR*, 120.

**20.** Adams, "Modified Divine Command Theory," 101.

**21.** Chandler, "Divine Command Theories," 231.

**22.** Hanink and Mar, "What Euthyphro Couldn't Have Said," 251.

**23.** Mann, "Modality, Morality, and God," 97.

**24.** Ibid., 96.

**25.** Wierenga, "Defensible Divine Command Theory," 395, and *Nature of God*, 221.

**26.** Forrest, "Argument," 3–5.

**27.** Wierenga, "Defensible Divine Command Theory," 394.

**28.** Ibid., 401, and idem, *Nature of God*, 221; Burch, "Objective Values," 291.

**29.** Mouw, *God Who Commands*, 30.

**30.** Kretzmann, "Abraham, Isaac, and Euthyphro," 44–46.

**31.** Cf. Hanink and Mar, "What Euthyphro Couldn't Have Said," 249. I do not say this in blame. "There are good Christian reasons," writes Mouw, "for nurturing a resistance to attempts to 'psyche God out' in too much detail in dealing with the issues of ethical theory" (*God Who Commands*, 42).

**32.** Mouw, *God Who Commands*, 6.

**33.** Hallett, *Essentialism*, 175–79.

**34.** Ibid., 19–22. I believe that the difficulties for the doctrine of rigid designation are still more serious than I and others have indicated, but I cannot spell them out here.

**35.** Adams, "Divine Command Metaethics Modified Again," 76 (paragraph break omitted).

**36.** Early in his argument for a divine-command theory, Peter Forrest makes this revealing "appeal to moral phenomenology": "Just as material objects are presented to me, *as a reality*, in much the same way, the wrongness of a wrong act is presented to me *as a reality*" ("Argument," 7). Is the act's being forbidden by God also presented to me, with equal immediacy?

**37.** Chandler, "Divine Command Theories," 236.

**38.** See Matt 5:45, Eph 4:24, Col 3:10, and note 14 in chapter 3; compare Lev 19:2, Ps 119:129, Wis 12:19.

**39.** *CMR*, 38–39.

**40.** Fisher, "Because God Says So," 357.

**41.** Forrest, "Argument," 3–4. Cf. Wierenga, *Nature of God*, 218–19.

**42.** Cf. Wierenga, "Utilitarianism," 313–14, and *Nature of God*, 233–34.

## *Chapter 6: Respect for Persons: Donagan*

**1.** Donagan, *Theory of Morality* (hereafter *TM*), 66. What follows, in this chapter, is a shortened, revised version of Hallett, "Christian Norms of Morality."

**2.** *TM*, 209.

**3.** *TM*, 30; cf. ibid., 3, 55.

**4.** *CMR*, 22–23.

**5.** *CMR*, 22, 26, 89–90.

**6.** *CMR*, 23.

**7.** *CMR*, 2.

**8.** See Garver, review, 304–5.

**9.** *TM*, 57.

**10.** *TM*, 7.

**11.** *TM*, 29. Donagan tends to equate the part of morality that does not depend on theistic beliefs with the part ascertainable by human reason. See, e.g., *TM*, 6. In this he is not true to the tradition he aims to represent.

**12.** Donagan's repeated references, without distinction or restriction, to "common morality" (as here and on 31), to "the fundamental principle of morality" (e.g., 57–58), to "the first principle of morality" (e.g., 59), and the like, though understandable as convenient shorthand, tend to obscure the limitations of his system and of its guiding principle.

**13.** *TM*, 30.

**14.** See Richards, "Alan Donagan," 321–24.

**15.** Stout, "Philosophical Interest," 189.

**16.** *CMR*, 71–72.

**17.** *TM*, 61.

**18.** *TM*, 64.

**19.** Farley, review, 236.

**20.** See chapter 3 and *CMR*, 114–15.

**21.** *TM*, 89.

**22.** Ibid.

**23.** "Respecting a being as a rational creature is respecting him as autonomous—as having the right, subject to the moral law, to decide for himself what his own good is, and how to pursue it" (*TM*, 77).

**24.** Farley, review, 235.

**25.** Stout, "Philosophical Interest," 177.

**26.** Wertheimer, review, 305.

**27.** Sartre, *Existentialism and Humanism*, 35–36.

**28.** "Kant was no less plagued by the notion that . . . human desires and purposes are hopelessly 'subjective' and relative, and hence not at all of a sort that can provide a basis for duties and obligations that are objectively binding upon all human beings" (Veatch, "Variations," 54–55).

**29.** *TM*, 225.

**30.** *TM*, 85.

**31.** Donagan envisages possible conflict between respect and beneficence (*TM*, 154–57), and not just between autonomy and beneficence, but does not explain how this is possible if beneficence is a requirement and test of respect, as dozens of passages in *TM* suggest (see those quoted later in the text).

**32.** *TM*, 62–63.

**33.** *TM*, 22.

**34.** *TM*, 23.

**35.** *TM*, 23–24.

**36.** *TM*, 237 (emphasis added). Cf. *TM*, 232: "Having this power to judge his producible ends, which as such, is a higher kind of power than brute animals possess . . . , human beings, as rational, are of a higher kind than any others they have yet encountered in nature. Nor can there be any creature higher in kind, although there may be some higher in degree."

**37.** See also, e.g., *TM*, 78–79, 82, 104, 152, 169, 173, 186–87.

38. *TM*, 64.
39. *TM*, 80.
40. *TM*, 86.
41. *TM*, 100.
42. *TM*, 111.
43. *TM*, 183.
44. *TM*, 242.
45. Wertheimer, review, 304. "Upon close examination," writes Stout ("Philosophical Interest," 182), "we find that Donagan's fundamental principle bears virtually no weight." Rawls, too, has stressed the indeterminacy of mere "respect for persons" and the impossibility of deriving specific precepts from so ill-defined a basis. See Rawls, *Theory of Justice*, 585–86.
46. Nielsen, *Ethics without God*, 94–95.
47. *TM*, 178.
48. *TM*, 179.
49. *TM*, 65.
50. *TM*, 66.
51. "Simplicity is the seal of truth."
52. *CMR*, 129–33.
53. *CMR*, 132.
54. *CMR*, 133–37.

## Chapter 7: Inviolable Goods: Grisez

1. For a succinct statement of Grisez's recent position and an annotated bibliography tracing the position's development and varied exposition, by him and others, see Grisez, "A Contemporary Natural-Law Ethics." For a similar bibliography, see the end of Grisez, Boyle, and Finnis, "Practical Principles."
2. Grisez, *Christian Moral Principles* (hereafter *CMP*), 2.
3. *CMP*, 141.
4. Ibid.
5. Ibid., 924.
6. Ibid., 184.
7. Ibid., 186.
8. Ibid., 185.
9. Ibid., 186.
10. Ibid., 205.
11. Ibid., 216.
12. Ibid., 217.
13. Finnis, Boyle, and Grisez, *Nuclear Deterrence, Morality and Realism*, 293. See *CMP*, 220; Grisez and Boyle, *Life and Death*, 368, 369.
14. *CMP*, 239.
15. Cf. *CMP*, 240, 297–98.
16. Kosnik et al., *Human Sexuality*, 89. With regard to the unconditional "demand that we respect in our judgment, in an equal way, *all* the elements

of the entire act if we formulate a normative proposition that is meant to be objective," Josef Fuchs remarks: "For this reason, the studies by Knauer and W. van der Marck, as well as those of B. Schüller, J. Fuchs, F. Böckle, L. Janssens, F. Scholz, R. McCormick, and others, have been fundamentally important" (*Christian Ethics*, 75).

17. Kosnik et al., *Human Sexuality*, 90.

18. Finnis, Boyle, and Grisez, *Nuclear Deterrence, Morality and Realism*, 291. Cf. Grisez, *CMP*, 267, and "Methods of Ethical Inquiry," 166.

19. Grisez et al., "'Open to New Life,'" 368. Cf. ibid., 370.

20. Ibid., 378.

21. Ibid., 399.

22. Ibid., 401.

23. Ibid., 401–2.

24. Gerard Hughes has pointed out to me that a phrase such as "*the* baby's coming to be" in an argument like Grisez's is not entirely innocent; it sounds as though there were *a* baby which was an individual who could be maltreated or undervalued.

25. Grisez et al., " 'Open to New Life,' " 390.

26. Ibid.

27. Ibid., 373.

28. Grisez, *Contraception and the Natural Law*, 91.

29. Talk of "practical hatred" is ambiguous. "Practical" suggests a behavioral sense, "hatred" an attitudinal sense. The first reading is needed for truth, the second for relevance. Conflated, they suggest a strong argument.

30. Cf. Grisez et al., " 'Open to New Life,' " 373.

31. Ibid., 377. Cf. ibid., 379 ("And they think that the future in which the baby does not live is better. It certainly seems so to them").

32. Ibid., 401.

33. Ibid., 379.

34. Ibid., 400–1.

35. Ibid., 402.

36. "They do not have to judge that the possible future without the baby will be rationally preferable to a possible future with it. For their choice to abstain need not be contrary to any reason, and so, assuming it is not, they need not try to justify it by reasoning that their reason for abstinence is rationally preferable to the reason to have another baby—namely, the inherent goodness of a possible person's coming to be" (ibid., 403–4).

37. Ibid., 405.

38. For a good illustration ("to kill a man who was spanking your child"), see Connery, "The Teleology of Proportionate Reason," 493–94 ("it would be pretty hard to maintain that the intention of the father was only to defend the child and that he was not venting his rage against the assailant").

## Chapter 8: *"Proportionate Reason": Knauer*

1. Knauer, "La détermination," 368–69; "Hermeneutic Function," 35; "Good End," 73, 85.

**2.** See Knauer, review of Hoose, *Proportionalism*, 474, and review of Pinckaers, *Ce qu'on ne peut jamais faire*, 150.

**3.** Failure to note this point explains, at least in part, the widespread inclusion of Knauer among "proportionalists." See, e.g., Hoose, *Proportionalism*, 81; McKeever, "Proportionalism as a Methodology," 212, 219–20; Pinckaers, *Ce qu'on ne peut jamais faire*, 76–77. Grisez sees Knauer's position as proportionalist ("restricted proportionalism") because he believes it entails the necessity of commensurating the incommensurable (*Christian Moral Principles*, 162); but Knauer sees things differently.

**4.** Knauer, "Good End," 73–74.

**5.** Knauer, "Hermeneutic Function," 24, 32; *Der Glaube kommt vom Hören*, 1978, 63–66; "Fundamentalethik," 329–31, 335, 336, 342, 348; "Good End," 85.

**6.** Knauer, "La détermination," 370; "Hermeneutic Function," 12; "Fundamentalethik," 333.

**7.** Knauer, "Hermeneutic Function," 12. Cf. ibid.: "In unmeasured desire there is sacrificed what alone would assure the greatest possible achievement of the end."

**8.** Ibid., 17. Cf. ibid., 28–29, 33–34.

**9.** Similarly, McCormick, characterizing Knauer's view which he came to adopt, speaks both of "the value realizable here and now" (*Ambiguity in Moral Choice*, 8; *Notes, 1965 through 1980*, 314) and of "the good end being sought" ("Commentary on the Commentaries," 223). However, the latter, subjective sense—suggested by the Thomistic tradition on object, circumstances, and end—dominates in his writings as in Knauer's.

**10.** Knauer, "Das rechtverstandene Prinzip," 129, 132; "Hermeneutic Function," 15 ("In this requirement what is meant by end is not a concrete fact but what in a particular fact makes it worth acting for, its *ratio boni*"). Sexual or contraceptive activity that subverts procreation overall and in the long run is deemed wrong, regardless of the partners' reason for engaging in it ("Überlegungen," 63, 68, 69, 71, 73; *Der Glaube kommt vom Hören*, 1978, 72).

**11.** See especially Knauer, "Fundamentalethik," 342, 346.

**12.** Knauer, "Überlegungen," 67; "Hermeneutic Function," 27; "Fundamentalethik," 326.

**13.** Knauer, "Hermeneutic Function," 35.

**14.** Ibid., 34.

**15.** Ibid., 35.

**16.** Knauer, "Good End," 75.

**17.** Knauer, "Hermeneutic Function," 16.

**18.** Knauer, "Fundamentalethik," 336.

**19.** Knauer, "Hermeneutic Function," 24.

**20.** Knauer, "Good End," 74. See idem, "Fundamentalethik," 329, 334; *Der Glaube kommt vom Hören*, 1978, 65; review of Pinckaers, 150.

**21.** Knauer, "La détermination," 369–70; "Fundamentalethik," 335.

**22.** Knauer, "La détermination," 368; "Fundamentalethik," 328; "Hermeneutic Function," 11–12; "Das rechtverstandene Prinzip," 117–18.

23. Knauer, "Fundamentalethik," 328.
24. Knauer, "La détermination," 368.
25. Knauer, "Das rechtverstandene Prinzip," 119; "Hermeneutic Function," 16; *Der Glaube kommt vom Hören*, 1978, 63.
26. Knauer, "Fundamentalethik," 328. For similar criticism, aimed at a different target (imposing the "higher" of two values), see also Knauer, "Hermeneutic Function," 17; "Good End," 76; and "Das rechtverstandene Prinzip," 121.
27. E.g., Fletcher, *Situation Ethics*, 82; Rahner, *Theological Investigations*, vol. 8, 146.
28. For a fuller response, see *CMR*, 75–78.
29. Levy, "Richard McCormick," 271. The closing quotation is from Knauer, "Hermeneutic Function," 143.
30. Levy, "Richard McCormick," 271–72.
31. Ibid., 272.
32. Kiely, "Impracticality of Proportionalism," 673: "James & Mann, in their extensive study of the psychology of decision-making . . . set aside the case of the decision involving only a single objective as being marginal and providing no useful model for the analysis of decisions in general (p. 10 and *passim*)."
33. Knauer, "Hermeneutic Function," 28. See idem, "Das rechtverstandene Prinzip," 129.
34. For a comparable case, see Schüller, "Die Bedeutung des natürlichen Sittengesetzes," 127.
35. Cf. Grisez, *Abortion*, 331: "The inadequacy of Knauer's position appears most clearly if we consider that it cannot exclude a fanatical dedication to any particular genuine value. A mad scientist would find support in Knauer's theory, so long as he was an intelligent and efficient investigator, for he could defend any sort of human experimentation, no matter how horrible its effects on the subjects, provided the experimental plan promoted the attainment of truth—on the whole and in the long run—in the most effective way."
36. McCormick, *Notes, 1965 through 1980*, 319.
37. McCormick, "Commentary on the Commentaries," 230.
38. Johnstone, "Meaning of Proportionate Reason," 246–47; Hoose, *Proportionalism*, 82–84.
39. Knauer, "Fundamentalethik," 350.
40. E.g., Knauer, ibid., 340–41; review of Pinckaers, 150.
41. Knauer, "Good End," 73.
42. Finnis, Boyle, and Grisez, *Nuclear Deterrence, Morality and Realism*, 277. Cf. Knauer, *Der Glaube kommt vom Hören*, 1978, 63: "Um etwas überhaupt wollen zu können, muss man es in irgendeiner Hinsicht als einen Wert ansehen können." In correspondence Knauer comments: "Mir geht es nur um das Recht des scholastischen Axioms, dass man nur 'sub ratione boni' überhaupt handeln kann." One reading of this axiom is tautologically true, the other false. Neither saves Knauer's position.
43. Knauer, *Der Glaube kommt vom Hören*, 1991, 99 (emphasis added). While still retaining his earlier, simpler criterion, Knauer anticipated this

amplification when he wrote: "If, in seeking a value, a person sacrifices other values without this sacrifice being truly necessary for the sought value, their loss enters directly into the realm of what is intended and determines the act as counterproductive to the extent that the loss tolerated for the sake of the value is not kept as small as possible. To a certain degree, this is a diminishment of the value itself" ("Hermeneutic Function," 28). More recognizably stated, this closing claim becomes the second, italicized clause of Knauer's new principle.

**44.** Knauer, *Der Glaube kommt vom Hören*, 1991, 98.

**45.** "Von der oben abgelehnten Theorie des 'Gütervergleichs' unterscheidet sich das hier vorgelegte Modell dadurch, dass nicht *verschiedene* Güter miteinander verglichen werden, sondern dass in bezug auf *ein und denselben* Wert gefragt wird, ob man ihm auf die Dauer und im Ganzen gerecht wird oder aber ihn in Wirklichkeit in der Weise des Raubbaus auf die Dauer und im ganzen nur untergräbt" (Knauer, "Fundamentalethik," 329–30; emphasis in the original). See also ibid., 336.

**46.** Grisez, *Christian Moral Principles*, 144. See ibid., 160; Attfield, "Toward a Defence of Teleology," 123; Connery, "Catholic Ethics," 235, 247; Cornerotte, "Loi morale," 519; Gallagher, *Time Past, Time Future*, 249–51; Janssens, "Norms and Priorities," 213; Keane, "Objective Moral Order," 265; Kiely, "Impracticality of Proportionalism," 657–58; Pinckaers, "La question," 188, 193; Quay, "Morality by Calculation of Values," 269; Walter, "Foundation," 129, and "Response to John C. Finnis," 187. For a fuller critique of this position than the present focus on Knauer permits, see Hallett, "Place of Moral Values," 131–40.

**47.** Hallett, "Place of Moral Values," 132–33.

**48.** Frankena, *Ethics*, 1973, 48–49; Connery, "Morality of Consequences," 258–59; Langan, "Direct and Indirect," 95; Curran, "Utilitarianism and Contemporary Moral Theology," 246; Lyons, *Forms and Limits of Utilitarianism*, 173.

**49.** Knauer, "Good End," 72.

**50.** Knauer, "Fundamentalethik," 325.

**51.** Ibid., 332.

**52.** Knauer, "Hermeneutic Function," 2.

**53.** Knauer, "Good End," 75. See ibid., 73 ("everything which can motivate the will can be seen as a value"); idem, "Fundamentalethik," 331. Cf. Walter, "Foundation," 129 ("Premoral values refer to those conditioned goods that we pursue for human and nonhuman well-being and flourishing").

**54.** Knauer, *Der Glaube kommt vom Hören*, 1978, 63 (note 76). Cf. idem, review of Hoose, 474.

**55.** See, e.g., the same note in *Der Glaube kommt vom Hören*.

**56.** Knauer, "La détermination," 376.

**57.** Walter provides a partial explanation: "When they emphasize the prefix 'pre' in premoral values and disvalues, proportionalists refer to the fact that these values/disvalues really do exist independently of our free will"—that is, independently of the prospective agent's willing the prospective act ("Foundation," 129; cf. Janssens, "Ontic Good and Evil," 80).

**58.** "Reducible" may be too strong a reading of Knauer's words, but seems required if they are to answer my objection. He writes (in correspondence): "Ich schliesse durchaus nicht 'moralische Werte' aus dem Kalkül aus, sondern meine nur, dass man moralische Werte *letzlich* immer auf einen bestimmten Umgang mit vormoralischen Werten zurückführen muss. Es gibt keine unmittelbar moralischen Werte, sondern alle moralischen Werte sind dies nur mittelbar, nämlich durch die Vermittlung vormoralischer Werte."

59. For fuller discussion, see *CMR*, 131, 135, and Hallett, "Place of Moral Values," 136–40.

### Chapter 9: Irreducible Rights: Thomson

1. McCormick, *Notes, 1965 through 1980*, 417.
2. Thomson, *Realm of Rights* (hereafter *RR*), 148 (paragraph break omitted). In Thomson's terminology, a claim is a right in the strict sense, that is, a right that is the correlative of a duty (ibid., 40–41).
3. *RR*, 135.
4. Ibid., 136.
5. Ibid., 137.
6. Ibid., 145.
7. Ibid., 146.
8. Cf. Nielsen, *Ethics without God*, 78–81, 86–89.
9. *RR*, 160–62.
10. Ibid., 182.
11. Ibid., 187.
12. Ibid., 189. See also, 190, 192. Marcus Singer agrees: "What good will it do him to survive in that way? He will feel sullied and soiled and polluted" ("Gewirth's Ethical Monism," 32).
13. *RR*, 184, 186.
14. Ibid., 181.
15. Layman, *Shape of the Good*, 150. See ibid., 149–53, 156. Cf. Pojman, "Ethics: Secular and Religious," 25: "Take away the idea that a just God will reward and punish us on the basis of how we have executed the law of love, and the sacrifices utility calls for seem unreasonable."
16. Hocutt, "Mutual Accommodation," 144.
17. *RR*, 146.
18. Ibid., 158.
19. Ibid., 168.
20. Ibid., 167–68.
21. *CMR*, 98.
22. *RR*, 148.
23. Ibid., 176.
24. Ibid., 176–77.
25. Ibid., 180.
26. Ibid., 181.
27. Ibid., 194–95.
28. Ibid., 193.

**29.** Ibid., 194.

**30.** It has been suggested that the justification of Thomson's inference from 2' to 3' might be sought in some kind of Rawlsian theory of justice ("self-interested rational consenters under a veil of ignorance which is arranged to guarantee impartiality"). Even if such a move had merit, it would entail a radical revision of Thomson's argument, not a mere refinement. And why set up the veil of ignorance in the morning rather than at noon?

**31.** *RR*, 181.

**32.** Ibid., 196.

**33.** Ibid.

**34.** Ibid., 124.

**35.** For Thomson's earlier solutions, see her "Killing, Letting Die, and the Trolley Problem" and "The Trolley Problem." For critiques of these and other solutions, see Fischer and Ravizza, *Ethics* (Introduction and Part 7); Fischer, "Tooley and the Trolley"; Fischer and Ravizza, "Quinn on Doing and Allowing"; Fischer, "Insiders and Outsiders."

**36.** Fischer, "The Trolley and the Sorites," 107.

**37.** Ibid., 106.

**38.** Ibid., 107–8.

**39.** Ibid., 125.

*Chapter 10: A Single Supreme Norm?*

**1.** Pincoffs, *Quandaries and Virtues*, 3.

**2.** Ibid., 2.

**3.** Cf. Brink, *Moral Realism*, 250 ("Based in large part on their criticism of utilitarianism, Thomas Nagel, Bernard Williams, and Charles Taylor all contend that we must abandon the search for a systematic and unified moral theory and recognize a variety of distinct moral considerations that are connected by no common principles").

**4.** Nagel, *Mortal Questions*, 136.

**5.** Ibid., 133.

**6.** Williams, *Ethics*, 127. Cf. Taylor, *Sources of the Self*, 98: "Isn't there a danger of ironing out too quickly what is paradoxical in our deepest moral sense, of reconciling too quickly the conflicts, making a synthesis of what cannot easily be combined, in short of making our moral predicament look clearer, more unified, more harmonious, than it really is?"

**7.** McCloskey, *Meta-Ethics and Normative Ethics*, 220.

**8.** Ross, *Right and the Good*, 24.

**9.** Ibid., 28. Compare Kant, *Metaphysik der Sitten*, quoted in Donagan, "Consistency in Rationalist Moral Systems," 274: "When two such grounds are in conflict, practical philosophy does not say that the stronger obligation holds the upper hand (*fortior obligatio vincit*), but that the stronger ground binding to a duty holds the field (*fortior obligandi ratio vincit*)."

**10.** Ross, *Right and the Good*, 41. Cf. Dyck, "Questions of Ethics," 460–61; Verstraeten, "From Just War," 305–6.

**11.** McCloskey, *Meta-Ethics and Normative Ethics*, 222.

**12.** Ibid., 245. Cf. Toulmin, *Examination*, 147 ("Given two conflicting claims, that is to say, one has to weigh up, as well as one can, the risks involved in ignoring either, and choose 'the lesser of the two evils'").

**13.** See, e.g., Hughes, "Is Ethics One or Many?", 194–95.

**14.** Donagan, "Consistency in Rationalist Moral Systems," 271–72.

**15.** Ibid., 272 (quoting Davidson, *Essays on Actions and Events*, 35).

**16.** Gewirth, *Reason and Morality*, 11. Compare Mill, *System of Logic*, 8th ed., bk. 6, chap. 12, sec. 7.

**17.** Singer, "Gewirth's Ethical Monism," 27.

**18.** Ibid., 28.

**19.** Rawls, *Theory of Justice*, 45. For other solutions, less interesting than Rawls's, see Sinnott-Armstrong, *Moral Dilemmas*, 32.

**20.** Rawls, *Theory of Justice*, 43.

**21.** Ibid., 63.

**22.** Layman, *Shape of the Good*, 115–17; Hallett, "Place of Moral Values," 142–43.

**23.** Gewirth, *Reason and Morality*, x.

**24.** Ibid., 48.

**25.** Gewirth, "Replies to My Critics," 198.

**26.** Gewirth, *Reason and Morality*, 333–38.

**27.** Ibid., 144.

**28.** Ibid., 205.

**29.** In *The Dialectical Necessity of Morality*, 15, Deryck Beyleveld makes this point more clearly than does Gewirth: "Use of the dialectically necessary method implies that Gewirth is not attempting to establish the PGC itself as a truth. What he attempts to establish as a necessary truth is the proposition 'A PPA [Prospective Purposive Agent] contradicts that it is a PPA if it does not accept/act in accordance with the PGC.'"

**30.** Gewirth, "Golden Rule Rationalized," 141.

**31.** Cf. Beyleveld, *Dialectical Necessity of Morality*, 42–45, 410–11; Nielsen, "Against Ethical Rationalism," 71–72; Gewirth, "Replies to My Critics," 207.

**32.** Lewis, *Values and Imperatives*, 75.

**33.** Ibid., 76–77. Cf. ibid., 110.

**34.** Ibid., 37 (emphasis deleted).

**35.** Ibid., 113–14.

**36.** Ibid., 183.

**37.** Mouw, *God Who Commands*, 33–34.

*Chapter 11: The Norm's Significance*

**1.** Gustafson, *Protestant and Roman Catholic Ethics*, 62.

**2.** See *CMR*, chapter 10 ("The Distinctiveness of Christian Moral Reasoning"), especially pages 205–6 ("Criteria"). This strong linkage, via VM, has elicited the remark that VM does not seem a particularly Christian norm.

Neither, in the same sense, is belief in God a particularly Christian belief. It may be worth noting, however, that "from this fundamental uniformity it follows . . . that Christian moral conclusions will and should diverge somewhat from those of non-Christians" (*CMR*, 205–6). More generally: "From viewpoint after viewpoint . . . —though less notably with respect to its overall criterion of right and wrong—Christian moral reasoning appears distinctive: in its conception of the acts to be judged; in the procedures by which it judges them; in its rules of preference; in the values it weighs and balances; in the beliefs that, directly or indirectly, codetermine the verdicts; in the broad horizons that guide detailed decision-making; in the precepts that ease the burden of analysis" (*CMR*, 221).

3. Hauerwas, *Character and the Christian Life*, 132 (on Bultmann), 140 (on Barth).

4. Barth, *Doctrine of Reconciliation*, 448.

5. Bultmann, *Existence and Faith*, 145.

6. Fletcher, *Situation Ethics*, 12.

7. McCormick, *Notes, 1981 through 1984*, 121 (on Daniel Maguire).

8. Taylor, *Sources of the Self*, 77.

9. Rorty, *Consequences of Pragmatism*, xiii.

10. Lewis, *Values and Imperatives*, 12. Cf. ibid., 15.

11. O'Neill, "Abstraction, Idealization and Ideology," 55. Cf. Lewis, *Values and Imperatives*, 111.

12. See *CMR*, 62–64. For reasoning like Cathrein's, see Healy, *Marriage Guidance*, 152.

13. Vermeersch, *De castitate*, 255. Cf. Hallett, *Darkness and Light*, 90–92.

14. Vacek, review of Smith, *Humanae vitae: A Generation Later*, 369.

15. Bender, "Organorum humanorum transplantatio," 147.

16. Hallett, *Christian Neighbor-Love*, 65–69.

17. Congregation for the Doctrine of the Faith, "Instruction," 707. Cf. Langan, "Catholic Moral Rationalism," 41–42.

18. Lewis, *Values and Imperatives*, 109. Cf. McGrath, "Natural Law and Moral Argument," 58–59; Adler, *Time of Our Lives*, 21.

19. McCormick, *Notes, 1965 through 1980*, 544. See ibid., 431.

20. Hughes, "Is Ethics One or Many?," 182. See Layman, *Shape of the Good*, 121–23.

21. Gustafson, "Moral Discernment," 20. Cf. Clark, "Abstract Morality, Concrete Cases," 42–43; Kiely, "Impracticality of Proportionalism," 673–75; Nagel, *Mortal Questions*, 135–36; Williams, *Ethics*, 116.

22. Nelson, *System of Ethics*, 8–9. Cf. Gewirth, "Replies to My Critics," 196, in answer to Bambrough, "Roots of Moral Reason," e.g., 41–42.

23. Thomson, *Realm of Rights*, 31.

24. On this sort of difficulty, see Annette Baier, *Postures of the Mind*, 242.

25. Gustafson, "Moral Discernment," 17.

26. Frankena, *Ethics*, 1973, 35, 39 (emphasis added).

27. McCormick, *Critical Calling*, 58–67.

28. Sumner, *Moral Foundation of Rights*, 165.

29. Urban, *Fundamentals of Ethics*, 159.

30. Gilleman, *Primacy of Charity*, 308.

31. Flick and Alszeghy, *Metodologia*, 76.

32. Ross, *Right and the Good*, 149–53. Cf. Campbell, "Moral and Non-Moral Values," 172–73; Ramsey, "Incommensurability," 90–91, 138–39.

33. Scheler, *Formalism in Ethics*, 94–96, 104–10.

34. *CMR*, 137–41.

35. In illustration, see Hallett, "The Place of Moral Values," 142–43, on the alleged serial relation between moral and nonmoral values.

36. Taylor, *Sources of the Self*, 79–80.

37. Adler, *Time of Our Lives*, 12–13.

38. Ibid., 13.

39. Ibid., 16–17.

40. Ibid., 39. Cf. ibid., 49, 53–54, 163, 167–69.

41. Hesburgh, *God, Country, and Notre Dame*, 215.

42. Adler, *Time of Our Lives*, 29.

43. Ibid., 169.

44. Ibid., 49.

45. Ibid., 49–50.

46. Ibid., 169 (emphasis added).

47. Ibid., 38 (emphasis added).

48. Grisez writes: "Consequentialism means that what one must be willing to do and to be to produce today's greatest net good can require one to be and to do something totally different tomorrow. No commitment can be permanent, no covenant indissoluble. A person or community which accepts consequentialism ought in all consistency to avoid any firm self-definition. The consequentialist ideal is that the person be a utensil, an all-purpose tool, available to be and to do whatever is necessary to bring about the 'greater good' " ("Against Consequentialism," 72). Implicit in this common objection (see Finnis, *Moral Absolutes*, 20–21, and Scheffler, *Rejection of Consequentialism*, 7–11, discussing Smart and Williams, *Utilitarianism: For and Against*, 116–17) is the answer to it. If commitment, stability, and self-definition are important values, as the objection clearly implies, then a norm like VM accords them importance, automatically. For it enjoins that value be maximized. Cf. Attfield, *Moral Theory*, 118–22; Brink, *Moral Realism*, 273–83; Feldman, *Doing the Best We Can*, 61–64.

49. Baier, *Moral Point of View*, 13–14. Cf. Nielsen, *Why Be Moral?*, 168.

50. Green, "Should We Return to Foundations?," 274.

51. Ibid., 278.

52. Norris, "Dolphins in Crisis," 35.

53. Ibid., 13.

54. Ramsey, "Kant's Moral Theology," 71. Cf. Knauer, "Fundamentalethik," 356–57 ("In unserer Sicht ist Normenfindung und Normenbegründung dasselbe").

55. Hoose, *Proportionalism*, 138. Cf. Hittinger, "After MacIntyre," 450–52.

56. Stocker, "Schizophrenia," 37.

**57.** Johann, *Building the Human*, 145. Cf. Finnis, "Consistent Ethic," 148.

**58.** Hauerwas, *Character and the Christian Life*, vii. Cf. Foot, *Virtues and Vices*, xi ("A sound moral philosophy should start from a theory of the virtues and vices"); Garcia, "Tunsollen," 274 ("At its heart, morals concern neither what actions someone ought to perform, nor what situations ought to exist, but what kinds of attitudes and cares people ought to have").

**59.** McCormick, *Notes, 1981 through 1984*, 125.

**60.** Pinckaers, "La loi nouvelle," 442.

**61.** Crossin, *What Are They Saying*, 8. Cf. Johann, *Building the Human*, 143.

**62.** Gustafson, *Ethics and Theology*, 62.

**63.** Murdoch, *Sovereignty of Good*, 99.

**64.** Keith Ward, *Ethics and Christianity*, 79. See Rashdall, *Good and Evil*, vol. 2, 299; Hauerwas, *Character and the Christian Life*, 8, 37.

**65.** Gilleman, *Primacy of Charity*, 35.

**66.** Gonsalves, *Fagothey's Right and Reason*, 76.

**67.** Aquinas, *Summa theologica*, 1–2, q.55.a.4.c.

**68.** Fagothey, *Right and Reason*, 182.

**69.** Schmitz, *Menschsein und sittliches Handeln*, 131.

**70.** Frankena, *Ethics*, 1963, 52.

**71.** Aquinas, *Summa theologica*, 1–2, q.71.a.3.

**72.** Montague, "Virtue Ethics," 54.

**73.** Johann, *Building the Human*, 145.

**74.** Janssens, "Norms and Priorities," 209.

**75.** E.g., Montague, "Virtue Ethics"; Clarke and Simpson, *Anti-Theory in Ethics*, 6–7; Grisez, Boyle, and Finnis, "Practical Principles," 129–30; Wallace, *Virtues and Vices*, 9.

**76.** Montague, "Virtue Ethics," 57.

**77.** MacIntyre, *After Virtue*, 152; Clarke, "Mature Conscience," 361; Grisez, "Logic of Moral Judgment," 71.

**78.** Meilaender, *Theory and Practice*, 31–32.

**79.** Louden, "Some Vices," 229–33.

**80.** Haughey, *Conspiracy of God*, 104.

# Works Cited

Adams, Robert Merrihew. "Divine Command Metaethics Modified Again." *Journal of Religious Ethics* 7 (1979): 66–79.

———. "A Modified Divine Command Theory of Ethical Wrongness." *Religion and Morality: A Collection of Essays*. Ed. Gene Outka and John P. Reeder, Jr. New York: Doubleday, 1973. 318–47. Rpt. in *Divine Commands and Morality*. Ed. Paul Helm. Oxford: Oxford University Press, 1981. 83–108.

———. *The Virtue of Faith and Other Essays in Philosophical Theology*. New York: Oxford University Press, 1987.

Adler, Mortimer J. *The Time of Our Lives: The Ethics of Common Sense*. New York: Holt, Rinehart and Winston, 1970.

Aertsen, J. A. "Natural Law in the Light of the Doctrine of Transcendentals." *Lex et Libertas: Freedom and Law According to St. Thomas Aquinas*. Ed. L. J. Elders and K. Hedwig. Vatican City: Libreria Editrice Vaticana, 1987. 99–112.

Alston, William P. "Some Suggestions for Divine Command Theorists." Beaty, *Christian Theism and the Problems of Philosophy*, 303–26.

Armstrong, R. A. *Primary and Secondary Precepts in Thomistic Natural Law Teaching*. The Hague: Martinus Nijhoff, 1966.

Attfield, Robin. *A Theory of Value and Obligation*. London: Croom Helm, 1987.

———. "Toward a Defence of Teleology." *Ethics* 85 (1974–75): 123–35.

Attridge, Harold W. *The Epistle to the Hebrews*. Ed. Helmut Koester. Hermeneia—A Critical and Historical Commentary on the Bible. Philadelphia: Fortress, 1989.

Baier, Annette. *Postures of the Mind: Essays on Mind and Morals*. Minneapolis: University of Minnesota Press, 1985.

Baier, Kurt. *The Moral Point of View: A Rational Basis of Ethics*. Ithaca: Cornell University Press, 1958.

Bambrough, Renford. "The Roots of Moral Reason." Regis, *Gewirth's Ethical Rationalism*, 39–51.

Barth, Karl. *The Doctrine of Reconciliation*. Vol. 4/1 of *Church Dogmatics*. Trans. G. W. Bromiley. Ed. G. W. Bromiley and T. F. Torrance. Edinburgh: T. & T. Clark, 1956.

Battaglia, Natale Anthony. *The Basis of Morals: A Study of Natural Law in Thomas Aquinas*. Ann Arbor, Mich.: University Microfilms, 1972.

Beaty, Michael D., ed. *Christian Theism and the Problems of Philosophy*. Notre Dame: University of Notre Dame Press, 1990.

Bender, L. "Organorum humanorum transplantatio." *Angelicum* 31 (1954): 139–60.

Bergmann, Frithjof. "The Experience of Values." *Revisions: Changing Perspectives in Moral Philosophy*. Ed. Stanley Hauerwas and Alasdair MacIntyre. Notre Dame: University of Notre Dame Press, 1983. 127–59.

Bergström, Lars. *The Alternatives and Consequences of Actions: An Essay on Certain Fundamental Notions in Teleological Ethics*. Stockholm: Almquist and Wiksell, 1966.

Beyleveld, Deryck. *The Dialectical Necessity of Morality: An Analysis and Defense of Alan Gewirth's Argument to the Principle of Generic Consistency*. Chicago: University of Chicago Press, 1991.

Black, Max. *Language and Philosophy: Studies in Method*. Ithaca: Cornell University Press, 1949.

Blank, Josef. "Zum Problem ethischer Normen im Neuen Testament." In Teichtweier and Dreier, *Herausforderung und Kritik der Moraltheologie*, 172–83.

Boice, James Montgomery. *Philippians: An Expositional Commentary*. Grand Rapids, Mich.: Zondervan, 1971.

Bourke, Vernon. "Is Thomas Aquinas a Natural Law Ethicist?" *Monist* 58 (1974): 52–66.

———. "El principio de la sindéresis: fuentes y función en la ética de Tomás de Aquino." *Sapientia* 35 (1980):615–26.

———. "The Synderesis Rule and Right Reason." *Monist* 66 (1983): 70–82.

Boyle, Joseph and Germain Grisez and John Finnis. "Incoherence and Consequentialism (or Proportionalism)—a Rejoinder." *American Catholic Philosophical Quarterly* 64 (1990): 271–77.

Brink, David O. *Moral Realism and the Foundations of Ethics*. Cambridge, England: Cambridge University Press, 1989.

Bruce, F. F. *The Epistle to the Hebrews*. 2nd ed. Grand Rapids, Mich.: W. B. Eerdmans, 1990.

Bruner, Frederick Dale. *Matthew*. 2 vols. Dallas: Word Publishing, 1987, 1990.

Bujo, Bénézet. *Moralautonomie und Normenfindung bei Thomas von Aquin: Unter Einbeziehung der neutestamentlichen Kommentare*. Paderborn: Schöningh, 1979.

Bultmann, Rudolf. *Existence and Faith*. Trans. Schubert M. Ogden. New York: World Publishing, 1960.

Burch, Robert. "Objective Values and the Divine Command Theory of Morality." *The New Scholasticism* 54 (1980): 279–304.

Campbell, C. A. "Moral and Non-Moral Values: A Study in the First Principles of Axiology." *Mind* 44 (1935): 273–99. Rpt. in *Readings in Ethical Theory*. Ed. Wilfrid Sellars and John Hospers. 2nd ed. New York: Appleton-Century-Crofts, 1970. 169–87.

Carney, Frederick S. "On McCormick and Teleological Morality." *Journal of Religious Ethics* 6 (1978): 81–107.

Chandler, John. "Divine Command Theories and the Appeal to Love." *American Philosophical Quarterly* 22 (1985): 231–39.

Charles, R. H. *A Critical and Exegetical Commentary on the Revelation of St. John.* Vol. 1. The International Critical Commentary. Edinburgh: T. and T. Clark, 1920.

Charlton, William. *Weakness of Will.* Oxford: Basil Blackwell, 1988.

Civit, Isidro Goma. *El Evangelio segun San Mateo.* Vol. 2. Madrid: Marova, 1976.

Clark, Stephen R. L. "Abstract Morality, Concrete Cases." *Moral Philosophy and Contemporary Problems.* Ed. J. D. G. Evans. Cambridge, England: Cambridge University Press, 1987. 35–53.

Clarke, Stanley G., and Evan Simpson, eds. *Anti-Theory in Ethics and Moral Conservatism.* Albany, N.Y.: State University of New York Press, 1989.

Clarke, W. Norris. "The Mature Conscience in Philosophical Perspective." *Conscience: Its Freedom and Limitations.* Ed. William C. Bier. New York: Fordham University Press, 1971. 357–68.

Collins, Raymond F. *Christian Morality: Biblical Foundations.* Notre Dame: University of Notre Dame Press, 1986.

Congregation for the Doctrine of the Faith. "*Donum vitae*: Instruction on Respect for Human Life in its Origin and on the Dignity of Procreation." *Origins* 16 (1986–1987): 697–711.

Connery, John R. "Catholic Ethics: Has the Norm for Rule-Making Changed?" *Theological Studies* 42 (1981): 232–50.

———. "Morality of Consequences: A Critical Appraisal." *Theological Studies* 34 (1973): 396–414. Rpt. in Curran and McCormick, *Readings in Moral Theology,* 244–66.

———. "The Teleology of Proportionate Reason." *Theological Studies* 44 (1983): 489–96.

Cope, Lamar. "Matthew XXV: 31–46—'The Sheep and the Goats' Reinterpreted." *Novum Testamentum* 11 (1969): 32–44.

Cornerotte, L. "Loi morale, valeurs humaines et situations de conflit." *Nouvelle Revue Théologique* 100 (1978): 502–32.

Crossin, John W. *What Are They Saying About Virtue?* New York: Paulist, 1985.

Curran, Charles E. "Utilitarianism and Contemporary Moral Theology: Situating the Debates." *Louvain Studies* 6 (1976–77): 239–55.

———, and Richard A. McCormick, eds.. *Readings in Moral Theology No. 1: Moral Norms and Catholic Tradition.* New York: Paulist, 1979.

D'Arcy, Eric. *Conscience and its Right to Freedom.* New York: Sheed and Ward, 1961.

Davidson, Donald. *Essays on Actions and Events.* New York: Oxford University Press, 1980.

Davies, W. D. and Dale C. Allison. *A Critical and Exegetical Commentary on the Gospel According to Saint Matthew.* Vols. 1 and 2. The International Critical Commentary. Edinburgh: T. and T. Clark, 1988, 1991.

Davis, Scott. "Ethical Properties and Divine Commands." *Journal of Religious Ethics* 11 (1983): 280–300.

Dedek, John F. "Intrinsically Evil Acts: An Historical Study of the Mind of St. Thomas." *Thomist* 43 (1979): 385–413.

Deidun, Thomas J. "Exceptionless Norms in New Testament Morality: A Biblical-Theological Approach." *Moral Theology Today: Certitudes and Doubts.* Saint Louis, Mo.: The Pope John Center, 1984. 165–81.

Demmer, Klaus and Bruno Schüller, eds. *Christlich Glauben und Handeln: Fragen einer fundamentalen Moraltheologie in der Diskussion.* Düsseldorf: Patmos, 1977.

Dodd, Charles Harold. "The Ethics of the New Testament." *Moral Principles of Action: Man's Ethical Imperative.* Ed. Ruth Nanda Anshen. New York: Harper, 1952. 543–58.

Donagan, Alan. "Consistency in Rationalist Moral Systems." *Journal of Philosophy* 81 (1984): 291–309. Rpt. in Gowans, *Moral Dilemmas,* 271–90.

———. "The Scholastic Theory of Moral Law in the Modern World." *Aquinas: A Collection of Critical Essays.* Ed. Anthony Kenny. Garden City: Doubleday, 1969. 325–39.

———. *The Theory of Morality.* Chicago: University of Chicago Press, 1977.

Donahue, John R. "Divorce: New Testament Perspectives." *Month* 242 (1981): 113–20.

———. "The 'Parable' of the Sheep and the Goats: A Challenge to Christian Ethics." *Theological Studies* 47 (1986): 3–31.

Dyck, Arthur J. "Questions of Ethics." *Harvard Theological Review* 65 (1972): 453–81.

Ellingworth, Paul. *The Epistle to the Hebrews: A Commentary on the Greek Text.* The New International Greek Testament Commentary. Grand Rapids, Mich.: W. B. Eerdmans; Carlisle, England: Paternoster, 1993.

Elter, E. "Norma honestatis ad mentem Divi Thomae." *Gregorianum* 8 (1927): 337–57.

Evans, C. F. *Saint Luke.* TPI New Testament Commentaries. London: SCM; Philadelphia: Trinity Press International, 1990.

Fagothey, Austin. *Right and Reason: Ethics in Theory and Practice.* 3d ed. Saint Louis, Mo.: C. V. Mosby, 1963.

Farley, Margaret A. Review of *The Theory of Morality,* by Alan Donagan. *Religious Studies Review* 7 (1981): 233–37.

Feldman, Fred. *Doing the Best We Can: An Essay in Informal Deontic Logic.* Dordrecht: D. Reidel, 1986.

Fenton, J. C. *The Gospel of St Matthew.* The Pelican New Testament Commentaries. Harmondsworth, England: Penguin, 1963.

Finnis, John. "The Consistent Ethic: A Philosophical Critique." *Consistent Ethic of Life.* Ed. Thomas G. Fuechtmann. Kansas City, Mo.: Sheed and Ward, 1988. 140–81.

———. *Fundamentals of Ethics.* Washington: Georgetown University Press, 1983.

———. *Moral Absolutes: Tradition, Revision, and Truth.* Washington: Catholic University of America Press, 1991.

———. *Natural Law and Natural Rights.* Oxford: Clarendon, 1980.

———, and Joseph M. Boyle, Jr., and Germain Grisez. *Nuclear Deterrence, Morality and Realism*. Oxford: Clarendon, 1987.

Fischer, John Martin. "Insiders and Outsiders." *Journal of Social Philosophy* 24 (1993), no. 3: 155–60.

———. "Tooley and the Trolley." *Philosophical Studies* 62 (1991): 93–100.

———. "The Trolley and the Sorites." *Yale Journal of Law and the Humanities* 4 (1992): 105–26.

———, and Mark Ravizza, eds. *Ethics: Problems and Principles*. Fort Worth: Harcourt Brace Jovanovich, 1991.

———, and Mark Ravizza. "Quinn on Doing and Allowing." *Philosophical Review* 101 (1992): 343–52.

Fisher, Carlton D. "Because God Says So." Beaty, *Christian Theism and the Problems of Philosophy*, 355–77.

Fitzmyer, Joseph A. *The Gospel According to Luke (X–XXIV)*. The Anchor Bible. Garden City, N. Y.: Doubleday, 1985.

Fletcher, Joseph. *Situation Ethics: The New Morality*. Philadelphia: Westminster, 1966.

Flick, Maurizio and Zoltan Alszeghy. *Metodologia per una teologia dello sviluppo*. Brescia: Queriniana, 1970.

Foot, Philippa, ed. *Theories of Ethics*. Oxford: Oxford University Press, 1967.

———. *Virtues and Vices and Other Essays in Moral Philosophy*. Berkeley: University of California Press, 1978.

Forrest, Peter. "An Argument for the Divine Command Theory of Right Action." *Sophia* 28 (1989), no. 1: 2–19.

Frankena, William K. *Ethics*. Englewood Cliffs, N.J.: Prentice-Hall, 1963, 1973.

Fuchs, Josef. *Christian Ethics in a Secular Arena*. Trans. Bernard Hoose and Brian McNeil. Washington: Georgetown University Press; Dublin: Gill and Macmillan, 1984.

Furger, Franz. "Zur Begründung eines christlichen Ethos— Forschungstendenzen in der katholischen Moraltheologie." *Theologische Berichte*. Vol. 4. Ed. Josef Pfammatter and Franz Furger. Zürich: Benziger, 1974. 11–87.

Gallagher, John A. *Time Past, Time Future: An Historical Study of Catholic Moral Theology*. New York: Paulist, 1990.

Garcia, J. L. A. "The *Tunsollen*, the *Seinsollen*, and the *Soseinsollen*." *American Philosophical Quarterly* 23 (1986): 267–76.

Gardner, Richard B. *Matthew*. Believers Church Bible Commentary. Scottdale, Pa.: Herald, 1991.

Garver, Newton. Review of *The Theory of Morality*, by Alan Donagan. *Ethics* 90 (1979–80): 301–5.

Gewirth, Alan. "The Golden Rule Rationalized." *Midwest Studies in Philosophy*, vol. 3: *Studies in Ethical Theory*. Ed. Peter A. French, Theodore E. Uehling, Jr., and Howard K. Wettstein. Minneapolis: University of Minnesota Press, 1980. 133–47.

———. *Reason and Morality*. Chicago: University of Chicago Press, 1978.

———. "Replies to My Critics." Regis, *Gewirth's Ethical Rationalism*, 192–255.

Gilleman, Gérard. *The Primacy of Charity in Moral Theology.* Trans. William F. Ryan and André Vachon. Westminster, Md.: Newman, 1959.

Gonsalves, Milton A, revisor. *Fagothey's Right and Reason: Ethics in Theory and Practice.* St. Louis, Mo.: Times Mirror/Mosby, 1985.

Gooding, David. *According to Luke: A New Exposition of the Third Gospel.* Grand Rapids, Mich.: W. B. Eerdmans, 1987.

Gowans, Christopher W., ed. *Moral Dilemmas.* New York: Oxford University Press, 1987.

Green, Ronald M. "Should We Return to Foundations?" *Knowing and Valuing: The Search for Common Roots.* The Foundations of Ethics and Its Relationship to Science 4. Ed. H. Tristram Engelhardt, Jr., and Daniel Callahan. Hastings-on-Hudson, N.Y.: The Hastings Center, 1980. 269–82.

Grelot, Pierre. *Problèmes de morale fondamentale: Un éclairage biblique.* Paris: Cerf, 1982.

Grisez, Germain. *Abortion: The Myths, the Realities, and the Arguments.* New York: Corpus, 1970.

———. "Against Consequentialism." *The American Journal of Jurisprudence* 23 (1978): 21–72.

———. "Are There Exceptionless Moral Norms?" *The Twenty-Fifth Anniversary of Vatican II: A Look Back and a Look Ahead.* Braintree, Mass.: The Pope John Center, 1990. 117–35.

———. "Choice and Consequentialism." *Proceedings of the American Catholic Philosophical Association* 51 (1977): 144–52.

———. *Christian Moral Principles.* Vol. 1 of *The Way of the Lord Jesus.* Chicago: Franciscan Herald Press, 1983.

———. "Christian Moral Theology and Consequentialism." *Principles of Catholic Moral Life.* Ed. William E. May. Chicago: Franciscan Herald Press, 1980. 293–327.

———. "A Contemporary Natural-Law Ethics." *Moral Philosophy: Historical and Contemporary Essays.* Ed. William C. Starr and Richard C. Taylor. Milwaukee: Marquette University Press, 1989. 125–43.

———. *Contraception and the Natural Law.* Milwaukee: Bruce, 1964.

———. "The First Principle of Practical Reason: A Commentary on the *Summa theologiae*, 1–2, Question 94, Article 2." *Natural Law Forum* 10 (1965): 168–201.

———. "The Logic of Moral Judgment." *Proceedings of the American Catholic Philosophical Association* 36 (1962): 67–76.

———. "Methods of Ethical Inquiry." *Proceedings of the American Catholic Philosophical Association* 41 (1967): 160–68.

———. "The Structures of Practical Reason." *Thomist* 52 (1988): 269–91.

———, and Joseph M. Boyle, Jr. *Life and Death with Liberty and Justice: A Contribution to the Euthanasia Debate.* Notre Dame: University of Notre Dame Press, 1979.

———, Joseph Boyle, and John Finnis. "Practical Principles, Moral Truth, and Ultimate Ends." *The American Journal of Jurisprudence* 32 (1987): 99–151.

————, and others. "'Every Marital Act Ought to Be Open to New Life': Toward a Clearer Understanding." *Thomist* 52 (1988): 365–426.

Gula, Richard M. *Reason Informed by Faith: Foundations of Catholic Morality*. New York: Paulist, 1989.

Gustafson, James M. *Ethics and Theology*. Vol. 2 of *Ethics from a Theocentric Perspective*. Chicago: University of Chicago Press, 1984.

————. "Moral Discernment in the Christian Life." In Outka and Ramsey, *Norm and Context in Christian Ethics*, 17–36.

————. *Protestant and Roman Catholic Ethics*. Chicago: University of Chicago Press, 1978.

Hallett, Garth L. *Christian Moral Reasoning: An Analytic Guide*. Notre Dame: University of Notre Dame Press, 1983.

————. *Christian Neighbor-Love: An Assessment of Six Rival Versions*. Washington: Georgetown University Press, 1989.

————. "Christian Norms of Morality." *The Philosophical Assessment of Theology: Essays in Honour of Frederick C. Copleston*. Ed. Gerard J. Hughes. Washington: Georgetown University Press; Tunbridge Wells, England: Search, 1987. 187–209.

————. *Darkness and Light: The Analysis of Doctrinal Statements*. New York: Paulist, 1975.

————. *Essentialism: A Wittgensteinian Critique*. Albany: State University of New York Press, 1991.

————. "The 'Incommensurability' of Values." *Heythrop Journal* 28 (1987): 373–87.

————. *Language and Truth*. New Haven: Yale University Press, 1988.

————. "The Place of Moral Values in Christian Moral Reasoning." *Heythrop Journal* 30 (1989): 129–49.

————. *Reason and Right*. Notre Dame: University of Notre Dame Press, 1984.

————. "'Whatever You Loose Shall Be Loosed.'" *America* 133 (1975): 188–90.

Hanink, James G. "A Theory of Basic Goods: Structure and Hierarchy." *Thomist* 52 (1988): 221–45.

———— and Gary R. Mar. "What Euthyphro Couldn't Have Said." *Faith and Philosophy* 4 (1987): 241–61.

Harrington, Daniel J. *The Gospel of Matthew*. Sacra Pagina Series, 1. Collegeville, Minn.: The Liturgical Press, 1991.

Hauerwas, Stanley. *Character and the Christian Life: A Study in Theological Ethics*. San Antonio: Trinity University Press, 1975.

————. *Vision and Virtue: Essays in Christian Ethical Reflection*. Notre Dame: Fides, 1974.

Haughey, John. *The Conspiracy of God: The Holy Spirit in Men*. New York: Doubleday, 1973.

Healy, Edwin F. *Marriage Guidance*. Chicago: Loyola University Press, 1948.

Hesburgh, Theodore M., with Jerry Reedy. *God, Country, Notre Dame*. New York: Doubleday, 1990.

Hittinger, Russell. "After MacIntyre: Natural Law Theory, Virtue Ethics, and Eudaimonia." *International Philosophical Quarterly* 29 (1989): 449–61.

Hocutt, Max. "Toward an Ethic of Mutual Accommodation." *Humanist Ethics: Dialogue on Basics.* Ed. Morris B. Storer. Buffalo: Prometheus Books, 1980. 137–47.

Hofmann, Rudolf. *Moraltheologische Erkenntnis- und Methodenlehre.* Handbuch der Moraltheologie 7. Munich: Max Hueber, 1963.

Hoose, Bernard. *Proportionalism: The American Debate and Its European Roots.* Washington: Georgetown University Press, 1987.

Hughes, Gerard J. "Is Ethics One or Many?" *Catholic Perspectives on Medical Morals: Foundational Issues.* Ed. Edmund D. Pellegrino, John P. Langan, and John Collins Harvey. Dordrecht: Kluwer, 1989. 173–96.

———. "Philosophical Debate on Nuclear Disarmament." *Heythrop Journal* 29 (1988): 222–31.

Idziak, Janine Marie. "Divine Command Morality: A Guide to the Literature." *Divine Command Morality: Historical and Contemporary Readings.* Ed. Janine Marie Idziak. New York and Toronto: Edwin Mellen, 1979. 1–38.

Janssens, Louis. "Norms and Priorities in a Love Ethic." *Louvain Studies* 6 (1976–1977): 207–38.

———. "Ontic Good and Evil—Premoral Values and Disvalues." *Louvain Studies* 12 (1987): 62–82.

Johann, Robert O. *Building the Human.* New York: Herder and Herder, 1968.

Johnstone, Brian V. "The Meaning of Proportionate Reason in Contemporary Moral Theology." *Thomist* 49 (1985): 223–47.

Kagan, Shelly. *The Limits of Morality.* Oxford: Clarendon, 1989.

Keane, Philip S. "The Objective Moral Order: Reflections on Recent Research." *Theological Studies* 43 (1982): 260–78.

Kelleher, Stephen J. *Divorce and Remarriage for Catholics?* Garden City, N.Y.: Doubleday, 1973.

Kerber, Walter. "Grenzen der biblischen Moral." In Demmer and Schüller, *Christlich Glauben und Handeln,* 112–23.

Kiely, Bartholomew M. "The Impracticality of Proportionalism." *Gregorianum* 66 (1985): 655–86.

Kirk, Albert and Robert E. Obach. *A Commentary on the Gospel of John.* New York: Paulist, 1981.

Knauer, Peter. "La détermination du bien et du mal moral par le principe du double effet." *Nouvelle Revue Théologique* 87 (1965): 356–76.

———. "Fundamentalethik: Teleologische als deontologische Normenbegründung." *Theologie und Philosophie* 55 (1980): 321–60.

———. *Der Glaube kommt vom Hören: Ökumenische Fundamentaltheologie.* 1st ed. Graz: Styria, 1978. 2nd ed. Freiburg im Breisgau: Herder, 1991.

———. "A Good End Does Not Justify an Evil Means—Even in a Teleological Ethics." Trans. Jan Jans. In Selling, *Personalist Morals,* 71–85.

———. "The Hermeneutic Function of the Principle of Double Effect." *Natural Law Forum* 12 (1967): 132–62. Rpt. in Curran and McCormick, *Readings in Moral Theology,* 1–39.

———. "Das rechtverstandene Prinzip von der Doppelwirkung als Grundnorm jeder Gewissenentscheidung." *Theologie und Glaube* 57 (1967): 107–33.

———. Review of *Ce qu'on ne peut jamais faire: La question des actes intrinsèquement mauvais*, by Servais Pinckaers. *Theologie und Philosophie* 63 (1988): 149–50.

———. Review of *Proportionalism: The American Debate and its European Roots*, by Bernard Hoose. *Theologie und Philosophie* 65 (1990): 473–75.

———. "Überlegungen zur moraltheologischen Prinzipienlehre der Enzyklika 'Humanae vitae.'" *Theologie und Philosophie* 45 (1970): 60–74.

Korff, Wilhelm. *Norm und Sittlichkeit: Untersuchungen zur Logik der normativen Vernunft*. Mainz: Matthias-Grünewald, 1973.

Kosnik, Anthony, and others. *Human Sexuality: New Directions in American Catholic Thought*. New York: Paulist, 1977.

Kretzmann, Norman. "Abraham, Isaac, and Euthyphro: God and the Basis of Morality." *Hamartia: The Concept of Error in the Western Tradition*. Ed. Donald V. Stump and others. New York: Edwin Mellen, 1983. 27–50.

Lane, William L. *The Gospel According to Mark*. The New International Commentary on the New Testament. Grand Rapids, Mich.: W. B. Eerdmans, 1974.

Langan, John. "Catholic Moral Rationalism and the Philosophical Bases of Moral Theology." *Theological Studies* 50 (1989): 25–43.

———. "Direct and Indirect—Some Recent Exchanges between Paul Ramsey and Richard McCormick." *Religious Studies Review* 5 (1979): 95–101.

Layman, C. Stephen. *The Shape of the Good: Christian Reflections on the Foundation of Ethics*. Notre Dame: University of Notre Dame Press, 1991.

Lehu, Léonard. *La raison: Règle de la moralité d'après saint Thomas*. Paris: Gabalda, 1930.

Levy, Sanford S. "Richard McCormick and Proportionate Reason." *Journal of Religious Ethics* 13 (1985): 258–78.

Lewis, Clarence Irving. *An Analysis of Knowledge and Valuation*. La Salle, Ill.: Open Court, 1946.

———. *Values and Imperatives: Studies in Ethics*. Ed. John Lange. Stanford, Cal.: Stanford University Press, 1969.

Lottin, Odon. *Le droit naturel chez Saint Thomas d'Aquin et ses prédécesseurs*. 2nd ed. Bruges: Beyaert, 1931.

———. "L'ordre moral et l'ordre logique d'après saint Thomas d'Aquin." *Annales de l'Institut Supérieur de Philosophie* 5 (1924): 301–99.

———. *Psychologie et morale aux XIIe et XIIIe siècles*. Vol. 2: *Problèmes de morale*. Part 1. Louvain: Abbaye du Mont César; Gembloux: J. Duculot, 1948.

Louden, Robert B. "On Some Vices of Virtue Ethics." *American Philosophical Quarterly* 21 (1984): 227–36.

Luz, Ulrich. *Matthew 1–7: A Commentary*. Trans. Wilhelm C. Linss. Minneapolis: Augsburg Fortress, 1989.

Lyons, David. *Forms and Limits of Utilitarianism*. Oxford: Clarendon, 1965.

McCloskey, H. J. *Meta-Ethics and Normative Ethics*. The Hague: Martinus Nijhoff, 1969.

McCormick, Richard A. *Ambiguity in Moral Choice*. Milwaukee: Marquette University Press, 1973.

———. "A Commentary on the Commentaries." In McCormick and Ramsey, *Doing Evil to Achieve Good*, 193–267.

———. *The Critical Calling: Reflections on Moral Dilemmas since Vatican II*. Washington: Georgetown University Press, 1989.

———. *Notes on Moral Theology: 1965 through 1980*. Washington: University Press of America, 1981.

———. *Notes on Moral Theology: 1981 through 1984*. Lanham, Md.: University Press of America, 1984.

———, and Paul Ramsey, eds. *Doing Evil to Achieve Good: Moral Choice in Conflict Situations*. Chicago: Loyola University Press, 1978.

McGrath, P. J. "Natural Law and Moral Argument." *Morals, Law and Authority: Sources and Attitudes in the Church*. Ed. J. P. Mackey. Dayton, Ohio: Pflaum, 1969. 58–78.

McHugh, John A. and Charles J. Callan. *Moral Theology: A Complete Course Based on St. Thomas and the Best Modern Authorities*. 2 vols. New York: Joseph F. Wagner, 1929–1930.

McInerny, Ralph. *Ethica Thomistica: The Moral Philosophy of Thomas Aquinas*. Washington: Catholic University of America Press, 1982.

———. "On Knowing Natural Law." *The Ethics of St. Thomas Aquinas*. Ed. L. J. Elders and K. Hedwig. Rome: Libreria Editrice Vaticana, 1984. 133–42.

MacIntyre, Alasdair. *After Virtue: A Study in Moral Theory*. 2nd ed. Notre Dame: University of Notre Dame Press, 1984.

McKeever, Paul E. "Proportionalism as a Methodology in Catholic Moral Theology." *Human Sexuality and Personhood*. St. Louis, Mo.: Pope John Center, 1981. 211–22.

McKim, Robert and Peter Simpson. "On the Alleged Incoherence of Consequentialism." *New Scholasticism* 62 (1988): 349–52.

McKinney, Ronald H. "The Quest for an Adequate Proportionalist Theory of Value." *Thomist* 53 (1989): 56–73.

McNamara, Vincent. "The Use of the Bible in Moral Theology." *Month* 20 (1987): 104–7.

Mackin, Theodore. *Divorce and Remarriage*. New York: Paulist, 1984.

Mahoney, John. *The Making of Moral Theology: A Study of the Roman Catholic Tradition*. Oxford: Clarendon, 1987.

Malcolm, Norman. *Knowledge and Certainty: Essays and Lectures*. Englewood Cliffs: Prentice-Hall, 1963.

Mangan, Joseph T. "An Historical Analysis of the Principle of Double Effect." *Theological Studies* 10 (1949): 41–61.

Mann, William E. "Modality, Morality, and God." *Nous* 23 (1989): 83–99.

Marshall, I. H. *The Gospel of Luke: A Commentary on the Greek Text*. New International Greek Testament Commentary. Grand Rapids, Mich.: W. B. Eerdmans, 1978.

May, William E. *Moral Absolutes: Catholic Tradition, Current Trends, and the Truth*. Milwaukee: Marquette University Press, 1989.

Meier, John P. *Matthew.* New Testament Message, 3. Wilmington, Del.: Glazier, 1980.

Meilaender, Gilbert C. *The Theory and Practice of Virtue.* Notre Dame: University of Notre Dame Press, 1984.

Mercken, H. Paul F., ed. *The Greek Commentaries on the Nichomachean Ethics of Aristotle.* Vol. 1. Corpus Latinum Commentariorum in Aristotelem Graecorum 6, 1. Leiden: Brill, 1973.

Milhaven, John G. "Towards an Epistemology of Ethics." *Theological Studies* 27 (1966): 228–41.

Mill, John Stuart. *Utilitarianism.* 1861. Indianapolis: Hackett, 1979.

Moellering, H. Armin. *1 Timothy.* Concordia Commentary. St. Louis, Mo.: Concordia, 1970.

Montague, Phillip. "Virtue Ethics: A Qualified Success Story." *American Philosophical Quarterly* 29 (1992): 53–61.

Morris, Leon. *The Gospel According to John.* Grand Rapids, Mich.: W. B. Eerdmans, 1971.

———. *The Gospel According to Matthew.* Grand Rapids, Mich.: W. B. Eerdmans; Leicester, England: Inter-Varsity, 1992.

Mouw, Richard J. *The God Who Commands.* Notre Dame: University of Notre Dame Press, 1990.

Murdoch, Iris. *The Sovereignty of Good.* New York: Schocken, 1971.

Murphy-O'Connor, Jerome. *1 Corinthians.* New Testament Message, 10. Wilmington, Del.: Glazier, 1979.

Murray, Michael V. *Problems in Ethics.* New York: Holt, 1960.

Nagel, Thomas. "The Limits of Objectivity." *The Tanner Lectures on Human Values,* 1. Ed. Sterling M. McMurrin. Salt Lake City: University of Utah Press, 1980. 75–139.

———. *Mortal Questions.* Cambridge, England: Cambridge University Press, 1979.

Nelson, Leonard. *System of Ethics.* Trans. Norbert Guterman. New Haven: Yale University Press, 1956.

Nielsen, Kai. "Against Ethical Rationalism." In Regis, *Gewirth's Ethical Rationalism,* 59–83.

———. *Ethics without God.* Buffalo: Prometheus; London: Pemberton, 1973.

———. *Why Be Moral?* Buffalo: Prometheus, 1989.

Noonan, John T., Jr. *Contraception: A History of Its Treatment by the Catholic Theologians and Canonists.* Cambridge: Belknap/Harvard University Press, 1965.

Norris, Kenneth S. "Dolphins in Crisis." *National Geographic Magazine* 182 (1992), no. 3: 2–35.

O'Connell, Timothy E. *Principles for a Catholic Morality.* New York: Seabury, 1978.

O'Connor, D. J. *Aquinas and Natural Law.* London: Macmillan; New York: St. Martin's, 1968.

O'Neill, Onora. "Abstraction, Idealization and Ideology in Ethics." *Moral Philosophy and Contemporary Problems.* Ed. J. D. G. Evans. Cambridge, England: Cambridge University Press, 1988. 55–69.

Outka, Gene H. and Paul Ramsey, eds. *Norm and Context in Christian Ethics.* New York: Scribner's, 1968.

Pinckaers, Servais. *Ce qu'on ne peut jamais faire: La question des actes intrinsèquement mauvais.* Fribourg: Éditions Universitaires; Paris: Éditions du Cerf, 1986.

————. "La loi nouvelle et la permanence des lois morales." *Universalité et permanence des Lois morales.* Ed. Servais Pinckaers and Carlos Josaphat Pinto de Oliveira. Fribourg: Éditions Universitaires; Paris: Éditions du Cerf, 1986. 442–54. [The title in the table of contents: "L'universalité et la permanence des lois morales dans la Loi évangélique."]

————. "La question des actes intrinsèquement mauvais et le 'proportionnalisme.'" *Revue Thomiste* 82 (1982): 181–212.

Pincoffs, Edmund L. *Quandaries and Virtues: Against Reductivism in Ethics.* Lawrence, Kans.: University Press of Kansas, 1986.

Pius XI. *On Christian Marriage.* New York: Barry Vail, 1931.

Pojman, Louis P. "Ethics: Religious and Secular." *Modern Schoolman* 70 (1992): 1–30.

Porter, Jean. *The Recovery of Virtue: The Relevance of Aquinas for Christian Ethics.* Louisville, Ky.: Westminster/John Knox, 1990.

Quay, Paul M. "The Disvalue of Ontic Evil." *Theological Studies* 46 (1985): 262–86.

————. "Morality by Calculation of Values." *Theology Digest* 23 (1975): 347–64. Rpt. in Curran and McCormick, *Readings in Moral Theology,* 267–93.

Quinn, Philip L. "The Recent Revival of Divine Command Ethics." *Philosophy and Phenomenological Research* 50 (1990), supplem.: 345–65.

Rahner, Karl. *Theological Investigations.* Vol. 8. Trans. David Bourke. London: Darton, Longman, and Todd; New York: Herder and Herder, 1971.

Ramsey, Paul. "The Biblical Norm of Righteousness." *Interpretation* 24 (1970): 419–29.

————. "Incommensurability and Indeterminancy in Moral Choice." In McCormick and Ramsey, *Doing Evil to Achieve Good,* 69–144.

————. "Kant's Moral Theology or a Religious Ethics?" *Knowledge, Value, and Belief.* The Foundations of Ethics and Its Relationship to Science, 2. Ed. H. Tristram Engelhardt, Jr., and Daniel Callahan. Hastings-on-Hudson: The Hastings Center, 1977. 44–74.

Rashdall, Hastings. *The Theory of Good and Evil: A Treatise on Moral Philosophy.* 2nd ed. 2 vols. Oxford: Oxford University Press; London: Humphrey Milford, 1924.

Ratzinger, Joseph. "Dissent and Proportionalism in Moral Theology." *Origins* 13 (1983–84): 666–69.

Rawls, John. *A Theory of Justice.* Cambridge: Harvard University Press, 1971.

Regis, Edward, Jr., ed. *Gewirth's Ethical Rationalism: Critical Essays with a Reply by Alan Gewirth.* Chicago: University of Chicago Press, 1984.

Reicke, Bo. *The Epistles of James, Peter, and Jude.* The Anchor Bible. Garden City, N.Y.: Doubleday, 1964.

Rescher, Nicholas. *Ethical Idealism: An Inquiry into the Nature and Function of Ideals.* Berkeley: University of California Press, 1987.

Richards, Jerald H. "Alan Donagan, Hebrew-Christian Morality, and Capital Punishment." *Journal of Religious Ethics* 7 (1979): 302–29.

Rienecker, Fritz. *Das Evangelium des Lukas.* Wuppertal: Brockhaus, 1966.

Rorty, Richard. *Consequences of Pragmatism (Essays: 1972–1980).* Minneapolis: University of Minnesota Press, 1982.

Ross, W. D. *The Right and the Good.* New York: Oxford University Press, 1930.

Sartre, Jean-Paul. *Existentialism and Humanism.* Trans. Philip Mairet. London: Methuen, 1948.

Scheffler, Samuel. *The Rejection of Consequentialism: A Philosophical Investigation of the Considerations Underlying Rival Moral Conceptions.* Oxford: Clarendon, 1982.

Scheler, Max. *Formalism in Ethics and Non-Formal Ethics of Values: A New Attempt toward the Foundation of an Ethical Personalism.* Trans. Manfred Frings and Roger L. Funk. 5th ed. Evanston, Ill.: Northwestern University Press, 1973.

Schierse, Franz Joseph. "Das Scheidungsverbot Jesu. Zur schriftgemässen Unauflöslichkeit der Ehe." *Die öffentlichen Sünder oder Soll die Kirche Ehen scheiden?* Ed. Norbert Wetzel. Mainz: Matthias Grünewald, 1970. 13–41.

Schmitz, Philipp. *Menschsein und sittliches Handeln: Varnachlässigte Begriffe in der Moraltheologie.* Würzburg: Echter, 1980.

Schnackenburg, Rudolf. *The Gospel According to St John.* Vol. 2. Trans. Cecily Hastings, Francis McDonagh, David Smith, and Richard Foley. New York: Seabury, 1980.

Schüller, Bruno. "Die Bedeutung des natürlichen Sittengesetzes für den Christen." In Teichtweier and Dreier, *Herausforderung und Kritik der Moraltheologie,* 105–30.

———. "The Double Effect in Catholic Thought: A Reevaluation." McCormick and Ramsey, *Doing Evil to Achieve Good,* 165–92.

———. "Neuere Beiträge zum Thema 'Begründung sittlicher Normen.'" *Theologische Berichte.* Vol. 4. Ed. Josef Pfammatter and Franz Furger. Zürich: Benziger, 1974. 109–81.

———. "Zur Problematik allgemein verbindlicher ethischer Grundsätze." *Theologie und Philosophie* 45 (1970): 1–23.

Schuster, Johann. "Von den ethischen Prinzipien: Eine Thomasstudie zu S. Th. IaIIae, q. 94, a. 2." *Zeitschrift für Katholische Theologie* 57 (1933): 44–65.

Schweizer, Eduard. *The Good News According to Luke.* Trans. David E. Green. Atlanta: John Knox, 1984.

Seidl, Horst. "Natürliche Sittlichkeit und metaphysische Voraussetzung in der Ethik des Aristoteles und Thomas von Aquin." *The Ethics of St. Thomas Aquinas.* Ed. L. J. Elders and K. Hedwig. Rome: Libreria Editrice Vaticana, 1984. 95–117.

Selling, Joseph A., ed. *Personalist Morals: Essays in Honor of Professor Louis Janssens.* Leuven: University Press; Uitgeverij Peeters, 1988.

Simon, René. *Fonder la morale: Dialectique de la foi et de la raison pratique.* Paris: Seuil, 1974.

Singer, Marcus G. "Gewirth's Ethical Monism." Regis, *Gewirth's Ethical Rationalism,* 23–38.

Sinnot-Armstrong, Walter. *Moral Dilemmas*. Oxford: Basil Blackwell, 1988.

Smart, J. J. C. and Bernard Williams. *Utilitarianism: For and Against*. Cambridge, England: Cambridge University Press, 1973.

Stein, Robert H. *Luke*. The New American Commentary, 24. Nashville, Tenn.: Broadman, 1992.

Stevens, Gregory. "The Relations of Law and Obligation." *Proceedings of the American Catholic Philosophical Association* 29 (1955): 195–205.

Stocker, Michael. "The Schizophrenia of Modern Ethical Theories." *Journal of Philosophy* 73 (1976): 453–66. Rpt. in *The Virtues: Contemporary Essays on Moral Character*. Ed. Robert B. Kruschwitz and Robert C. Roberts. Belmont, Cal.: Wadsworth, 1987. 36–45.

Stout, Jeffrey. "The Philosophical Interest of the Hebrew-Christian Moral Tradition." *Thomist* 47 (1983): 165–96.

Stump, Eleonore. "Intellect, Will, and the Principle of Alternate Possibilities." Beaty, *Christian Theism and the Problems of Philosophy*, 254–95.

Sumner, L. W. *The Moral Foundation of Rights*. Oxford: Clarendon, 1987.

Swinburne, R. G. "Duty and the Will of God." *Canadian Journal of Philosophy* 4 (1974–1975): 213–27. Rpt. in *Divine Command Morality: Historical and Contemporary Readings*. Ed. Janine Marie Idziak. New York: Edwin Mellen, 1979. 287–304.

Talbert, Charles H. *Reading Corinthians: A Literary and Theological Commentary on 1 and 2 Corinthians*. New York: Crossroad, 1987.

Taylor, Charles. *Sources of the Self: The Making of the Modern Identity*. Cambridge: Harvard University Press, 1989.

Taylor, Paul W. *Normative Discourse*. Englewood Cliffs, N.J.: Prentice-Hall, 1961.

Teichtweier, Georg and Wilhelm Dreier, eds. *Herausforderung und Kritik der Moraltheologie*. Würzburg: Echter, 1971.

Thomson, Judith Jarvis. "Killing, Letting Die, and the Trolley Problem." *Monist* 59 (1975–76): 204–17.

———. *The Realm of Rights*. Cambridge: Harvard University Press, 1990.

———. "The Trolley Problem." *Yale Law Journal* 94 (1985): 1395–1415.

Toulmin, Stephen Edelston. *An Examination of the Place of Reason in Ethics*. Cambridge, England: Cambridge University Press, 1950.

Urban, Wilbur Marshall. *Fundamentals of Ethics: An Introduction to Moral Philosophy*. New York: Holt, 1930.

Vacek, Edward. "Proportionalism: One View of the Debate." *Proceedings of the Jesuit Philosophical Association*, 1984, 41–76.

———. Review of *Christian Moral Reasoning: An Analytic Guide*, by Garth L. Hallett. *Theological Studies* 45 (1984): 187–89.

———. Review of *Humanae vitae: A Generation Later*, by Janet E. Smith. *Theological Studies* 53 (1992): 368–70.

Veatch, Henry B. "Are There Non-Moral Goods?" *New Scholasticism* 52 (1978): 471–99.

———. "Variations, Good and Bad, on the Theme of Right Reason in Ethics." *Monist* 66 (1983): 49–70.

Vermeersch, Arthur. *De castitate et de vitiis contrariis tractatus doctrinalis et moralis.* 2nd ed. Rome: Università Gregoriana; Bruges: Beyaert, 1921.

Verstraeten, Johan. "From Just War to Proportionate Defense: A Critical Reassessment of a Significant Tradition." In Selling, *Personalist Morals,* 302–18.

Von Hildebrand, Dietrich. *Fundamental Moral Attitudes.* Trans. Alice M. Jourdain. New York: Longmans, Green, 1950.

Wallace, James D. *Virtues and Vices.* Ithaca: Cornell University Press, 1978.

Walter, James J. "The Foundation and Formulation of Norms." *Moral Theology: Challenges for the Future.* Ed. Charles E. Curran. New York: Paulist, 1990. 125–54.

———. "Response to John C. Finnis: A Theological Critique." *Consistent Ethic of Life.* Ed. Thomas G. Fuechtmann. Kansas City, Mo.: Sheed and Ward, 1988. 182–95.

Ward, Keith. *Ethics and Christianity.* New York: Humanities; London: George Allen and Unwin, 1970.

Weber, Helmut. "Historisches zum Utilitarismus." In Demmer and Schüller, *Christlich Glauben und Handeln,* 223–42.

Wertheimer, Roger. Review of *The Theory of Morality,* by Alan Donagan. *Nous* 17 (1983): 303–8.

Wierenga, Edward. "A Defensible Divine Command Theory." *Nous* 17 (1983): 387–407.

———. *The Nature of God: An Inquiry into Divine Attributes.* Ithaca: Cornell University Press, 1989.

———. "Utilitarianism and the Divine Command Theory." *American Philosophical Quarterly* 21 (1984): 311–18.

Williams, Bernard. *Ethics and the Limits of Philosophy.* Cambridge: Harvard University Press, 1985.

Wolter, Allan B., ed. *Duns Scotus on the Will and Morality.* Washington: Catholic University of America Press, 1986.

# Index

abortion, 48
action(s): value intrinsic to, 13–14,
    46; end of, 8–9, 91–98, 101–4,
    106–8, 180; understandings of,
    10–11, 47–48; and last end, 53–54;
    necessary conditions of, 134–35
Adams, Robert, 37, 64–73, 169, 174
Adler, Mortimer, 149–52
Aertsen, J. A., 172
Albert, St., 57
Allison, Dale, 167
Alston, William, 64
Alszeghy, Zoltan, 147
alternatives, 15–17
altruism, 22–23. See also love
Anselm of Laon, 59
Aquinas, St. Thomas, 37, 44, 52–63,
    78, 87, 142, 169
Aristotle, 53–54, 59
Attfield, Robin, 30, 32
Attridge, Harold, 168–69
Augustine, St., 44–45

Baier, Kurt, 153, 165
Barth, Karl, 139
Bender, L., 142
Bergström, Lars, 15
Beyleveld, Deryck, 184
Black, Max, 6
Boice, James, 168
Bourke, Vernon, 172
Brink, David, 183

Broad, C. D., 83–84
Bruce, F. F., 168, 169
Bruner, Frederick, 167
Bultmann, Rudolf, 139

Carney, Frederick, 161
Cathrein, Viktor, 142
Chandler, John, 70
charity. See love
Charles, R. H., 169
choice, 21–23
Civit, Isidro, 167
Connery, John, 178
consequences, 1, 13–14, 47–48, 105,
    162–63
consequentialism, 1, 13–14, 163
contraception, 93–98, 141–42
counsel, 11–13, 75, 142. See also obli-
    gation; supererogation
criterion, criteria: of right and
    wrong, 2–5; defined, 2; versus
    method, 2–3, 89, 145–47; shift-
    ing, 2–3, 67–69; moral, 2–3; deci-
    sive for method, 3–4; one or
    many, 4; epistemological primacy
    of, 71–72. See also linguistic

D'Arcy, Eric, 172
Davidson, Donald, 164
Davies, W. D., 167
Deidun, Thomas, 169

dilemmas (moral), 18
divine-command theories, 64–73
divorce and remarriage, 48–49, 142, 170
Dodd, Charles, 166
Donagan, Alan, 37, 74–88, 142, 169, 176
Donnellan, Keith, 68

Ellingworth, Paul, 168
Evans, C. F., 168

Farley, Margaret, 79
Feldman, Fred, 162–63
Finnis, John, 20–21, 40–41, 165, 170
Fischer, John, 125–27
Fletcher, Joseph, 66, 174
Flick, Maurizio, 147
Foot, Philippa, 187
Forrest, Peter, 72, 175
Frankena, William, 146
Fuchs, Josef, 178

Gallagher, John, 171
Garcia, J. L., 187
Gardner, Richard, 166
Geach, Peter, 32
Gewirth, Alan, 132–35
Gilleman, Gérard, 62
God, 35, 50, 53, 64–73
Gonsalves, Milton, 156
Good. *See* values
Gooding, David, 168
Gowans, Christopher, 164
Grisez, Germain: on good, 8; on consequentialism, 18, 47, 186; objections to proportionalism, 20–24; on value-incommensurability, 23–24, 43; on intrinsically evil acts, 47; on divorce and remarriage, 48; on Aquinas's first principle, 56, 172; system of, 89; conception of proportionalism, 89; on

inviolable goods and the eighth "mode of responsibility," 90–91; on morality and intention, 90–98, 169; implicit challenge to proportionalism, 91–95; on contraception, 93–98; on Knauer, 180
Grosseteste, Robert, 44
Gustafson, James, 139, 145–46

Hales, Alexander of, 173
Hanink, James, 175
Hare, R. M., 32
Harrington, Daniel, 166–67
Hofmann, Rudolf, 166
Hoose, Bernard, 154–55
Hugh of St. Victor, 59
Hughes, Gerard, 178

Idziak, Janine, 174
intention, 9–10, 46. *See also* action: end of; motive
"intrinsically evil" acts, 49–50

Jesus, 35–36, 78, 159, 166
John Paul II. *See Veritatis splendor*
justice, 14, 110

Kant, Immanuel, 79, 81, 87, 119, 136–37, 142, 183
Kiely, Bartholomew, 180
Kirk, Albert, 168
Knauer, Peter, 37, 46, 100–112, 163, 169, 179–82, 186
Kripke, Saul, 68

Lane, William, 167–68
Levy, Sanford, 102–3
Lewis, C. I., 7, 23, 31, 135–37, 140–41, 143, 165

linguistic: usage, 2–3, 12, 33, 67–68; criteria, 2–3, 71–72; variations, 2–3, 5, 11, 44–45, 47–49, 67–69, 162, 165; meanings, 3, 46–47, 49–50; contexts, 5, 68, 108; borders, 12–13; aptness, 33, 50, 82–83; indefiniteness, ambiguity, 56–60, 66, 148–49; rigidity, 64, 68–69, 163; terminology, 91. *See also* criterion, criteria; objective focus; prospective focus

Lottin, Odon, 53–54
love, 35, 62, 66
Loyola, St. Ignatius, 78
Luz, Ulrich 167
lying, 79–80

McCloskey, H. J., 128–32
McCormick, Richard, 105, 113, 144, 146–47, 179
McGrath, P. J., 55–56
McInerny, Ralph, 172
Mackey, J. P., 78
Mahoney, John, 172
Mar, Gary, 175
Maritain, Jacques, 78
Marshall, I. H., 168
means (evil), 40–41, 43–45
Meier, John, 167
method: versus norm or criterion, 2–5, 89; multiple, 3–4
Mill, John Stuart, 66
Moellering, H. Armin, 168
Moore, G. E., 128
Morris, Leon, 36, 167
motivation, motive, 8–10, 46, 117, 152–54. *See also* act: end of; intention
Mouw, Richard, 138
Murdoch, Iris, 155
Murphy-O'Connor, Jerome, 168
Murray, Michael, 172

Nagel, Thomas, 8, 138, 161
natural-law ethics, 52–53, 171
Niebuhr, Reinhold, 78
Nielsen, Kai, 86
norms: versus methods, 4, 132; exceptionless, 45–50, 62–63; supreme, 128–38

Obach, Robert, 168
objective focus, 6–10, 105–6
obligation, 11–13, 102, 124–25, 137–38
O'Connor, D. J., 53, 171
O'Neill, Onora, 141

Paul, St., 39–42, 78, 104, 119
Philip the Chancellor, 173
Pincoffs, Edmund, 128
Pius VI, 50
Pius XI, 50
Plato, 152
Pojman, Louis, 182
probability, 5–6
proportionalism: varieties of, 1, 100, 109; not a method, 2–4; narrow definition of, 100, 109. *See also* consequentialism; VM (Value-Maximization)
prospective focus, 5–6, 75
Putnam, Hilary, 68

Quay, Paul, 162

Rahner, Karl, 78
Ramsey, Paul, 35, 78, 142, 154
Rawls, John, 133–34, 177
Reicke, Bo, 169
Rescher, Nicholas, 26
respect for persons, 74–88
Rienecker, Fritz, 168

right and wrong: criterion of, 2; different senses of, 3, 5, 68
rights, 113–27, 142
Rorty, Richard, 140
Ross, W. D., 83–84, 128–32
rule-utilitarianism, 116, 132, 146

Sartre, Jean-Paul, 81
Scheler, Max, 147
Schnackenburg, Rudolf, 35–36
Schüller, Bruno, 162, 165
Schuster, Johann, 172
Schweizer, Eduard, 168
Seidl, Horst, 172
Simon, René, 172
Singer, Marcus, 132–33
Smith, Janet, 142
Stein, Robert, 168
Stout, Jeffrey, 76, 80, 177
suicide, 61–62
Sumner, L. W., 147, 161
supererogation, 12–13, 75, 100–2.
  *See also* counsel; obligation
Swinburne, Richard, 7–8

Talbert, Charles, 168
Taylor, Charles, 138, 140, 149, 183
Teilhard de Chardin, Pierre, 78
Thomson, Judith, 37, 113–27, 169
Toulmin, Stephen, 184

universality (principle of), 135–37
utilitarianism, 1, 66, 84, 128, 146, 169, 183. *See also* rule-utilitarianism

Vacek, Edward, 142, 169
values: objective, 8, 21, 30–33, 106–7; varieties of, 13–14; moral, 14, 109–13, 181–82; comparability of, 23–29, 83–86, 101–2, 164–65, 167–69; ordering of, 24, 147–49; relation to action, 32–33, 121; "inviolable," 90–91; "ontic" or "premoral," 109–11; and claims, 120–21; and obligations, 130–31; and principles, 133–34; system of, 147–49. *See also* VM (Value-Maximization)
Veatch, Henry, 32, 176
*Veritatis splendor*, 41–42, 45–51
Vermeersch, Arthur, 142
virtue, 154–58
VM (Value-Maximization): formulated, 2; explained, 2–19; relation to morality, 2–3, 11–13; versus method, 2–5, 46, 145–47; and obligation, supererogation, 11–13, 75, 100–2, 124–25, 137–38; objections to, 20–21, 114–15, 162–63; positive case for, 30–51; in the New Testament, 34–42; and love, 35; in Christian tradition, 42–51, 169–70; and principle of universality, 136–37; significance of, 138–59; modes of thinking in conflict with, 141–43; and ways of life, 149–52, 186; and motivation, 152–54; epistemological primacy of, 157–58; Christian character of, 184–85. *See also* proportionalism

Walter, James, 181
Weber, Helmut, 169
Wertheimer, Roger, 80, 86–87, 177
will (defective), 95–99
Williams, Bernard, 138